THE FIGHTING 69th

ALSO BY SEAN MICHAEL FLYNN

Land of the Radioactive Midnight Sun:
A Cheechako's First Year in Alaska

THE FIGHTING 69th

One Remarkable National Guard Unit's
Journey from Ground Zero to Baghdad

SEAN MICHAEL FLYNN

VIKING

VIKING

Published by the Penguin Group

Penguin Group (USA) Inc., 375 Hudson Street, New York, New York 10014, U.S.A. • Penguin Group (Canada), 90 Eglinton Avenue East, Suite 700, Toronto, Ontario, Canada M4P 2Y3 (a division of Pearson Penguin Canada Inc.) • Penguin Books Ltd, 80 Strand, London WC2R 0RL, England • Penguin Ireland, 25 St. Stephen's Green, Dublin 2, Ireland (a division of Penguin Books Ltd) • Penguin Books Australia Ltd, 250 Camberwell Road, Camberwell, Victoria 3124, Australia (a division of Pearson Australia Group Pty Ltd) • Penguin Books India Pvt Ltd, 11 Community Centre, Panchsheel Park, New Delhi – 110 017, India • Penguin Group (NZ), 67 Apollo Drive, Rosedale, North Shore 0632, New Zealand (a division of Pearson New Zealand Ltd) • Penguin Books (South Africa) (Pty) Ltd, 24 Sturdee Avenue, Rosebank, Johannesburg 2196, South Africa

Penguin Books Ltd, Registered Offices: 80 Strand, London WC2R 0RL, England

First published in 2007 by Viking Penguin, a member of Penguin Group (USA) Inc.

10 9 8 7 6 5 4 3 2 1

Photographs from the United States Government

LIBRARY OF CONGRESS CATALOGING-IN-PUBLICATION DATA

Flynn, Sean Michael.
The fighting 69th : one remarkable National Guard Unit's journey from Ground Zero to Baghdad / Sean Michael Flynn.
        p. cm.
Includes index.
ISBN 978-0-670-01843-7
1. New York (State). National Guard. Infantry Regiment, 69th--History. 2. September 11 Terrorist Attacks, 2001. 3. Iraq War, 2003—Personal narratives, American. 4. Iraq War, 2003—Participation, Irish American. 5. Iraq War, 2003—Participation, Puerto Rican. 6. New York (N.Y.)—Ethnic relations. 7. New York (N.Y.)—History, Military. I. Title.
UA363.569th .F59 2008
356'.113097471--dc22   2007040436

Printed in the United States of America
Designed by Carla Bolte • Set in Scala

FOR THE SOLDIERS, FAMILIES, AND FRIENDS

OF NEW YORK'S OWN

69th INFANTRY REGIMENT

I'm going to go home and decompress. I'm going to clean up my equipment. I'm going to make contact with my chain of command, and I'm going to get ready to go. Because right below the pain that I feel is a burning fucking desire to kill something. And somebody just needs to give the 69th a chance and that somebody is going to get a belly full.

—Lieutenant Colonel Geoffrey Slack,
Commander of the Fighting 69th, September 17, 2001, New York City

CONTENTS

AUTHOR'S NOTE

The commander of the Fighting 69th called me in February 2006 and asked if I would write a narrative history of the National Guard unit's involvement in the Global War on Terror from September 11, 2001, to September 11, 2005. As an aficionado of the regiment's long history and as a veteran of the unit's duty at Ground Zero and Iraq, I was quick to sign on to the project.

I commanded two rifle companies in the 69th from 2001 to 2006, and had a firsthand appreciation of the unit's struggles and its triumphs. But the scope of the story dictated that I leave my foxhole and chronicle the regiment's history as more a journalist than an infantryman. With the commander's blessing, I set out to collect reams of historical data on the unit, including operations orders, unit newsletters, photos, videos, combat journals, and anything else I could get my hands on. I also began a round of interviews with the unit's principals in an effort to capture their recollections before they slipped away. The resulting narrative is the nexus of key individuals and events that I believe most shaped the Fighting 69th's experience from Ground Zero to Baghdad.

All the events and people in the book are real. All quoted dialogue and situations are based on re-creations from the soldiers I interviewed or my own recollection. Some names have been changed out of respect for the individuals' privacy.

AN INFANTRY PRIMER

The infantry generally consists of foot soldiers, often referred to as grunts, whose primary mission is to close with and kill the enemy by shooting and moving. When one thinks of World War II or Vietnam films, these are guys fighting with just guns, grenades, and a lot of foul language. In Iraq, most infantry units maneuver in armored Humvees, Bradley Infantry Fighting Vehicles, or Stryker Infantry Carrier Vehicles. Infantry units today are generally broken down in the following manner:

- **Team or Crew**: Four soldiers, including one junior sergeant team leader.
- **Squad**: Two teams lead by a more senior sergeant (nine men).
- **Platoon**: Three or four squads lead by a lieutenant (20 to 40 men).
- **Company**: Three or four platoons lead by a captain (about 130 men).
- **Battalion**: Four or five companies lead by a lieutenant colonel (500 to 700 men).
- **Task Force**: A battalion augmented for a specific mission or deployment.
- **Brigade**: Three or more battalions lead by a colonel (1500 to 2000 men).
- **Brigade Combat Team**: A brigade augmented for a specific mission or deployment.
- **Infantry Regiment**: Historically, similar in size to a brigade. U.S. infantry regiments today are not functional headquarters. Rather, they represent a given battalion's history.
- **Division**: Multiple brigades lead by a two-star general.

The 1st Battalion, 69th Infantry Regiment (The Fighting 69th) consisted of six companies totaling around 500 soldiers during peacetime and four companies totaling up to 700 soldiers during its tour in Iraq. During homeland defense duty from 2001 through 2003, the Fighting 69th reported to the 3rd Brigade of the 42nd Infantry Division, New York Army National Guard. For deployment to Iraq, the Fighting 69th was reorganized as Task Force Wolfhound and reported to the 256th Brigade Combat Team from the Louisiana Army National Guard. The 256th reported to the 1st Cavalry Division for the first half of its deployment to Iraq and the 3rd Infantry Division for the second half.

PROLOGUE

OCTOBER 1991

New York Army National Guard Captain Geoff Slack drove his tired pickup truck through the Queens Midtown Tunnel toward Manhattan with nothing to look forward to when he came out on the other side. No units would be standing in formation. No sergeants would be calling cadence. No soldiers would be cleaning their rifles. There would be nothing to satisfy the hunger of the patriotic warrior that stirred restlessly just below his civilian clothes, searching for a target, listening for the sound of the guns. Slack took a long drag from an unfiltered Camel, smoking it down to the brown stains on his leathered thumb and middle finger. He was headed to the 69th Regiment Armory, home to what was, as far as he was concerned, the worst unit in the National Guard, the laughingstock of the Army.

The Guardsman flicked the cigarette out the window and then lit another as he pulled into the night and made his way through the East Side, where ethnic toughs wearing first-generation hip-hop gear were waiting to be recruited and led out of the darkness and over the ramparts, where aimless yuppies who should have been at officer candidate school stumbled in and out of bars, and where middle-aged men wearing ties and cuff links sped toward Nassau, Westchester, and Jersey in shiny German and Japanese sedans that burned Detroit autoworkers at the same rate as Arabian oil. At a red light at Lexington Avenue he flipped on his left turn signal, taking another long drag on

1

the Camel to help the time pass. He was just ten blocks away from the armory, yet light-years from where he thought he should be. If Geoffrey James Slack had controlled his own fate, he would have been, at that very moment in late 1991, blazing across an open field atop an American infantry fighting vehicle near some contested border. The Bushmaster on his M2A2 Bradley would be loaded with 25-millimeter armor-piercing and high-explosive rounds. His M16A2 assault rifle would be loaded with a 30-round magazine of NATO 5.56-millimeter ball-and-tracer bullets. He'd be a major, just a step away from commanding a battalion in his own right. He'd be wearing the Combat Infantryman Badge that he would have earned during Schwarzkopf's hundred-hour blitzkrieg in the desert. Below the badge, inside his chest pocket, he would have a Cuban cigar that his operations sergeant major would have picked up for him in a third world bodega that sold everything a primal man could ever want. If at age thirty-four Geoff Slack from Mastic Beach, Long Island, was where he thought he should be—indeed, where Saint Michael, the Archangel himself, intended—he'd be cradled in the cold steel of the military-industrial complex, defending America from evil and smiling from ear to ear like a kid who had just scored the prom queen.

But Captain Slack wasn't one who could compromise his values simply to satisfy his own selfish needs. Family came first, just ahead of the Army, and the life of an infantry officer in the U.S. Army in the late '70s and early '80s had placed a strain on Slack and his newly-wed. Not far from his romantic visions of martial service were the grim realities of life as a soldier. While he might one day get command of an infantry battalion, Slack also reasoned there was a good chance the stress of the Army would leave him divorced, estranged from his wife and children, and suckling on a whiskey bottle alone in the bottom of his closet, only moments after the armored vehicles were parked in the motor pool. Slack couldn't risk it. He opted instead for the perfect family and a vision of a white picket fence and green lawn where Ward and the Beaver could play catch for an hour before June called them in for dinner. He moved to suburbia and took over his father's landscaping business. It all seemed like the right thing to do—for a while, anyway. But by the late 1980s Slack's inner warrior began to stir. After five years of living as just a regular old guy—Mr. Slack, if you will—he decided to put the uniform back on, but this time only for one weekend a month and two weeks every summer.

The light turned green, and the citizen-soldier headed south on Lexington Avenue, down a slight hill and into a hostile bunker of drug dealers, junkies, thieves, and a veritable platoon of hookers. Their numbers increased as he got closer to the armory, which stood between Twenty-fifth and Twenty-sixth. Some were walking the streets, others used parked cars, and many leaned against the very walls of the building, their well-worn heels rising from a sidewalk sprinkled liberally with used condoms. Business was good, and even more rubbers would have accumulated by the time Slack left the armory later that night, including two soiled specimens stuck to the side of his car.

Slack was repulsed by the scene outside the soot-and-piss-stained armory and hurried into the fortresslike structure, where he expected some sense of proper military decorum. Not so. In its cavernous spaces garbage cans overflowed onto the floors, spilling sludge in small rivers across the hallways. Empty beer bottles and stacked ashtrays rested on most level surfaces. Slack had known before he arrived that the unit was in rough shape, but this was far worse than he imagined. Gotham's 69th Infantry—the so-called Fighting 69th featured in the 1940 James Cagney film of the same name—was an absolutely demoralizing pigpen of an operation.

Stepping around piles of garbage, the captain made his way to the massive drill hall, a hangarlike edifice with a 130-foot-high arched roof hovering over a football field–sized wooden floor. Only one light of the dozens that hung over the hall worked. The place echoed with the screams and rants of the alcohol- and drug-crazed homeless women who were housed on the armory's fourth and fifth floors. Slack wondered how any unit could train for war in such an environment and then quickly concluded that it wasn't possible. Any soldier tasked to train in the 69th Regiment Armory was set up for failure, a result the captain had witnessed firsthand. While assigned to another unit, Slack and his men used to lean against their jeeps and watch the 69th stumble into the field blaring hip hop and salsa music like a ghetto version of the Keystone Kops.

In Slack's estimation 69th men were inevitably unprofessional. Their equipment was always broken, and when they trained, they loaded their trucks with alcohol, hibachis, and boom boxes instead of Army supplies. The Fighting 69th embodied all the negative stereotypes held in the military about the National, or "Nasty," Guard. They were true weekend warriors, wayward Boy Scouts old enough to drink but not really interested in low-crawling through an obstacle course. And if you asked them, unit members would tell you that is exactly what they wanted. They got the uniforms and the rank and a dozen weekends away from the home, the job, the wife and kids—and they never had to worry about getting shot at (by the enemy, anyway). It was an instant fraternity complete with camping trips, institutionalized hazing, and a bar well stocked with dollar bottles of beer. The 69th hadn't gone to war in fifty years, and the overwhelming consensus was that they weren't about to go anytime soon. Except for the risk of catching a venereal disease at a unit party, duty in the Fighting 69th was probably the safest and easiest duty in the Army. The running joke among the soldiers of the outfit was that a Russian tank regiment would have to be crossing the George Washington Bridge into Manhattan before the Fighting 69th got the call—and then only maybe.

For a gung ho soldier like Captain Slack, service in a group as unmilitary and operationally irrelevant as the 69th was especially depressing. He believed the sole purpose of an Army organization, whether active or Guard, was to move toward combat. If a soldier or a unit wasn't doing that, then what was the point of being a soldier? Why waste the taxpayers' dollars? The Army had recently called up three National Guard infantry brigades for Desert Storm, and Slack believed every unit should strive to be the next one in the queue. He had brought that philosophy to his first National Guard company command, in the 71st Infantry Regiment, based on Long Island. Instead of hanging around their armory, Slack pushed his men to the field. Instead of riding buses, Slack ordered road marches and instructed his troops to load rocks into their rucksacks to simulate the weight of extra ammunition. They were taken aback by the aggressive captain, and many of them concluded that the former active-duty officer from the Big Army was crazy. One soldier who didn't care for his leadership style tried to run him down with a Humvee. But if anything, this attempt on his life only reinforced Slack's desire to train harder and rid his unit of the laziness, ineptness, and at times criminal behavior he had observed in other Guard outfits—the Fighting 69th in particular. He had no regard whatsoever for the 69th and believed the unit should be disbanded, its flags sent to a museum, and its armory sold off to make way for a new Trump high-rise.

Accordingly, when he learned that the Pentagon's post–cold war drawdown meant that a National Guard infantry battalion in the New York Metro area would have to be closed, Slack was certain it would not be his unit, the 71st; they were just too good. Instead, he assumed the Fighting 69th would get the axe—and good riddance.

But that was easier said than done. The 69th Regiment was not just a horrible Army unit, it was *New York City*'s horrible Army unit, a quintessential element of Big Apple identity and culture. It included soldiers from all five boroughs. It led New York's annual Saint Patrick's Day Parade. It was the subject of books and films and corruption investigations. One could no sooner shutter the 69th than one could move the New York Yankees to California. Moreover, the senior Army officer in the state of New York, Major General Lawrence Flynn, an Irish American from Queens whose relatives had served in the Fighting 69th in the Civil War and World War I, refused to let the regiment be closed on his watch. Against the recommendations of many of his own staff officers and a squad of politicians, Flynn directed the more competent 71st Regiment be closed. End of discussion.

Slack thought the decision was a travesty and was aghast when he learned he would be transferred to the 69th. The captain, who had a tendency to make decisions based on his emotions and often engaged his mouth before his brain, told his commander he would quit the National Guard before going to the city unit. But his normally gentle commander chewed him out, calling him immature and selfish. "You don't serve for yourself. You serve where the Army needs you!"

The positive side of Slack's gut decision-making process was that one always knew where he stood on a given issue. The negative side was that Slack had had his ass kicked halfway off his body by any number of captains and colonels throughout his career. But he wasn't one to sit in the mud and cry about it. After each good reaming Slack began immediate battle-damage repair. Roger, sir, he told his commander at the 71st Infantry. What he really meant to say was, "Of course I'll go and work for the 69th."

Slack would take over the 69th's Headquarters Company. As he walked through the halls of his new duty station for the first time, Slack wondered if the 69th could really be as bad as he had feared. An optimist by nature, he searched for signs of hope. Then, as he looked closer at the armory, beyond the mounds of garbage and felled plaster, Slack began to see traces of the old Fighting 69th—a plaque here, a painting there. In a sixteen-foot-tall display case, hidden under a dirt-caked pane of glass, was a collection of the unit's battle flags. He walked up to the case and began to rub away some of the grime so he could make out the inscription next to one of the standards: IRISH COLOR, 69TH STATE VOLUNTEERS, FIRST REGIMENT, IRISH BRIGADE, 1861–1863. Next to that flag was another from the Battle of Cold Harbor, and then a dozen more, all from the unit's legendary Civil War campaigns. Slack was standing just inches from the very flags that the young, brave Paddy Yanks of the Union Army had carried amid the carnage of war. How many soldiers had rallied around those flags? How many soldiers had died carrying them, because of them? Slack could almost see those fearless boys standing before him. They were immigrant patriots who had yet to enjoy their adopted country, but they still carried a rifle, still pushed forward against the enemy, and still fought like hell against insurmountable odds for their mates and for those flags. The glass case might as well have been a mirror, for in his soul, Slack was one of them. The boys who carried those shredded flags into salvo after salvo of deadly fire were his brothers.

But the platoons of gaunt Irish faces in Union Blue faded from Slack's mind as the sounds of the screaming homeless residents grew louder in the littered halls. The captain turned away from the battle flags and looked toward the direction of the commotion in time to see two foul naked women spill down a flight of stairs. They were locked in combat and punched, kicked, and pulled each other's hair for several moments before one of them broke away, grabbed her crotch with her right hand, and screamed, "Eat me!"

Slack should have walked out of the armory right then and never returned. All he had heard about the 69th was spot on. The unit was in desperate shape and well beyond the help of any one officer, let alone a dozen. Nobody would truly blame him if he turned his back on the unit. It was not a matter of selfishness; it was a matter of hopelessness, and there was simply no hope for the Fighting 69th.

But Slack wasn't thinking clearly. Instead of marching out the door to his salvation, he turned again to the display case. The boys in Union Blue reappeared, this time joined by shell-shocked doughboys fresh from the trenches of France and dogface grunts right off the beaches of the South Pacific. Those troopers had truly been up against hopeless situations. The Confederate positions they charged during the Battle of Fredericksburg were so strong that every member of the 69th who attacked was killed or wounded. A third died going "over the top" against entrenched Germans in World War I. And they faced such determined defenders in World War II on Okinawa and Saipan that the Army concluded that the only way to defeat the Japanese was with the atom bomb. Who the hell was Geoff Slack to walk away from the Fighting 69th just because the armory was a shambles? Who the hell was one captain to question centuries of U.S. Army wisdom?

Slack believed the modern-day 69th Infantry had dishonored its proud history. The unit had run itself into the ground, and it made the captain angry. He could make it better. If he did nothing more than screw in some lightbulbs and apply a coat of paint, the captain could leave the 69th a brighter place than he found it. He owed as much to the U.S. Army.

BOOK I

HOMELAND DEFENSE

MARCH 2001–FEBRUARY 2004

1: WEEKEND WARRIORS

SAINT PATRICK'S DAY 2001

"The battle flags of many regiments are celebrated in American history," film director Cecil B. DeMille announced gravely at the start of a radio play about the 69th Infantry Regiment in 1942. "But none is more famous than the 69th New York, the Fighting 69th of glorious memory." Founded by Irish immigrants in 1851, the 69th Infantry Regiment of lore stands at the forefront of both New York and American martial heritage. Once closely tied to the Irish independence movement—earning notoriety for its refusal to parade in honor of the visiting Prince of Wales in 1860—the 69th became one of the most well-known regiments to fight in the Civil War, earning its nickname "the Fighting 69th" from its respected adversary, Confederate General Robert E. Lee. The regiment later mobilized for the Spanish-American War and the Mexican border campaign before becoming one of the first U.S. Army units to steam for France in World War I. The Irish American unit earned three Medals of Honor in that war, including one for its commander, William "Wild Bill" Donovan, who later went on to found the Office of Strategic Services (OSS), precursor to the Central Intelligence Agency. The regiment earned another Medal of Honor in World War II, where it served in the Pacific at Makin Atoll, Saipan, and Okinawa. General Douglas MacArthur declared "no greater fighting regiment has ever existed." The U.S. Army relied on the Fighting 69th so heavily in the late nineteenth and early twentieth centuries that the regiment had earned more battle credits than any other in the world except the Black Watch out of Scotland. To make room for all the battle rings on its flag staff, the U.S. Congress passed a measure to extend the shaft by twelve inches. No other American unit before or since has ever been given such an honor.

More than twenty books have been written about the unit and its members. Folk singers and rock bands have written songs about the regiment. In World War II the Fighting 69th was so well known that a group of reporters that included Andy Rooney and Walter Cronkite was dubbed "The Writing 69th" in a reference to the famous regiment. In 1963 President Kennedy presented one of the 69th's battle flags to the Irish Parliament in Dublin. That flag and scores of other 69th artifacts are still displayed in Ireland today, where the early history of the "Irish 69th" is only somewhat less serious a school subject than math.

But times change. By 2001 the Fighting 69th was no more Irish than the Notre Dame football team and had been relegated to water boy status for the Big Army.

Once the busiest Army unit in the United States, the Fighting 69th was not a member of the two Guard divisions called for Korea; it sat on the bench with the preponderance of National Guard units during Vietnam, and it was far too unprepared for service in the Persian Gulf War. Indeed, its only official task in support of Desert Storm was to man a hot dog distribution point for the regular Army soldiers marching in the welcome-home ticker-tape parade on Fifth Avenue. Now most of its soldiers were immigrant kids and Nuyoricans from the lower economic classes of inner-city New York. Most had no prior military experience and no intention of serving their country any longer than it took to get a paycheck or college credit or job training. Their uniforms were often incomplete and worn to look better in the hood than in the wood—black Tupac bandanas instead of helmets, unbuttoned fatigue shirts, low-riding camouflage pants, unlaced combat boots. There were sergeants among them, but it was hard to tell who was who, since many wore no rank or sideways rank or upside-down rank. When they marched, it was more of a pimp roll or gangster limp. If they didn't feel like doing Army duties, they'd tell you to stick it. Rank didn't seem to make much difference. Most of the sergeants were noncommissioned officers in name only; although they wore stripes on their sleeves, many of them had never led soldiers anywhere beyond the Non-commissioned Officers' Club. Most had no active-duty experience, and the handful that had seen combat had done so in Vietnam. While these veterans' wisdom was solid, their knees, their backs, and their stomachs were not. The officers—the few that were there—were rarely better. While many aspired to a career in the National Guard, they would have been more suited to leading a Boy Scout troop than an infantry company. Relief for cause was not an uncommon fate for many company commanders in the unit then. One of them had brought hookers inside the building for liberal use by his soldiers at a unit party. The captain was sacked for the incident but would probably have gotten away with it had he simply invited his supervisor.

If the men were sketchy, their equipment was downright derelict. Machine guns were missing parts. Rust-laden trucks sprouted flower beds and served as makeshift shelters for the homeless. Soldiers talked on radios that were so old they couldn't communicate with anybody else in the Army. In many cases, they couldn't even talk to one another. They fired the earliest version of the M16 assault rifle whenever they shot, which was supposed to be once a year, but did not always take place that often.

The oldest of the Fighting 69th's subordinate units, Alpha Company, traced its roots back to New York Irishmen who fought in the Revolutionary War. But despite its proud heritage, one would have been hard-pressed to find many Celtic faces in the unit's ranks on March 17, 2001. With the exception of a handful of officers and soldiers from suburban units on Long Island, most of the soldiers in the unit were Hispanic or African American—even the battalion's last commander was Chinese—and had little interest in getting up before dawn to march in the Saint Patrick's Day Parade, especially when it would ruin a perfectly good weekend. Gone were the days of the "Irish 69th" when the smattering of non-Irish soldiers claimed they were "Irish by adoption, Irish by association or Irish by conviction." None-theless, here they were to honor New York's Fighting Irish for the unit's sesquicentennial year. The men had been handed clippings of boxwood to tuck into their headgear as a reminder of the doomed Irishers who tucked a green sprig in their caps just before their sui-cidal attack against Marye's Heights at the Battle of Fredericksburg in 1862. The overwhelming majority of the soldiers had no clue as to the meaning of that symbol, and if they did, they didn't care. One asked his buddy if he thought you could smoke the green stuff.

The 69th spilled out of its armory at 6:15 a.m. to prepare for its an-nual unit day. Some of the troops wore helmets, others carried them under their arms. A handful of sergeants attempted to urge the men on with as many shouted insults as instructions. Most of the soldiers ignored the goading and gaggled about in cliques, eventually gravitat-ing on their own schedule to their proper place in the ranks. It took ten minutes longer than planned for the Fighting 69th to organize itself. Then, with a barely audible command of "Forward, march," the three-hundred-soldier-strong battalion set off to march a mile north to Saint Patrick's Cathedral on Fiftieth Street and Fifth Avenue, where the archbishop, Edward Cardinal Egan, would offer his first Mass in honor of New York's famous Fighting Irish Regiment in advance of the parade.

At about that same time, twenty-six-year-old Specialist Jay Olmo, a Hispanic independent contractor and sometimes machine-gunner in Alpha Company's second platoon, woke up in his bed across the East River in Queens. He glanced at the clock, realized he was late for the parade, and decided without hesitation to go back to sleep.

Jay Olmo was a conscientious objector when it came to marching on Saint Patrick's Day. In his mind the Hispanics and blacks that made up the preponderance of the Fighting 69th had no place in the festivities. Olmo himself was half Mexican and half Puerto Rican, and didn't care in the least about the 69th's Irish heritage. He thought the unit should have been marching in the Puerto Rican Day Parade and suggested as much to his first sergeant, Richard Acevedo. Acevedo was also Hispanic and told Olmo it sounded like a good idea and therefore would never happen.

Fuck that, Olmo thought. *When they change their fuckin' minds and want to march in the fuckin' Puerto Rican Day Parade then I'll get my fuckin' ass out of bed. Until then, they can go fuck their mother. I'm not doin' nothin'.*

Raised in the Pomonok Houses, a public project next to Queens College in Flushing, Olmo was typical of the inner-city soldiers who enlisted in the Fighting 69th around the turn of this century. Streetwise and always looking for an angle, Olmo viewed the military as an opportunity to get ahead. His older brother had joined the Coast Guard to establish himself, and Jay figured it would work for him, too. But instead of the Coast Guard, the fast-talking and cocksure kid would join the real military, rack up a stack of medals, and show his brother who was more of a man. Fueled by youth, machismo, and a large cache of Sylvester Stallone and Chuck Norris war films, Olmo, whose short five feet, eight inches was offset by a steady, forward-leaning, in-your-face posture and a "don't fuck with me" scowl, set his sights on the infantry when he met the recruiters in 1993.

"You want the infantry?" the recruiter asked. "No problem. But since you only have a GED the Army won't take you right off the streets. You have to join the National Guard first, put in six months of good duty, and then you can transfer to the regular Army. What do you say?"

"What the fuck do I know?" Olmo answered. "I'm only fuckin' eighteen."

Olmo shipped off to basic and advanced individual training, where the Army taught him to be an artilleryman—or pretty much the exact opposite of John J. Rambo. He may as well have joined the Coast Guard. But it didn't really matter: Private Jay Olmo was in the system. If everything worked out as the recruiter assured, Olmo would be out of the National Guard and in the Big Army earning a steady paycheck and shooting machine guns in no time. *Say hello to my little friend!* But anyone who has ever joined the military will tell you that the Army never quite works out exactly how the recruiters sell it. In the case of Olmo, there were official and self-inflicted barriers that blocked his ascension to active duty. The Army delayed the process month after month for two full years, and when they finally did say, "Follow me," Olmo got into a bad, 128-stitches-in-your-face car wreck after he and his Coastee brother downed a gallon of Bacardi at a send-off party. So instead of becoming a macho, snake-eating infantry killer, Olmo became one of Gotham's weekend warriors—first with the 258th Field Artillery in Jamaica, Queens, and then with the Fighting 69th in Manhattan.

Truth be told, one weekend a month and two weeks every summer with the National Guard in New York wasn't bad duty. In fact, it wasn't really duty at all. When Olmo drilled in the city, he and his mates were usually able to sign in to a roster and then slip away for a day on the town. There was so little control of the unit that the guys could play hooky undetected. For married or otherwise committed soldiers, it was the perfect opportunity to skip out for beers with their guy friends or trysts with their girlfriends. And if their wives wondered where they were, the soldiers had a legitimate excuse. Some Guardsmen became so adept at using the system that they told their significant others that they had Guard duty on *two* weekends a month: "But don't call the armory, honey. The guys won't know anything about it because it's a special operations mission." On more than one occasion, Olmo got a call from a fellow soldier who quickly warned him, "If my wife calls, I was with you doin' Army shit yesterday." Sure enough, the wife phoned, and Olmo toed the party line like a good pal.

When the unit went for their annual two-week stint in the field, the soldiers found ways to drink just as much but tossed around a football in lieu of chasing women. The officers tried to impose some level of discipline but could never seem to outsmart them. When one lieutenant took Olmo's football away, the soldiers wrapped a roll of toilet paper in duct tape to make a new one. When they confiscated that, Olmo and the guys simply abandoned any pretense of training and went to sleep in the woods instead. And when that got too boring, the soldiers stole their commander's Humvee for showers and a beer run back at the base. During one two-week training event at Fort Drum near the Canadian border, Olmo "missed" his unit's move to the field altogether and opted to spend the next week by himself, alternating between the barracks, the Post Exchange, and the post swimming pool. Nobody seemed to notice his absence.

Olmo took pride in his repeated and successful efforts to get over on the system.

And why not get over? This was just the National Guard. Even the most junior private knew that nobody would be calling up the unit to actually fire its weapons against a real foe. So why train hard? Why pretend the National Guard was relevant or important or even necessary when it clearly wasn't? The soldiers believed that anyone who took the Guard seriously was out of his mind. Further, any soldier who followed the guy taking it seriously was an ass kisser trying to curry favor with the system for a promotion or other special treatment. Jay Olmo and his fellow soldiers grew up in a place where one didn't seek favor with the establishment to get ahead. They were independent thinkers who were raised to take care of themselves and their families first. They joined the National Guard or the Army either because of the enlistment bonus, or for college tuition, or for a paycheck. They intended the Army to be merely a launching pad for their journey through life, not the be-all and end-all. While the men loved America and New York without qualification, few soldiers if any joined the military out of an overwhelming sense of patriotism. They had lived hard lives and didn't believe they owed anything to the flag beyond the minimum standard. And if they could get away with less, they would. Guys who could get over without finding themselves in major trouble were practically folk heroes in their units. "You fuckin' hung out at the pool while we were fuckin' sweating in the fuckin' field? No fuckin' way! You're the fuckin' *man*!"

By March 2001 Jay Olmo knew well his left and right limits, what he could and could not get away with. Skipping the Saint Patrick's Day Parade was not a big deal, so long as he showed up at the armory later and claimed that someone had told him he was on the stay-behind detail, which is exactly what Olmo did. By the time the Fighting 69th concluded its march up Fifth Avenue and headed for an exclusive Irish- and American-flagged number 6 subway train that would return the unit downtown, Olmo was back in the good graces of the Army. He even volunteered to mix and test the regimental cocktail, which, at one part Irish whiskey to three parts champagne, was pretty darn good for noon on a Saturday.

For all the things he hated about Saint Patrick's Day—the parade, the bagpipes, the speeches by jerk-off politicians—Olmo enjoyed the regimental cocktail and the kegs of beer without reservation. In that regard he seemed to be in line with the hard-drinking stereotype of the handful of Irish Americans who were still in the unit as well as the tens of thousands who had served in the Fighting 69th since its founding in 1851. In fact, Jay Olmo, as well as his fellow Hispanic, black, and Asian soldiers, had a lot more in common with the 69th's famous hardscrabble Irish veterans than first met the eye.

Peter Quinn, an author and chronicler of the Irish American experience, has characterized the typical Irish American members of the Fighting 69th in the late nineteenth and early twentieth centuries as fast-talking, profane, sarcastic, tough, combative, and "derisive of everyone in authority." The men were cool and walked with a swagger that announced their ownership of the mean streets of New York. They viewed as treasonous any attempt by their peers to rise above their station and achieve middle-class respectability. They viewed the economy as a rigged game that kept them at the bottom of the rung, which caused the Micks to view the border between legal and illegal as a question of convenience rather than morality. The only unforgivable offense "was to be boring or colorless," as Quinn wrote in *Looking for Jimmy: A Search for Irish America.*

Quinn's archetype of the Irish American soldier in the Fighting 69th is Joe Hennessy, who was featured in Albert Ettinger's World War I memoir, *A Doughboy with the Fighting 69th*. Ettinger describes Hennessy as a "con artist and wiseacre." " 'Fuck you. If you got any sisters, fuck them, too.' That was Hennessy." Such "fuck you" attitude and beliefs were not so much Irish American, however, as they were New York Urban—a style that the Irish themselves invented and James Cagney epitomized in films like *The Public Enemy, Yankee Doodle Dandy,* and *The Fighting 69th,* in which he played World War I Private Jerry Plunkett, a New York tough who bucked military authority at every turn. "Whoever the streets belong to gets to define what it takes to belong," Quinn explained, and because the Irish owned New York it was they who defined the city dweller's edge. As subsequent waves of immigrants moved into New York City, they watched Cagney on the big screen and adopted the same confident swagger, sarcastic countenance, and rapid-fire New Yorkese. Jewish immigrants picked it up. Italian immigrants picked it up, and later Puerto Ricans. When Specialist Jay Olmo confidently rolled into the 69th Regiment Armory several hours late on Saint Patrick's Day in 2001, he might as well have been Joe Hennessy or the fictional Jerry Plunkett in 1917.

A parade spectator with a green-painted face from Westchester or Suffolk County might look at the 69th as it marched up Fifth Avenue, see guys like Jay Olmo, and might well wonder what happened to the Good Ol' Fighting Irish of yesteryear. In other words, where are all the pale white Irish faces like mine? But while this green beer–drinking "Irish American" might root for Notre Dame, listen to the bagpipes, and have a shamrock tattooed on his ass, he usually didn't think, sound, or act anything like Joe Hennessy or his latter-day descendant Jay Olmo.

The modern-day Fighting 69th was a hell of a lot more brown than white. But in truth, few members of the 69th Regiment from New York had ever looked like that chubby parade watcher, who had likely driven a Lexus into the city from the suburbs that morning. The majority of the men who served in the Fighting 69th throughout America's history were poor, lean, and well muscled from the labor of day-to-day life. The hard edges etched into their faces reflected their immigrant background and a tremendous struggle against prejudice, sickness, poverty, and conflicts with other races and ethnic groups, to use Quinn's words.

But more than anything else, the soldiers of the 69th Infantry Regiment throughout its history have reflected the yearning of masses of people trying to earn credibility and dignity in America. While the Irish were the first to immigrate en masse to New York City and were responsible for founding the 69th, echelons of immigrants and dispossessed from other states and countries soon followed them down the path they blazed. During the Civil War virtually all the regiment's soldiers were born in Ireland or claimed Irish ancestry. The figures slipped to 90 percent in World War I and 70 percent in World War II. By 2001 only about 13 percent of the soldiers could be considered Irish American to some degree or another. But the overwhelming majority of the unit was still comprised of immigrants and second-generation Americans like Jay Olmo, New Yorkers with the stomach for a good brawl and an innate desire to prove themselves along the road less taken.

Most of the Irish Americans who were members of the 69th in 2001 came from families that had long since ascended to middle-class America. More than 80 percent lived in the suburbs and had completed or were enrolled in college. Lieutenant Mike Drew, the commander of Delta Company on Long Island, was typical. Like Jay Olmo, the New York City police officer had grown up in Queens. But unlike Olmo, who had joined the military for a job and an opportunity to get ahead, Drew simply believed he had an obligation to serve his country, and the Army sounded like a fun way to do it. He earned his commission through the Reserve Officer Training Corps (ROTC) program at Villanova University. When it came time for selecting an infantry unit to fulfill his eight-year service commitment, Drew looked to the 69th for three reasons. First, it was based in New York, where he wanted to live. Second, his father had served as a Guardsman in the unit. Finally, the 69th had an Irish heritage, a factor that played a significant role for many of its Irish American soldiers. For them the 69th was often more than just a place to fulfill a military obligation. The 69th was a significant part of their cultural identity. As a result, when the going got tough, officers with an Irish American background were more likely than non-Irish officers to stick with the unit. Consequently, about 41 percent of the regiment's officers claimed Irish American roots.

Of course if you observed all of that to Olmo, especially after he had had a few shots of regimental cocktail, he'd wonder what the hell you were smoking. (And could he get some?)

FAILURE TO LAUNCH

While Olmo attended to his bartending duties, the main body of the 69th Regiment exited the subway and reassembled outside the armory to begin the second phase of their Saint Patrick's Day drill event—a pass-in-review inside. The officers broke from the group and dashed ahead of the unit to line the stairwell of the building's great entrance and greet each company as it advanced. Unit by unit the soldiers of the Fighting 69th marched into the vaulted edifice to the shouts of the officers and other onlookers. "Three cheers for Alpha Company: Hip Hip—Hooray! Hip Hip—Hooray! Hip Hip—Hooray!"

In the 1970s this process would have taken the better part of an hour. With its ranks swollen by soldiers who had joined the National Guard to avoid the draft and service in Vietnam, the 69th consisted of two full battalions—more than fourteen hundred soldiers. As it was based in the middle of the largest population center on the East Coast, everyone was trying to get into the regiment, which numbered in its ranks many of the New York Knicks. With the end of the draft, however, the unit had shrunk in size with each successive year, so that by 2001 the 69th was down to a single battalion with a paltry three hundred soldiers marching. It took the unit less than twenty minutes to enter the building.

Lieutenant Colonel Geoff Slack cheered as the unit passed through the foyer of the armory. He had just concluded his first march in command of the Fighting 69th, and though his forty-four-year-old legs were a little stiff behind the knees from the stop-and-go stepping, the aches paled in comparison to the pain he had suffered as an officer with the unit over the past ten years.

When he first joined the battalion in 1991, it was in desperate shape. Not only was it hobbled by poor equipment, facilities, and leadership, but it had been ordered to trade in its rifles for Stinger missiles: after 140 years as an infantry unit, the regiment was to become an air defense artillery (ADA) battalion. To Slack, a dyed-in-the-wool military romantic, the Army was all about the foot soldiers of the infantry, and if you weren't one of them then there was something wrong with you. He inwardly railed against the very idea of becoming an air defender, but orders were orders.

Though he shuddered at the thought of being an artilleryman, he came to view the change as an opportunity to reestablish some level of credibility to the broken unit, which had long been the butt of jokes in New York. But few soldiers saw it the way he did. Instead of embracing the challenges of converting from infantry to ADA, scores of men fled in the early 1990s. The exodus was hardest felt in the noncommissioned officer (NCO) ranks. Like Slack, the sergeants of the Fighting 69th had been trained as infantrymen and wanted nothing to do with air defense. But unlike Slack, whose sense of duty usually trumped his other five senses, the sergeants ran for the doors. Those with enough points to retire hung up their boots, while the younger, machismo-fueled sergeants transferred en masse to other infantry units in the metro area. Slack didn't blame them; he would have done the same thing if given the chance. Practically overnight, the battalion's already thin pool of experienced leadership was gone. In a civilian corporation it would have been as if every manager below the level of vice president walked out the door. The CEO might wind up running the mailroom instead of leading his company, which is exactly what Slack tried to do. He jumped into the morass as a motivated captain and tightened the reins to try and bring his Headquarters Company under control. But the harder he pulled back, the more his soldiers bucked. Troopers like Jay Olmo just didn't see the point in taking the National Guard seriously.

In addition to the exodus of competent sergeants, the 69th Air Defense faced other obstacles. To qualify as an air defender, a soldier needed a secret clearance. To get a secret clearance, a soldier had to be a U.S. citizen. Some 20 percent of 69th soldiers, however, were immigrants, most of whom had not yet earned citizenship. Another percentage had a criminal record or other skeletons in their past that prevented them from obtaining clearance. Further, the Army expected all the unit's current soldiers to retrain into the ADA within three years—yet there were a limited number of slots available for the necessary training every year. Those slots often went to the sergeants, many of whom ultimately bailed because they were treated like privates at the air defense school and concluded they wanted nothing to do with the program.

After this initial experience at the armory in 1991, Slack had thought that the Fighting 69th could only get better. Instead, it began to tailspin into anarchy. Units had no idea what equipment they owned and couldn't keep track of even their high-dollar items like night-vision goggles. They had no idea which soldiers were actually on their books. The troops often signed in to the armory and then disappeared, skipping training for quickies with the hookers on Lexington Avenue or heading down to the local dive for cocktails. Nobody seemed to be in charge. Slack's first year in the battalion was so ugly it was enough to make a camel puke.

Nobody would have blamed Slack had he walked away from the assignment. In fact, he considered it on a regular basis and even wrote out his resignation several times. But he couldn't bring himself to submit it. He was a young, idealistic military romantic, and the myth of the Fighting 69th, coupled with an unfaltering love for the Army, had taken root in his soul and then spread like a cancer, causing the officer all sorts of ailments. He bitched and cursed about the unit on a regular basis to his superiors. He smoked more and more. He even attempted to physically beat one of his peers who seemed to be stifling the regiment. But no matter how hard the duty, no matter how sick he felt, Slack lowered his shoulder and drove on.

The commander was both selfless and stubborn, traits he learned from his Depression-generation father. A World War II veteran, the elder Slack was a dedicated family man who worked countless hours to put food on the table at endless sacrifice to his own life. When the going got tough, he put his head down like an old plow mule and just kept pulling, which he did until the day he died. The father's actions left a deep impression on the son, shaping his philosophy on life, work, and the Army: If you love something, just do it, and that's all there is to it. Shrug off the small stuff, roll with the punches, keep your chin high, and drive on. Slack summed the philosophy up in one phrase: *stay frosty.*

To get his work done, Slack started drilling two weekends per month, even though he was paid for only one. His zeal for the mission seemed fanatical to many of his superiors, not to mention his wife, who was ready to throw him out of the house. But the more he struggled with the unit, the more Slack came to love the work and the Fighting 69th. He and a small group of other loyalists stayed frosty and refused to let the unit die. For as bleak as the 69th's outlook was, he had come to believe that the Army's byzantine logic would one day become clear, that some reward would be awaiting him after his purgatory at the 69th Air Defense.

His gut proved correct. The first harbinger of better times came in 1994, when U.S. marshalls seized the Kenmore Hotel on Twenty-third Street, two short blocks from the armory, which had become a "bizarre warehouse for crack dealers, prostitutes, robbers and extortionists," according to the *New York Times*. With the Kenmore shut down, the men had one fewer temptation to skip out on drill. But the real turnabout came in 1996, when the Army acknowledged that the air defense plan had been a disaster and declared the Fighting 69th would henceforth be an infantry unit again. Despite the hours of work they had put into the air defense program, Slack and the other officers rejoiced. In 1997 they cut the insignia of the Air Defense Artillery branch off their uniforms and again sewed on the crossed rifles of the infantry. For Slack, it was as if the most famous of 69th veterans, World War I chaplain Father Francis Duffy, had reached down from heaven and picked him up off the ground, brushed away the layers of frustration, and encouraged him forward.

Slack was elated. Then, like any soldier who's been around the block a couple of times, he got back to business: there was no time for gloating if he ever hoped to get the 69th back in fighting trim. By now, however, with a few exceptions, the 69th had no more infantrymen. The air defenders and signalmen who made up the unit's ranks were usually old or overweight or didn't know basic soldier tasks. The infantry was anathema to them, and Slack wondered if some soldiers knew which end of a rifle to look down.

But by March 2001, Slack believed that his unit had made significant progress and was indeed frosty. Not only were his soldiers starting to look like infantrymen, but the unit was planning to conduct its first live fire maneuvers in more than ten years. It was a significant milestone in Slack's mind, one that would bury the air defense legacy once and for all, and return a shred of credibility to the 69th. As Colonel Slack watched his soldiers march into the armory that Saint Patrick's Day, he couldn't help but think it was fate that had brought his passion, frostiness, and vision to a unit that needed them all so badly.

But Slack also knew that every visionary needs loyal, smart, and hardworking operators to make his dreams a reality. As his unit marched through the front doors of the armory after the parade, Slack looked over at Captain Chris Daniels. As usual, the captain's uniform was wrinkled and his boots scuffed. Yet despite Daniels's general lack of spit and polish, Slack had anointed him his top foot soldier and the key to a successful resurgence for the Old Fighting 69th by naming him commander of his Headquarters and Headquarters Company, the HHC. The massive unit was comprised of nearly half the 69th's soldiers and contained all the support staff and equipment that made an infantry unit viable. But it was in a truly horrible state. No matter how good a line infantry company was, a battalion would just be pissing in the wind without an effective HHC. The only problem was that Daniels had already concluded that the 69th would never truly evolve into anything more than a well-oiled drinking club that thought it was cool to wear fatigues.

MISSIONARIES, MERCENARIES, AND MISFITS

With no regard for propriety, a vocabulary dependent on four-letter words, and a physique that seemed more paunch than punch, Chris Daniels did not fit the image of a well-groomed officer and gentleman. He had a constant wad of Cherry Skoal tobacco under his lip, a nicotine patch on his arm, a Marlboro Light in his left hand, and—when on light duty—a Budweiser or tumbler of Jameson in his right hand. With a mischievous grin, the officer resembled a skinnier version of John Belushi. Yet in contrast to the career frat boy he appeared to be, the Long Islander was actually a successful Manhattan accountant and one of the most competent leaders the Fighting 69th had seen in years. Daniels was a "Mustang," an officer who had come up from the enlisted ranks. He had spent time in reserve component Special Forces units, had graduated from Ranger School, and had been a successful platoon leader in the defunct 71st Infantry. When his Special Forces unit in upstate New York shut down in 1998, an officer at the 69th urged Daniels to come aboard.

"The reason why I love it is that we'll never deploy—ever," the officer told Daniels. "We'll never go anywhere."

It wasn't exactly the most motivating pitch one could have made to an infantry officer who had been trying to earn his Green Beret, but since the end of the cold war, National Guard units had been closing shop in New York state at breakneck speed, and Daniels was thankful that he could find a new home anywhere. But after a short time with the Fighting 69th, he quickly concluded that the battalion simply couldn't make things happen. Only three months into his assignment, and still a lieutenant, Daniels was ordered by a colonel to fire his company commander and take over. Nothing he had learned about the Army in other units was at play in the 69th. On weekend drills his soldiers acted as if they were on a camping trip. The moment the sun went down, the men stopped training, popped up their civilian tents, and built a bonfire to roast hot dogs. By the end of his first year, Daniels threw his hands up in frustration. *So I guess this is the way it's gonna be. But so what? It's not as if we're ever gonna deploy for war. So why fight it?* As it had for his colleagues, the National Guard became a hobby for Chris Daniels, one that got him out of the house with the boys a couple of times a month without causing a major row with his wife.

That all changed when Slack phoned Daniels one night in October 2000 while he was on a business trip in France. The call came at 2:00 a.m. Paris time, and Slack asked him to take command of the HHC. Daniels quickly said yes, hoping that would be the end of the conversation and he could go back to sleep. Instead, Slack kept him on the phone for an hour, outlining the year ahead and stressing the importance Daniels would play in it. The length of the call was the junior officer's first indication that his new job would require more than the accustomed one weekend a month.

Daniels had led Charlie Company on Long Island before assuming responsibility for the HHC. Though separated by only fifty miles, the two units were worlds apart. Charlie Company and the other Long Island outfits were largely white, middle class, and populated by experienced sergeants who were generally settled in their communities. The HHC and the other city units were populated by a transient group of minority teenagers and twentysomethings trying to figure out what to do in life.

The Islanders had joined the Guard for old-fashioned camaraderie, esprit de corps, and a place to drink cheap beer with their mates. When unit flags changed, they maintained their loyalties to their neighborhood armory. Whether they were infantry or signal or air defense didn't make much of a difference, so long as somebody lit the smoking lamp at 4:00 p.m. Bravo Company in Bay Shore, Long Island, was a prime example. In the course of a single generation the armory had housed an armor troop, three different infantry companies, and an air defense battery. Yet neither the unit bar nor the men sitting alongside it changed much. At his armory in Freeport, Daniels was able to tap into NCOs who were sergeants in the old 71st Infantry who had been retrained as signalmen during the mid-1990s and who were now back in the infantry. The drawback, however, was that many were old, fat, and not generally interested in running around in the woods.

By contrast, the city units had been gutted of experienced leaders in the 1990s and struggled to recruit and retain quality soldiers. Most young men who sought Army service in New York were attracted to better-funded units that had the latest equipment and that traveled to Puerto Rico, Germany, and Iceland for training. Meanwhile, the 69th could offer new recruits only a rusted and aging fleet of vehicles and the chance to march in a parade full of white guys. Selling the 69th over other units was like selling a teenager a rusted minivan over a shiny new Lexus. As a result the 69th was seriously short of soldiers, leading recruiters to push for quantity over quality. It didn't matter how out of shape, how intelligent, or how ethical the recruits were. Soldiers who were kicked out of the Big Army for drug use or criminal activity were signed up with a waiver by Guard recruiters who were under pressure to produce. Candidates who had trouble passing the entrance exams were coached. Even the unit's officers and soldiers were pressed into recruiting duty, and since Daniels's first day in command, finding new recruits and convincing his existing troops to stick around had been his primary job. This made it difficult to both motivate and discipline the existing units. To motivate, commanders needed to train, yet instead of training, soldiers were sent out on recruiting missions. To discipline, commanders needed a hammer, yet if a commander punished a wayward GI, the soldier may well quit the battalion. And losing a single soldier—even a worthless slug—was considered a failure in the eyes of the State Headquarters. Daniels found the environment stifling. If he wanted to take a stripe from a soldier for skipping a drill or stealing beer from the unit bar, he didn't think anybody in New York would have backed him, and he was right. The senior officers of the battalion ran into the same problem. They needed to get rid of dozens of slipshod officers and men, but the system wouldn't have permitted them to wholesale fire everybody. If they had done so, they would have been fired themselves. The Fighting 69th was rife with examples of soldiers who should have been jailed—if not sacked, at the very least. Instead of receiving a court-martial, a sergeant who tried to run over the command sergeant major with a truck was simply reassigned. Instead of jail time, a soldier who attacked an NCO with a tire iron was scolded—though not too badly.

But by March 2001, even with the relentless emphasis on recruiting, Daniels found he was short more than two hundred soldiers in his company alone. The 69th Infantry Regiment was a sieve. For every new recruit the unit brought on, it seemed two more walked out the door for any of a hundred reasons. Crappy leadership. Disgusting facilities. Broken payroll systems. Competent officers who promised to be the future of the 69th left when they didn't see progress. Frustrated soldiers who missed promotions because of paperwork snafus found more competent units. Experienced sergeants, whom the battalion needed more desperately than anything else, turned in their jerseys after watching the 69th fall all over itself weekend after weekend. At times it seemed a wonder that any soldiers stayed in the Fighting 69th at all.

Specialist Jay Olmo was one of those who threatened to quit the battalion all the time. He hated the armory. He hated the annual sojourn to Fort Drum for summer camp. Most of all he hated Saint Patrick's Day. Olmo now perched in the seating area that ringed the interior walls of the armory, twenty-five feet above the drill floor. As the unit marched onto the wooden pitch to conduct its pass-in-review, he remembered again why life in the Fighting 69th was miserable. Olmo had grown up in a mixed neighborhood, populated by whites, blacks, Hispanics, Asians—you name it. About the only thing he was prejudiced against was stupidity. And what could be more stupid than a bunch of grown men marching around as if they were back at basic training? But Olmo never did quit. God knows he never hesitated to skip out on a training event or sneak a regimental cocktail before it was served, but he drew the line at going AWOL for any significant period of time. His father had done that—quit on the family, leaving Olmo's mom to support two little boys. Olmo grew up watching his mother work until her hands and feet were raw. She was tough, cursed like a sailor, and seemed far older than her age. It didn't have to be that way. If his dad had stuck around, Olmo's mom could have had an easier life. But his father's failings were Olmo's strengths. The soldier followed his mother's example and refused to walk away from any challenge. Whether it was a job or an athletic event or the Army, Olmo was going to see it through—on his own terms, anyway. As for the 69th, the citizen-soldier planned to suffer through all the bullshit in hopes of someday kicking some ass with the Big Army. His attitude was a little like the old New York State Lottery motto: You've got to be in it to win it.

Others had their own reasons for staying, but whatever they were, Olmo and a core of other missionaries, mercenaries, and misfits stuck faithfully with the Fighting 69th. It was a motley crew, to say the least. But by March 2001, the two key ingredients needed for a comeback run were in place—inspired leadership from Slack and Daniels, and a small pool of aggressive men like Olmo who managed to stay frosty during the worst of times. While the young Hispanic trooper wasn't the type of soldier who would ever earn a good-conduct medal, both Slack and Daniels recognized he might be the kind of man who would willingly charge into an enemy machine-gun nest if he needed to—a far-fetched possibility for a National Guardsman, to be sure, but Slack didn't rule the possibility out. In fact, he even thought it likely.

When he ascended to battalion command in a formal ceremony in October 2000 at Fort Dix, New Jersey, Slack had caused a good deal of concern among his men. First, the new leader directed his men to sing along with the playing of the National Anthem. (As if tough guys like Jay Olmo would ever do that!) Second, and perhaps more disconcerting, Slack stood in front of his battalion straight as a flagpole, helmet strapped tight, sun glinting off his large wire-rimmed glasses, creases pressed into his fatigues, and told his men to get their acts together because they were going to go to war. More than one of the soldiers concluded Slack was absolutely out of his mind, and even Daniels couldn't imagine anything more absurd. But in Slack's mind, no matter how peaceful the New World Order was, if a soldier didn't think war was a possibility, then he was the one who was actually crazy. Because when it came right down to it, there was only one purpose on earth for an infantry battalion, to move to the sound of the guns. Geoff Slack had prepared his entire life for that eventuality, and when the bell tolled for New York City six months later, Slack was ready—even if the Old Fighting 69th was not.

2: MINUTEMEN

A NEW PARADIGM

Slack stared at the ground, squinting through the shroud of ash and smoke to get a better look at what he had just stumbled across. Next to his dust-covered boots was a shoe that still contained a foot. He crouched down and blinked tears over his dry, burning eyes to make sure of what he was looking at. There was no mistaking it. Though he had already encountered dozens of horrific sights, nothing else he had seen at the World Trade Center defined what had happened earlier that morning more completely than that shoe. He reached out with his left hand and picked it up. It was a light blue pump, and though her foot was sheared off through the ankle, Slack could picture the woman who had put it on that morning. She had driven to the train for the commute into Manhattan on the Long Island Rail Road. It was a crowded ride, but she managed to get a window seat and stared out into the bright September day, isolated in her own thoughts about work, an overdue oil change for her car, and her beautiful children, who would have already finished their breakfast and begun the trip to school. When she got into the city, she rode the subway to the World Trade Center and purchased a banana and a bottle of juice at the newsstand before riding the elevator to her office high up in the tower. Then she and thousands of other people—innocent civilians, people sitting at their desks, having a cup of coffee, going to their offices—were murdered by some filthy terrorists who had deluded themselves through a twisted psychology into thinking that what they were doing was a noble act. It wasn't noble. It was murder—senseless, pitiful murder. Slack needed to do something, but what? He wanted to help, but how? After several moments of struggling with feelings of uselessness, he decided that all he could do for the moment was to try to give that woman back some dignity and respect. Slack rose from his crouch, opened the right cargo pocket on his camouflage uniform, and gently slid her foot and her shoe—slid her—inside for protection until he could find someplace proper to lay her down again.

He walked over toward his executive officer and second in command, Major Joe Obregon, who scanned the West Side Highway in stunned disbelief. It was dark as night at street level. An airborne slurry of concrete dust and soot filled the air and covered every surface, as if an apocalyptic blizzard had swept over the city. Obregon had never seen or imagined anything so horrible. What would later be called Ground Zero reminded Slack of the photographs of what was left of Hiroshima after the atomic bomb was dropped. Where the towers once soared were a couple hundred feet of skeletal remains projecting from the ground like stakes. The remainder of the 110-story structures and their outlying buildings seemed to have pancaked into one dense pile. Flames shrouded vehicles and buildings at every turn. A group of firefighters stood around one of their own burning trucks, holding hands in prayer for the souls of their comrades who had never made it out of the vehicle.

When another fire truck about a block away exploded, the concussion of the blast jerked Slack and Obregon back to their job at hand—a reconnaissance of the attack site. The commander forced from his mind the human tragedies that were unfolding all around him and started thinking like a soldier. He hadn't received any specific orders and he wasn't certain exactly how, but he knew his part-time Fighting 69th was going to be in whatever fight would come. He needed to get clear and accurate situational awareness of the attack site so he could

plan for what would come next. Where and when would the next attack occur? Where and how will I deploy my battalion?

By rushing to Ground Zero to conduct a reconnaissance, Slack had
already exceeded the efforts of the entire National Guard in the wake
of the 1993 terrorist bombing of the Trade Center. Following that first
attack, Slack waited in vain for orders to move to the site, convinced
that the Guard should have at least assessed the situation and developed contingency plans. But in the absence of orders, the Fighting
69th did nothing. Slack was ashamed by their inaction—by his own
inaction—and vowed not to repeat it. Within minutes of watching the
second plane strike the towers, the battalion commander left his
house seventy miles outside the city and sped to the Fighting 69th's
motor pool at Farmingdale, Long Island. There he traded in his green
Ford Ranger pickup for his camouflage Humvee, which would allow
him to bypass all the police checkpoints and get into the city quickly.
Along the way he called his wife, Debbie, and asked her to grab his
alert roster and start calling all the 69th's company commanders, first
sergeants, and other key leaders. She passed on Slack's instructions
to the men as she reached them in turn: "Report to your armories and
assemble your men." After running down dozens of traffic cones and
signs with his speeding vehicle, Slack arrived at the Lexington Avenue
Armory just after noon, where Obregon and Captain Daniels, who
was among the first soldiers to arrive at the armory after the attack,
brought the commander up to speed. Basically, Daniels said, the fucking State had its collective fucking head up its fucking ass.

Daniels had bolted like a Minuteman from his office in Midtown
Manhattan when the second plane hit. He could see the World Trade
Center burning as he drove south on Fifth Avenue toward the Fighting 69th's headquarters. As he pulled up to the building, southern
Manhattan disappeared in a cloud of black smoke and gray concrete
dust. The South Tower had collapsed. Daniels ran inside the armory,
opened his company arms room, and passed out rifles and ammunition to whatever soldiers were there. He posted them at the corners
of the building, shutting down pedestrian and vehicular traffic. As the

HHC commander, Daniels also owned the battalion's motor pool in Farmingdale, where Slack had picked up his Humvee. The captain called the motor sergeant there and told him to bring into the city every vehicle that had wheels and would actually run for more than five minutes. He gave another soldier his credit card and sent him to nearby stores to buy all the maps of Manhattan he could find. The commander next instructed his clerk to call in everyone else—though that seemed unnecessary, as scores of soldiers in the unit had already traded their civilian clothes for their fatigues and begun reporting to the armory without orders.

A casual observer might think Daniels's actions that morning were in keeping with the official homeland defense plan used by the 69th. But in truth, there *was* no homeland defense plan, and certainly nothing that covered what was unfolding as a multiple-target terrorist attack against the United States. The only recent scenario that the men of the Fighting 69th had war-gamed that even approached the scale of 9/11 was the Y2K "Millennium Bug" contingency plan, which itself was culled together from disparate instructions designed for a response to a hurricane on Long Island. In the hours after the attack, several elements of the New York National Guard began implementing aspects of that plan, including an Air Force major on Long Island who called the 69th and directed it to bring its trucks out to Westhampton Air Base, seventy-five miles from the eye of the storm, in the event troops assembled there and needed transportation. Daniels took the call and reasoned with him with his trademark expletive-laden common sense.

"Sir, how many dead bodies do you have out at Westhampton Air Base right now?" Daniels asked. "How many soldiers do you think you're gonna have out at Westhampton Air Base in the next hour? I'll tell you—none. So why the hell do you think you need my fucking vehicles out at Westhampton Air Base? This is not fucking Y2K. The war is here in the city, and I need all my vehicles here now."

The Air Force officer was only the first of several Guardsmen taken aback by Daniels's actions that morning. When a colonel from upstate

New York called for an update he got Daniels on the phone. "Right now, sir, it's mass chaos," Daniels reported. "All the soldiers are coming in, and we're getting prepared to deploy wherever the State needs us or to possibly go down to the World Trade Center just to help down there with the recovery efforts."

"Stop right there," the colonel said. "You have no authorization to bring soldiers into the armory. Send everyone home right now. This is a local police matter." Daniels said, "Roger-out, sir." In other words—and with all due respect—*Fuck off.* He hung up the phone and continued gathering soldiers for duty.

Even at the armory Daniels's actions caused some raised eyebrows. Major Obregon cringed when he learned that Daniels had posted armed guards outside the building. "Chris, what are you doing?" Obregon asked.

"Jesus, we're under fucking attack!" Daniels said. "I'm defending the fucking armory right now."

"You can't give these guys guns," Obregon insisted. He told Daniels to wait until they received orders to issue ammunition. Daniels disagreed but followed Obregon's instructions. *Maybe I am going a little overboard.* However, when the second tower collapsed and the scope of the attacks became clear, Obregon called and told him, "Chris, put the weapons back out there now."

The problem with waiting for orders to mobilize soldiers or to issue ammunition was that every echelon of command above the 69th was also waiting for orders. To deploy National Guardsmen in support of civil authorities in New York, someone first has to issue a formal request. And in the case of 9/11, many of those someones were otherwise engaged. But assuming that such a request for Guard support is made, it must then be validated by the State Emergency Management Office (SEMO). SEMO then sends the validated request to the headquarters of the New York Army National Guard, which would then draw up an official order. Of course all of this takes time. Under these circumstances, Daniels wasn't willing to wait, and he knew that Slack would back him 100 percent.

While Slack and Daniels were doing what infantrymen were trained to do—move to the sound of the guns—some bureaucrats at the State Headquarters were already prepping their CYA—cover your ass—memorandums: "At 9:30 a.m. on September 11, 2001, Colonel Pickshisnose ordered the 69th to cease and desist any actions that might be construed as martial in nature." When Daniels notified Slack that he had been ordered to stand down, Slack told him to drive on. In the commander's opinion, many of the officers at the State Headquarters were careerists, people who didn't like sticking their necks out for fear a misstep would cost them their next promotion. *Fuck them,* Slack thought. *They had been punched in the nose four times and still didn't realize they were in a fight.* Later that day one high-ranking civilian employee of the National Guard told Slack to send everyone home or be prepared to pay the salaries of all the soldiers he brought in, because the State hadn't authorized it. Slack hung up on him.

"How dare you hang up on me!" the bureaucrat shouted at Slack when he called back. "Who do you think you are?"

Colonel Slack wondered the same thing about the civilian. The battalion commander took orders only from his chain of command in the 42nd Infantry Division, and most of them were at an exercise in Kansas. They had not issued any instructions, so Slack filled the vacuum the only way he knew how—like an infantry officer. He hung up on the bureaucrat again and instructed his staff not to take any more of his calls. The commander of the Fighting 69th had by then earned a reputation in the State Headquarters as a loose cannon and a difficult person to work with. He had no patience for bureaucrats and was, by his own admission, hotheaded, short-tempered, and very demanding and aggressive. He acted on gut instinct and had tried throughout his career to surround himself with like-minded officers and sergeants, who preferred to beg for forgiveness after the fact rather than ask for permission beforehand when it came to fulfilling the Army's mission. He had no use for careerists who were worried about their next assignments, preferring leaders who were fully cognizant that they were in the Army for the short term. That awareness enabled them to think outside the box and do what seemed right for the mission at hand, rather than what played well for their careers. The 69th officers and NCOs were free to stick their necks out and then look Slack square in the eye and say, "Well, I dare you to tell me that what I did was wrong, because that was the choice that I had, and I acted on it. All right, so there were some mistakes involved, but God dammit, what else would you have had me do?" Slack had built a team of freethinkers who were willing to act extemporaneously, perhaps even hastily. It made the Fighting 69th bold and at times downright frightening to outsiders.

One risky decision some of Slack's officers had made prior to 9/11 was already paying off. The officers were charged with securing hundreds of rifles and machine guns in their poorly secured armories. Yet according to New York State policy, they weren't authorized to keep any ammunition at their armories to protect the cache. It was a catch-22 the men weren't willing to tolerate. After every trip to the firing range, the officers squirreled away a few bullets here and a few there so that when someone did attack, they would be able to arm their soldiers. Of course, if Slack had found out about the secret store of ammunition, he would have ripped the troopers a new one. At the same time, Slack would have loved and respected the men for having the moxie to take the risk.

As Slack reconnoitered Ground Zero, he came across another of his leaders who had charged without orders to the attack site. First Sergeant Acevedo from Alpha Company had taken all the 69th's medics he could get his hands on, loaded them in the back of his pickup truck, and rushed them down to Ground Zero, where they provided both medical support and Spanish-language translation for paramedics from the New York Fire Department. Slack was immeasurably proud.

But not all the 69th's leaders were able to cut loose from work to get into the armory. Dozens of his senior men were already committed to responding in their civilian roles as police officers and firefighters. Battalion Logistics Officer Captain Pat Macklin was a city cop working at the NYPD Operations Unit at 1 Police Plaza; he wouldn't leave his station for days. Bravo Company Commander First Lieutenant Cliff Mason was also in the NYPD; he was assisting with evacuation efforts near the New York Stock Exchange. Delta Company Platoon Leader Second Lieutenant Alfred Trentalange was a firefighter based in Midtown; he was sifting through the pile in search of his comrades. His Army boss, Delta Company Commander First Lieutenant Mike Drew, another police officer, was loading his cruiser with oxygen tanks, blankets, and blood from NYU Medical Center to rush down to the Beekman Street Hospital, a medical facility four blocks from Ground Zero that had been established in response to a 1920 terrorist bombing on Wall Street that claimed the lives of thirty-eight civilians and left four hundred more wounded.

Mike Drew got word that the second tower had collapsed while he was still gathering supplies. He knew that many of his police and firefighter friends had already headed downtown; he feared the worst. He thought about the boys from Engine 8, Ladder 2. Drew had halted traffic outside their station earlier to speed their trip to the towers. He could still see the face of one of the firefighters who had given him a wave and a thumbs-up as the truck passed by. The prospects of what happened to them pissed him off, his anger eventually spilling out onto a handful of civilians far from the danger zone who complained to him about not having a way to get home. *You're worried about getting home? How about you worry about the cops and firefighters down at the fucking Trade Center!* Another woman walked up to Drew, presumably to ask him another selfish, stupid question. He snapped at her. "What do you want!"

"I can't find my husband. I don't know if he was still . . . what do I do?"

Up until then Drew hadn't really thought about the civilians in the building, so focused was he on the rescue workers. But the woman's words struck him in the face like a bat. She was a slight professional woman in her early fifties with gray-streaked brown hair. She could have been Drew's mom, and all she wanted to do was find her husband.

He directed the woman to a Red Cross worker, and then got the hell out of there.

Drew pulled his cruiser onto the FDR Drive and headed downtown. Although it was normally crowded with six lanes of civilian cars, only one lane was now open for emergency vehicles. The rest of the highway was crowded shoulder-to-shoulder with thousands of ash-coated and bloodied civilians walking north. Among the mass of people were a dozen more Fighting 69th men who had survived the attack as citizens and then set off on foot for the armory to report for duty as soldiers.

They weren't alone. All across the metro area soldiers from the National Guard had watched the towers fall and concluded independently that there was only one thing to do. Jay Olmo was installing a kitchen in a house on Long Island when the TV switched to live coverage of the attack. *If there was ever a time to report for Army duty, this was it,* he thought. Olmo collected his tools and left for the city.

The scene at the armory was chaotic. The locker rooms were packed with soldiers donning their uniforms and checking their equipment, while other troops tested radios in the hallways. Civilian workers were literally running in and out of the drill floor as they struggled to break down a trade show that had been set up in the massive space, which usually doubled as a sort of civic center for the art community. Another group of civilians with conspicuously short haircuts loitered around the armory looking for a mission. These were other Guardsmen, reservists, and active-duty soldiers, Marines, sailors, and airmen from all over the country who were in New York on business or pleasure. Since they were away from their units they reported to the 69th Regiment Armory to await follow-on instructions. They were joined by another score of former and retired military personnel, often in incomplete and ill-fitting uniforms, who had also shown up and asked, "How can I help?"

Olmo's first sergeant, Rich Acevedo, had already left for the Trade Center with the medics when Olmo arrived at the armory. So without other instructions, the soldier joined a squad of men that was checking in with Captain Daniels. The officer was organizing the battalion's actions while Slack and Obregon conducted their recon. He was sitting at a desk in Obregon's office when the soldiers walked in.

"Who's got a five-ton license?" Daniels asked as they walked through the door. Olmo and the other soldiers looked at one another. "A fucking *truck* license—who's got a fucking five-ton truck license?"

"I've got one, but it's out-of-date," Olmo said.

"Do you still know how to drive?"

"Roger."

Daniels grabbed the license, a computer-generated document that listed all the vehicles Olmo was qualified to operate. Daniels reached for a pencil, rubbed out the old expiration date, scribbled in a new one, and signed his name.

"Congratulations, you can drive again," he said. "Go find a truck and get ready to move."

"Move where?" Olmo asked.

"You didn't see two big fucking buildings collapse?"

Slack had called back from the attack site and told Daniels he wanted to start getting platoon-sized elements down to the Trade Center as they reported in for duty. The battalion commander had drawn three conclusions from his recon: the police department needed more people to provide security, the fire department needed more people to help with the recovery effort, and perhaps most striking, nobody seemed to be in charge of the site. Slack decided that the National Guard could fill the vacuum. After his conversation with Daniels, Slack called in his observations to his boss in Buffalo. The 3rd Brigade commander had already heard from his chain of command and informed Slack that the governor had ordered the entire 69th Infantry to duty.

Not that he needed the affirmation, but Slack's decision to call in his soldiers was now officially validated. But before he could get any of his men on the ground, he received another order that placed him under the control of the 53rd Troop Command, which had elements operating out of the Park Avenue Armory on Manhattan's Upper East Side. The 53rd Troop Command was a collection of support units that did not typically lead operational missions. According to the provisions of the New York National Guard natural disaster plan, Slack's maneuver battalion would fall under the operational command of this outfit, stereotypically a group of men and women not known for decisive action. In addition to the 69th, two other 3rd Brigade units in New York City were cut to the supporters: the 1st Battalion, 101st Calvary Regiment, based on Staten Island; and the 1st Battalion, 258th Field Artillery Regiment, based in Queens. Slack linked up with the other two unit commanders and headed for the Park Avenue Armory, where he expected to be told to stop pushing forward. But the general in charge of the Troop Command had not yet arrived, and afraid to commit to a course of action without him, the senior officer at Park Avenue said he'd call Slack later. Given the state of emergency, Slack and the other two commanders declined to wait for further guidance and returned to the 69th Regiment Armory to draw up a plan.

When the commander of the Troop Command did make contact the next day, he lauded the colonels' actions. Brigadier General Edward Klein, a retired New York City cop, knew it was a life-or-death situation downtown and thanked God that he had three aggressive battalion commanders making the decisions on site—not some general or politician farther up the Hudson River. He contemplated how bad the situation could have been if Slack and the other battalion commanders—Lieutenant Colonel Mario Costagliola of the 101st and Lieutenant Colonel Frank Candiano of the 258th—had been paralyzed by fear, afraid to make a decision. Imagine if they had had to tell some frantic fire, police, or hospital official that, "This has to go through my headquarters, and I can't do it; sorry." Klein told the colonels to continue with what they were doing: "If you make a good, common-sense decision, as long as I'm the commander and I'm wearing the star and I'm in the National Guard, I'll back you."

By 6:00 p.m. Slack and the other commanders had reconvened at the 69th Armory in a makeshift operations center the staff had established in the unit's ornate regimental room, which was decorated with a silk flag that grateful Irish citizens of New York had presented in gratitude to the roguish 69th after it had refused to march in support of the Prince of Wales in 1860. In front of the flag, Slack's staff had set up an easel with a crude map of Lower Manhattan. The three National Guard commanders huddled around the sketch. Under the watchful gaze of a massive portrait of General Douglas MacArthur, the colonels war-gamed different courses of action until they agreed on a plan. Before returning to their individual units, the men stared at one another for a moment in silence. To the staff officers who watched from a distance, their collective gazes seemed to say, "Ready or not, here we come!"

BEIRUT-ON-HUDSON

The Fighting 69th unloaded from a small fleet of city buses at Battery Park around 6:30 on the morning of September 12. Thick smoke still rose out of Ground Zero several blocks to the north, but the scene at the Battery was deathly quiet. Several inches of ash and dust covered the ground and trees, and, it seemed, the air itself. Whenever the soldiers took a step, the powder puffed up to knee level, turning their green, brown, and black woodland camouflage pants a ghostly gray. Women's shoes, discarded briefcases, computer disks, and sheets of paper lay scattered like snow-covered leaves. Cars were abandoned with their doors open and keys in the ignition. Hot dog carts sat untended in the middle of the street. Baby strollers rested on their sides. The men gagged on the putrid stench of concrete, melted plastic, and other carnage. Those who had them put on cloth face masks and stared blankly for a moment before getting under way.

The company commanders had conducted a reconnaissance with Slack in the early morning hours when the only sound coming out of Ground Zero was water from the broken pipes and fire engines splashing onto asphalt and metal. When their troops arrived, they marched the soldiers into their various appointed sectors. The level of destruction increased violently as they moved closer to Ground Zero. Echo Company Commander Captain John Colombo, normally a DEA agent, stared at a destroyed fire engine about five hundred yards from where he set up his command post. The truck engine was still running, but water spewed from the vehicle in every direction. Colombo thought the vehicle looked like a wounded and dying animal just trying to hold on. A car nearby had been split in half lengthwise, as if by a giant axe, a pool of blood still wet in the passenger's seat. Other cars were crushed flat. A little farther north, a group of Colombo's soldiers huddled around a debris-covered flowerbed that had once separated north- and southbound traffic on the West Side Highway. It was now the resting place for a young girl who Colombo later learned had fallen from one of the airplanes. The soldiers, tough inner-city kids who would never show fear or emotion on the streets of New York, fell upon each other in tears, lamenting the loss as if she were their own sister. Other soldiers encountered similar scenes as they marched into security positions around Ground Zero.

Slack and the other two battalion commanders had devised a security plan in concert with the NYPD wherein the National Guard, with its roughly twelve hundred soldiers, would establish a cordon around Ground Zero. In general, actions inside the cordon would be under the jurisdiction of the fire department, while actions outside it would be controlled by the NYPD. Because more soldiers were needed during daylight operations, the colonels opted to use one battalion as the night force and two battalions as the day force. Since most of the 258th's soldiers had reported for duty in the city itself—as opposed to the 69th and the 101st, both of which also had companies outside the city—the 258th was first to head downtown. They deployed to Ground Zero at nightfall on September 11 and secured the perimeter until relieved at 7:00 a.m. September 12 by the 69th on the west side of the cordon and the 101st on the east side. Also at Ground Zero was Bravo Company of the 105th Infantry, one of the well-funded units to which many of the 69th's best soldiers had fled a decade earlier. The 105th guys screened relief workers at the base of the debris pile.

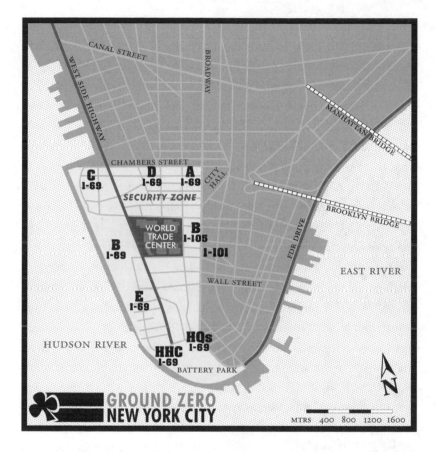

The 69th soldiers were in their standard-issue battle-dress uniform and black boots. For extra protection from falling debris, as well as the possibility of a secondary attack, the men also wore flak jackets, helmets, and leather gloves. They were issued flimsy white face masks to filter the air, but many took them off after they became filthy or just too much of a pain in the ass to use. The 101st Cavalry troopers upped their posture slightly by stationing a Humvee and an armored personnel carrier, both mounted with .50-caliber machine guns, in front of City Hall. But that didn't last long; the City and State of New York wanted a show of force, but the armor was a bit too showy.

In fact, the governor had directed that the National Guard respond without arms, causing a fair amount of consternation among the

69th's officers and men. All the company commanders thought the call was bullshit. "Are we securing an area or just providing more targets for the terrorists?" one of them chided. Sergeant Joe Minning, a Bravo Company soldier who had just transferred into the 69th from the elite 82nd Airborne Divison, wanted to know why he had to wear a flak vest and helmet in case of a second wave of attacks, but couldn't have a rifle to defend himself if they came. "What are we supposed to do if there is another attack, just tuck our tails between our legs and run?" In Alpha Company, Jay Olmo tried to be more pragmatic and asked, "What are you gonna do, shoot a plane out of the sky before it hits anything?" Slack entertained the strong opinions of his leaders, many of whom carried a gun in their civilian jobs. To a man, they wanted arms for self-defense. But Slack had his own serious concerns. In an e-mail to his brigade commander just a week before 9/11, Slack wrote, "We have a deep problem with shooting capability within this command. Most of my men never handle a rifle except when in uniform, and then mostly with blank ammo. This is not a part of the State that regularly handles weapons." Worried that an eighteen-year-old kid with limited shooting experience might get spooked and take out some civilians, Slack struck a compromise: He issued Beretta 9-millimeter pistols with one magazine to all his officers, since they generally had more training with the rules of engagement. In addition, he stockpiled his rifles and ammunition near his command post at Battery Park, easily accessible in case the situation changed.

The battalion intelligence officer, Captain Mike Dunn, concurred with Slack's decision. Dunn had given the commander his intelligence estimate in the hours after the first attack: The enemy's targets were clearly national symbols with significant media value. Dunn didn't expect suicide car bombers or other small-scale attempts and in his mind the only possibility was that the enemy might strike against the first responders. But even that seemed less likely as every minute passed. Dunn suggested the enemy had shot his load.

But weapons or not, the Fighting 69th represented the tip of the spear for the entire U.S. Army. In fact, many civilians assumed the soldiers they saw in New York or on the television news marching down to Ground Zero on September 12 were the Army's most elite troops. As one group of soldiers moved into position at dawn's early light, a civilian cheered from the sidewalk. He thought the men were paratroopers from the 82nd Airborne Division. "When did you guys get in?" he asked one of the troops. "Did you fly straight out of Fort Bragg?"

"Fort Bragg?" one citizen-soldier responded. "I'm from Queens."

The first soldiers at Ground Zero were, in fact, the nation's last line of defense. As a group they were generally undertrained, under-resourced, and underled. One of their own described them as "the Bad News Bears." They had been written off as a joke by the State and as a waste of resources by the Pentagon, and weren't even in the Big Army's war plan. But when the smoke started to clear from southern Manhattan, Americans saw Gotham's own weekend warriors, and the country breathed a sigh of relief.

Nobody was happier to see the troops arrive than the beleaguered police officers who had been in and around Ground Zero for nearly twenty-four hours. They viewed the National Guard as a relief force, as opposed to simple augmentation. From one post to the next cops were hopping in their cars and taking off to finally get some rest. Even police sergeants and lieutenants told their patrolmen that the military had control of the situation. Slack and Daniels spent much of their first day at Ground Zero trying to explain to various NYPD officers that the Guard was working for *them* and could do little without police backing. At each of their key positions inside the 69th's area of responsibility, the pair sought out patrolmen and asked how they could help. To a man the cops responded, "Hell, you're in charge now."

The situation eventually improved when the NYPD established a command post adjacent to Slack's headquarters at the tip of Battery Park. Whenever an Army commander had an issue, he would call Slack's command post—usually on his personal cell phone, as opposed to a military radio—and ask for help. A staff officer would then run across the street to the police trailer and relay the request, and the problem was usually fixed within minutes. As the day progressed and everybody learned the ground rules, both the NYFD and NYPD started asking the 69th for assistance.

One of its first missions was to help the fire department search rooftops near Ground Zero for human remains and aircraft parts. The 69th's Scout Platoon handled that task and indeed found both. More requests followed. The NYFD needed help at the debris pile itself. In the early days, when hope of finding survivors was high, no heavy equipment was used on the collapsed Trade Center. Instead, the fire department used "bucket brigades," lines of people passing pieces from the top of the pile to the bottom. The 69th provided as many men as possible to support that detail.

Soldiers were also asked to clear the area of journalists. At first Slack had wanted to ensure that reporters had free access to the site so the rest of America could understand the horrific nature of the attack as forcefully as he did, but some photographers began trying to aim their cameras toward human remains. "There's a difference between showing people what's happening and taking close-up shots of disemboweled women and children," he told his men. Slack believed the attack had robbed America of a lot of dignity, so as he had with the woman's foot the day before, he made it his battalion's mission to give some of that respect back to the victims of the attack, to give them privacy in death. After word spread of a photographer who had snuck into the morgue to take pictures, soldiers were more than happy to comply with the edict and escort media out of the secure area. And if the troops accidentally dropped a journalist's camera in the process, well, that wasn't necessarily a bad thing, either. Some soldiers chased away so many journalists and other carnage-seeking shutterbugs that their legs were cramped by the end of their first shift at Ground Zero.

The pictures that haunted the soldiers most, however, were not shot at Ground Zero. Some were taken in backyards, some at the office, others at school. But all were hanging on the walls of the 69th

Regiment Armory when the soldiers of the battalion pulled up to the headquarters late on September 12. The concrete-and-brick facade of the building had become an endless sea of white flyers, each featuring a photo of a smiling man, woman, or child, with the words "MISS-ING" or "LAST SEEN" or "HELP" typed out in large font. The home of the Fighting 69th had become a shrine—or, in the words of one soldier, a big graveyard of dead souls.

Standing along the walls in a line that stretched around the block were the thousands of people who had hung the photos. While the 69th was working at Ground Zero, the City of New York's Office of Community Affairs had turned the armory into the family bereavement center, the place people would come to register their missing children, spouses, parents, or friends. Men and women, old and young, were panicked, desperate, scared. One man grabbed a Guardsman by the shoulders as he got off the bus. "Have you seen my baby?" he cried. "Have you seen my little girl?" He fell into the soldier's arms. The civilians saw the GIs' legs covered in ash and dust and wanted to know what was happening at Ground Zero, how many people they had rescued, was there any hope? Did they see Patrick or Mary? Of course, the Guardsmen hadn't seen any of them, but they promised that they would look, and that they would do everything they could. Many of the troops cried with the civilians. Many more pushed past with their heads down because they had seen the remains of the World Trade Center and knew nobody was coming out alive.

The drill floor, which had housed a trade show on Tuesday morning, was now carpeted, air-conditioned, filled with two thousand chairs, dozens of desks and computers and fold-out tables covered with forms and booklets about how to deal with loss. Families sat alongside the desks providing information to volunteers, and on subsequent trips bringing DNA samples from combs or toothbrushes. In the days to come even more sheets of paper were taped to the outside walls, from ground level to the height of outstretched and shaking arms. Candles were lit on the sidewalks, and people huddled in prayer groups or stared alone into nothing.

Among the pleas hanging on the armory was one that contained a grainy picture of Gerard Baptiste, a veteran of the Fighting 69th who had served as Jay Olmo's first platoon leader in Alpha Company. First Lieutenant Baptiste, a firefighter based out of Greenwich Village, would later be discovered to have died in the South Tower while trying to rescue civilians. Tommy Jurgens, another veteran who had finished his last drill with the Fighting 69th just weeks before, was also killed in the attack. The former 69th specialist was a police officer in the city courthouse up the street from Ground Zero. He and several of his comrades jumped into a van and rushed to the tower. Four of the twelve perished. Other soldiers learned later that they had lost family and friends in the attack. The entire crew of the fire truck for which Lieutenant Drew had halted traffic on the morning of 9/11 was killed.

On the second floor of the armory the men slumped in chairs or lay on cots and tried to rest. But even their exhaustion wasn't always enough to induce sleep. Concern for their own families, the cries of the grieving downstairs, and the sights of the day kept many of them awake until the buses came to get them at 6:00 the next morning to take them back to Ground Zero.

3: THE STRATEGIC RESERVE

NOT READY FOR PRIME TIME

Slack reclined in his office chair on the first floor of the 69th Regiment Armory and let out a long breath. He was physically exhausted from five consecutive nights without sleep and from dozens of miles of foot patrols around Lower Manhattan. He closed his eyes and let some of the pressure of his command release. Guard units from upstate New York had relieved the 69th at Ground Zero, and for the moment Slack had no mission except to decompress. He had sent his soldiers home an hour earlier to do the same, which disappointed a team of Army mental-health counselors who had just arrived at the armory to help the men cope. But Slack told the team he wasn't overly worried about them; they were tough inner-city kids trained as combat-arms soldiers, and you couldn't crack them with a hammer. Sure, they had grieved during the past week; virtually all the men knew someone killed in the tragedy. But they grieved as a team, as a squad, and then went back to work. The men were determined to help their city and their unit move forward, and they had served brilliantly in that task. Slack conceded that some of his soldiers would likely have emotional difficulties now that they had left their support group. But that was normal, wasn't it? Their town and their friends had been attacked. They were going to have to suffer a little bit, every one of them.

Slack turned in his seat to look at one of the "missing" flyers for

Lieutenant Baptiste, which a soldier had found on the wall of the armory and passed along to him. The commander had a vision of Baptiste in the field. The young lieutenant sat smiling atop an armored personnel carrier full of soldiers. He was vibrant, confident, and had earned the respect of his men. Now he was gone—poof. For the first time in a week, raw emotion began to replace Slack's command clarity. He was overcome with pride in his soldiers and in men like Gerard Baptiste who had responded to the Trade Center. But he was also enraged. All week long people had been comparing the attacks to Pearl Harbor, but that had been an engagement between two armies. September 11 was just murder, and Slack felt a deep hatred for the type of men who could commit such a crime. A short-tempered and aggressive man by nature—in his younger days Slack wouldn't hesitate to pummel a rude or disrespectful stranger—the commander began to foster a burning desire to kill anyone affiliated with the terrorists, whether Bin Laden, his deputies, the Taliban, or any one of those bastards in the Middle East who cheered the destruction of the towers. *They came into the heart of our city! They killed our brothers and sisters!* The men in the battalion told the commander they felt the same. They were ready to fight like the Irish Wolfhounds the regiment was named for, to chase down the running terrorists. The purpose of an infantry battalion was to go to war, and the president had said earlier in the week that America was now at war. Someone just had to give New York's Ol' 69th Infantry Regiment a chance to fight again.

But when the United States began dropping big bombs on the heads of Al Qaida and the Taliban three weeks later on October 7, 2001, the 69th seemed far from the fight. Instead of combat, the staff of the Fighting 69th was back near Ground Zero, trying to determine whether to get lunch from the mobile Outback Steakhouse near the ferry terminal or the relief tent staffed with a squad of comely young women near the tip of Battery Park. They chose the latter, which they had affectionately nicknamed "the Hoochie Koochie" in honor of its volunteers.

Slack's respite in his office had been brief. Before releasing his men on the first Sunday after 9/11, he had told them he never wanted to return to Ground Zero. But instead of mobilizing for an action overseas, Slack went home only to receive follow-on orders for another two weeks of security in Lower Manhattan.

When the commander arrived back at Battery Park on October 6, he found Ground Zero to be a different place. While the pile of rubble that was the Trade Center looked about the same, the rest of the area had changed drastically. The 69th's ten-man headquarters run out of two Humvees was now occupied by scores of soldiers working out of tractor trailers that expanded into mobile command posts, complete with every cable channel Time Warner could give them. A dozen green tents were also set up throughout the park. Instead of shuttling back and forth to the 69th Regiment Armory, soldiers now ferried to Ground Zero on boats from a barracks on Governors Island, a former Coast Guard station and naval base. While only a thousand Guardsmen had been present during the first week, there were now close to five thousand. The civilian support structure had expanded as well. In the first few days, the soldiers ate Army rations or food from Red Cross trailers. Now they had the option of filet mignon or sandwiches from Tavern on the Green. Relief tents were so numerous that soldiers couldn't go a block without someone shoving food in their faces. All nature of services thrived. A virtual department store of donated construction gear was set up near the Hudson River. Clergymen of every faith wandered the area, comforting the workers. Massage therapists had set up their tables. Football players from the New York Giants toured the site, thanking the workers. The brigade commander found himself nestled between four Playboy Bunnies for a photo op. In the first days only Gothamites had gathered at Ground Zero. Three weeks after the attack, the full weight of American generosity had landed on the tip of Manhattan. The soldiers, along with the other rescue and recovery personnel, had become rock stars. Wherever they went, people cheered, waved flags, offered free food, free batteries, free socks, free paper, even free admission to strip clubs. One soldier who ventured into a Manhattan massage parlor found a letter of appreciation from an upstate National Guard colonel already taped to the wall.

Slack was amazed at how quickly America had mobilized in response to the attack. Trucks from all over the country arrived at the armory with pallet after pallet of food and equipment. Other vendors called the armory looking to donate items, and if they couldn't get an answer there, they tracked down Slack's home number and offered Debbie goods and services. One meat supplier wanted to send her forty-five thousand pounds of raw beef. Slack was impressed with the outpouring of support and personnel, but found much of it to be a distraction at Ground Zero.

More bothersome, however, was the presence of a higher headquarters. During the first week, the triumvirate of combat-arms officers was the sole source of martial leadership in New York City. Now the commander had to suffer some second-guessing and bureaucratic taskings from senior Guard officers. In addition to a new command structure, Slack also had to contend with a fresh batch of soldiers, for alongside 69th men were small detachments from around the state. Most were combat-arms soldiers, tankers, and engineers from Buffalo, but he also had a detachment of troops from the Naval Militia and a flight of Air Force National Guardsmen—and women. Slack was an old-fashioned soldier and didn't relish the responsibility of commanding women, especially airwomen who didn't have the proper equipment or training to stand a post for twelve hours. But he was also realistic. In addition to its being the twenty-first century, duty at Ground Zero in October was not as tense as it had been in September.

The mission had changed. In the week after the attacks, the 69th had secured the perimeter of Ground Zero, assisted police and fire officials with recovery efforts, and escorted the residents of apartment buildings near the Trade Center in and out of their homes to recover pets, medications, and other key personal belongings. But when the U.S. launched air strikes against Afghanistan, the 69th and other National Guard units assisted the police in securing all of Lower Manhattan. Platoons of soldiers left the Trade Center cordon and took positions at the entrances and exits of the bridges and tunnels leading from the boroughs into Manhattan. Soldiers established checkpoints to search vehicles (and in at least one instance to vomit after opening some poorly refrigerated trucks full of thawing chicken and gnawing rats headed downtown; some of the soldiers on loan to the 69th from Buffalo swore never to eat in New York City again). Other 69th soldiers were attached to the Federal Emergency Management Agency (FEMA) and tasked to stop organized crime from pilfering the bent steel girders being removed from the Trade Center. Tons of the sacred metal had already found its way to New Jersey scrap yards. Petty thieves were also caught looting in the buildings that surrounded the Trade Center, and to combat that threat, soldiers conducted roving foot and golfcart patrols through key areas, nailed plywood over smashed windows, and vectored police to any suspicious activity.

To the casual observer it might have looked like martial law had been declared in southern New York. But many of the soldiers were concerned they were little more than window dressing for a worried populace. The men didn't have guns or arrest authority, prompting one officer who was a city cop when in civilian life to worry. *God help us if we're attacked,* he thought. *We're nothing more than aiming points for the next terrorist.*

A lack of firearms was only one of the concerns. While the Fighting 69th had responded magnificently to the situation in New York, they were still the same unit that struggled to conduct realistic training, that was hobbled by broken and rusted equipment, whose armory was infested with rodents, and whose reputation for thievery and other mischief was so bad that other units put extra guards on their gear whenever 69th soldiers were around. Before September 11 many soldiers and officers believed the 69th would quit its bad habits if it was ever called for a real-world operation. But in a handful of cases, the men carried those same habits right down to Ground Zero. Several soldiers loaded up on clothes and other gear intended for rescue workers, while two were caught looting in vacated buildings. Two others were reprimanded for showing up too hungover for duty. One officer accepted a payment for escorting a civilian into his home. A company commander roughed up a photographer. Another commander was relieved after abandoning soldiers at a remote post.

But even with those warts, the 69th Infantry that responded to attacks in Lower Manhattan in 2001 was a much improved version of the 69th Infantry that had handed out hot dogs in Lower Manhattan to returning Desert Storm veterans in 1991, when Slack and other soldiers from his old unit had reluctantly joined the regiment.

First Sergeant Acevedo, a smooth-faced Hispanic Customs agent who never seemed without a fat cigar, had been in Slack's Long Island command in the 71st Infantry for a few months before that unit closed. When Acevedo was transferred to the 69th, the former Big Army NCO was shocked at the lawless, brawling nature of the unit. In short order he learned it was normal in the 69th to smoke marijuana or drink beer on the way to drill; it was customary for soldiers to tell sergeants to fuck off; it wasn't a surprise when leaders who were corrections officers in the civilian world would see their soldiers from the 69th processed into Rikers Island prison Monday only to report for Army duty Saturday. His first company commander in the 69th was relieved for using cocaine. Another soldier was arrested for rape. On one weekend Acevedo got into a fight with another sergeant that didn't break up until a tire iron and bayonet became the weapons of choice. Fighting was the standard method of settling disputes in the 69th in the 1990s. Ace recalled lieutenants duking it out in the woods. Even Slack got into the spirit of things: during one training event he chased down a fellow captain and gave him a well-deserved clobbering.

By 2001, however, Acevedo found that the 69th had largely grown out of that phase—or at least moved it underground. The number of soldiers "pissing hot" for drug use was lower, and Acevedo hadn't seen any high-ranking soldiers in a good fight since 1999, when Slack tried to chase Daniels down for a good ass-beating. Daniels was one step faster and wisely ran off into the darkness of Fort Dix.

There were pockets of progress throughout the battalion, and both Acevedo and Daniels (who never held a grudge against Slack's attempt to wring his neck) believed Slack had been the catalyst for change. Even before he took over the battalion outright, Slack was hammering the company commanders to develop battle rosters, to deliver operations orders, and—as basic as it sounds—to train like infantrymen. For years the battalion had been focused on finding new soldiers and keeping old ones. But when Slack took command, his philosophy was to train instead of recruit. *Damn the State. Let them fire me. This is the way I run my battalion.*

Daniels loved it. Even though the captain knew the 69th would itself never be posted anywhere, he believed he had the responsibility to train the younger soldiers, because one day they might decide to join the Big Army and wind up in a Middle East shithole fighting Islamic extremists or other bad guys. In addition, the new focus on training versus recruiting actually resulted in a larger unit. Good training is fun, and once the guys knew they would do something cool on the weekend, more of them decided to stick around when their enlistments were up.

Slack was also a stickler for standards. He lectured his commanders on the importance of training correctly, of wearing the uniform correctly, and of customs and courtesies like saluting. Some of the commanders resented his condescending lessons and his attention to minutia that the junior officers thought was outside his lane. But like it or not, the commanders and NCOs started enforcing standards that they wouldn't or couldn't enforce before.

"When you're one commander in the 69th, and there are no standards anywhere, you can't stand up in front of your company and say, 'This is the way it's gonna be,'" Daniels told another officer. "Everyone's gonna tell you to fuck off, and you're not gonna get any support from the top." But Slack gave Daniels and the other commanders all the top cover they needed. If nothing else, Daniels explained to his men that Slack was loony tunes, so they had all just better do what he said if they wanted to make it through the weekend alive.

Daniels had found it easy to train his infantrymen on Long Island. He had a core of old-timers to run the bar and a small group of young kids that liked to get dirty and do Army infantry stuff. But Daniels hardly knew where to start with his HHC, an urban cornucopia among which he was obliged to find the mechanics, fuelers, cooks, administrators, and the other flotsam and jetsam needed to support an infantry unit. He was slated to have 300 soldiers, but had only 165, of whom he had to discharge 65 immediately because they were habitually AWOL. Many of his remaining men didn't know what their jobs were, and if they did know, they had little equipment to work with. What wasn't lost was stacked haphazardly in dozens of dark corners of the armory basement. Daniels quickly concluded he had his work cut out for him, and Slack gave him all the leeway necessary to get the job done. Normally the head of internal auditing at Fimat, a global brokerage company, Daniels began to take one day off of work per week from his civilian job to begin sorting the mess. He asked his soldiers why they had joined the Army and sent them to retraining if necessary. He organized the men into squads and platoons. And he latched on to a young full-time clerk, whom he sent weekly to the State Headquarters armed with bottles of whiskey in an effort to grease the necessary palms to get what his men needed.

The strategy worked. Before long, rumor spread among the men in the 69th that the HHC was the place to be—especially if one wanted to get paid or promoted. Some soldiers sought transfer there from the line companies. Acevedo lost dozens of his Alpha Company men to Daniels, which wasn't necessarily a bad thing. Many of the soldiers who left were having trouble going along with the strict sergeant's Big Army rules and regulations. If a soldier didn't want to play Acevedo's way, then he was happy to facilitate a transfer to HHC. The same thing happened on Long Island. Out at Bravo Company, the commander, Lieutenant Cliff Mason, proclaimed he wanted no junior troops over age thirty-five. Daniels, who had scores of non-infantry jobs to fill, could care less how old or fat the men were so long as they could perform. Within nine months, Daniels found enough equipment and recruited enough misfits and castoffs from the line companies to boost the HHC to a ramshackle but somewhat functional level. After the battalion's annual training in July 2001, Slack commented in an e-mail to his commanders and staff that the "HHC showed just how really great a company it can be!"

But was it great enough to fend off a terrorist attack against the Brooklyn Bridge? Great enough to go to war?

The 69th had made definite strides since 1991, but their progress was dependent on the exceptionally hard work of a handful of soldiers. Daniels was physically rebuilding the Headquarters Company, but if he bled to death from a paper cut on his day job, the unit would have fallen to pieces. That was the case in every company in the battalion. Infantry units can function in battle only if the soldiers know and are prepared to do the job of the guy two ranks higher, but the Fighting 69th had no reliable bench. Even if the battalion had had any depth among its leadership, they'd have been lucky to get half the team to the game. The 69th's maintenance officer, Chief Warrant Officer Bill Solmo, described the unit's equipment in 2001 as a mere one on a scale of one to ten. It was "atrocious, neglected, and cannibalized, worse than any other unit's equipment in the state." The 69th was a mechanized infantry battalion, but in July it had made it to annual training on bubble gum repairs. There were vehicles whose tires were falling off and had no brakes, no seat belts, no windshield wipers, cracked windows, and no mirrors. "Exhaust systems and entire engines could literally fall out on the road," Solmo said. He thought the unit would be lucky to get out of its own way.

Ready for war? Specialist Jay Olmo, who was in Acevedo's Alpha Company, doubted it. Though he was spoiling for a fight like the rest of the battalion, he didn't think the 69th was ready for prime time. If Acevedo told Olmo that he would be going to a real shooting war with the 69th, the soldier knew what his answer would be. "Go fuck your mother. Not with you, not with the leadership we have. I wouldn't play paint ball with you guys. High ho, Canada, here I come!"

THE ROUGHNECKS

While the Fighting 69th as a whole was beginning to show signs of life under Slack's leadership, Alpha Company was floundering. When Olmo first joined, it was the largest of the 69th's four infantry units, topping out at near 120 soldiers of only 111 authorized. But by October 2001, the company had imploded.

Olmo had come to Alpha Company from the 258th Field Artillery in 1997. He had always wanted to be in the infantry and got the chance when the 69th dumped its Stingers. He was impressed the moment he walked in. Soldiers were hustling about, packing rucksacks and talking about messing around with the other units when they got the field. There was an energy about the place. Olmo wasn't sure what platoon he was supposed to be in, so he reported to Lieutenant Baptiste, the 1st Platoon leader. The officer grabbed Olmo by the collar and told him that since he was the new guy he would carry the radio, an antiquated PRC-77, which hadn't been taught in Army schools for years. But Olmo, who was good with his hands, figured the machine out quickly and fell in line behind Lieutenant Baptiste as the platoon went into the field. Carrying the officer's radio was more responsibility than Olmo had been given in his entire military career and he enjoyed it. Instead of drinking and fucking off, Baptiste led the platoon on multiple mock raids against other 69th units throughout the night. Though it might have been more fun with a buzz on, Olmo loved the Army duty and felt something new: for the first time, he was already looking forward to his next drill.

But the positive outlook didn't last. Over the next four years, three company commanders had got the boot by Slack. Six other lieutenants struggled with the platoons before leaving for greener pastures. What few enlisted leaders the company once claimed had retired or quit when they weren't promoted. Finally, Slack pulled Alpha Company's first sergeant, Pedro Sanchez, and reassigned him to the HHC with Daniels. Alpha could suffer changes in officers, but the loss of Sanchez broke the company's back. Many of his soldiers were slavishly loyal and followed him to the HHC. Those who stuck around ultimately fled shortly thereafter, when newly promoted First Sergeant Acevedo came to Alpha. While Sanchez had focused on soldier-care issues, Acevedo's priority was standards. Like Slack, he wanted his soldiers to look and act like active-duty soldiers, not extras in a hip-hop video. Olmo shuddered during Acevedo's first formation.

"This bullshit's going to stop!" Acevedo ordered. "I want boots shined! I want haircuts and pressed uniforms! You only come here one weekend a month. That's the way I want it. If you can't do that, I'm going to clean house and get rid of everybody."

Olmo and the other soldiers were put off. "This is the Guard, man. Relax. Who are we trying to look good for? We're an infantry unit, why the fuck do we need polished boots to go into the woods?" In addition, the soldiers were suspicious of Acevedo's rapid rise through the ranks. Though it had in fact taken him more than ten years, it seemed the child-faced Acevedo had advanced from staff sergeant to sergeant first class to first sergeant in a matter of months. "Who's fuckin' balls is he rubbing?" one soldier asked. If Acevedo really wanted to clean house, he wouldn't have to scrub too hard: after that first formation, soldiers scattered to other units like New York City cockroaches when the lights come on.

Olmo, however, was stuck. He had transferred into the Fighting 69th to be an infantry soldier, and there really weren't many other options. There were no true infantry jobs in Daniels's Headquarters Company; Acevedo and Alpha Company were it. Olmo decided to go with the flow. Others stayed, too—about 40 soldiers of the required 111. But when Olmo took his place with Alpha at Ground Zero, he discovered himself standing in a platoon-sized company of lower-ranking soldiers who looked more like the last kids chosen for the basketball team on the playground than the GI commandos who were once the backbone of the company. There was the Spanish-speaking specialist Miguel Luna, a short Weebles' wobble of a soldier who was so motivated and ready to kill that he spent all his spare time sharpening a Rambo knife. His running mate was Specialist Terzy Debniak, a fifty-something Polish-born immigrant who claimed he was once a sergeant major in the Polish army. There was Michael Delancey, a skinny Irish American cop who sported a perpetual sunburn and often sweated alcohol in the field. Speaking another language and seeming to laugh behind the backs of everyone else was a fire team of Asian immigrants earning money for college. There was hardly a sergeant among them, and certainly no platoon leaders. Alpha Company now consisted of Acevedo, the commander of the month, and a mass of soldiers, with no real leadership in between. The first sergeant looked over the formation and could think of only one moniker that accurately described them—the Roughnecks. Olmo had his own nickname for them—the Nut Jobs.

As rough and nutty as they were, however, Alpha Company came to represent the entire Fighting 69th at Ground Zero, if not the entire U.S. Army. By happenstance, its position in the cordon in the first days after the attack was in front of a pool of journalists. Dozens of photographers snapped the unit's picture as they marched in formation into position on September 12. At the time Jay Olmo was thinking, *Why the hell are we marching? This is not the time for drill and ceremony. There are dead bodies all around.* But to the public, the photos of the soldiers marching with their helmets, flack vests, and paper masks reassuringly seemed to say, "Everybody relax; the cavalry has arrived."

But if the Alpha Company Roughnecks and the rest of the Fighting 69th were viewed as the cavalry, they had attained that standing almost by accident. The Big Army never called on the Fighting 69th to respond to Ground Zero, as the Department of Defense had no jurisdiction in New York City. Besides, what good could four hundred unarmed weekend warriors do in a city with some forty thousand armed police officers? It was Geoff Slack who brought the Fighting 69th to Ground Zero, like a modern-day Minuteman with the disposition of Jeb Stuart. The State of New York caught up to him and the other maverick commanders, Costagliola and Candiano, only after the fact.

The Fighting 69th was never intended to be first responders for the U.S. Army, as the planners and policy makers at the Pentagon had designed the modern National Guard as more of a strategic reserve. The Guard was never meant to mobilize and deploy on short notice for a small regional conflict, like Desert Storm, or for a peacekeeping mission, like Bosnia. It was designed solely to be called up in the event of World War III: use it once, for the big one, and then throw it away. Guardsmen were the very last line of defense for the nation and were funded, trained, equipped, and manned appropriately. By design, little money was made available for facilities and training. Equipment consisted of hand-me-downs from the active component, and units were never staffed to full strength.

This institutionalized neglect was defined in the Pentagon's tiered readiness system.

Every unit in the Army was assigned a Force Activity Designator (FAD), which coincided with its likelihood to fight. The units most likely to engage in combat received the best recourses and highest designation, FAD-I. In football terms, FAD-I was the "first string," units that were in combat or expected to fight at any moment. They included rapid-response elements like the 82nd Airborne Division, Ranger regiments, and Special Operations forces, and large cold war armor and infantry formations stationed in Germany, Korea, and other frontline overseas locations.

FAD-I units essentially had a blank check for whatever they needed, and they chose their soldiers from the best the Army had to offer. FAD-II consisted of the balance of the Army's regular combat forces stationed in the continental United States. This "second string" was expected to be prepared to deploy within twenty-four hours. While the resourcing gap between FAD-I and FAD-II units was not that great, FAD-III units were provisioned at a much lower level. This is where the top National Guard units, called "round out" or "enhanced" brigades, made their debut. While the third string never got the latest gear, they were given top-flight equipment, more personnel, and more money for training than most Guard units. Designed to augment regular Army divisions, FAD-III–enhanced brigades were slated to deploy to the fight thirty days after being mobilized. Two of these combat-maneuver brigades trained for the Persian Gulf War, the 48th Brigade from Georgia and the 256th Brigade from Louisiana. However, the train-up for both units took longer than the Army expected, and the war ended before either brigade was ready to be shipped overseas.

At the very bottom rung of the Army heirarchy were the FAD-IV units, such as the Fighting 69th. These low-priority outfits were designed to be in the fight ninety days after mobilization. But with the collapse of the Soviet Union, nobody really expected the fourth-string combat elements of the Guard to ever get the call for anything more serious than a snowstorm or flood, events with which the Pentagon wasn't overly concerned, as it considered them State issues. In fact the Army had concluded in its own planning that FAD-IV units, which made up the majority of the National Guard's combat power, were no longer needed at all. In the 1997 Quadrennial Defense Review, the Army pledged to reduce the strategic reserve and transition its combat units to a support role. The Congress disagreed and continued to fund the FAD-IV combat units for use by the States. But the Big Army was not overly concerned with the health of units like the 69th. If they wanted to camp instead of bivouac, and drink beer instead of train, nobody at the Pentagon really cared.

But the planning documents that governed the Fighting 69th's role in the Army were effectively incinerated when American Airlines Flight 77 hit the Pentagon. In the wake of the attack, Big Army officers gave their commanders new intelligence estimates. They came to the same conclusion as the 69th's Captain Dunn had on September 11: Al Qaida was targeting America's national symbols of economic and military strength. While the civilian authorities focused on the economic symbols, the Army needed to secure its military ones, places like the Pentagon. And there was only one military symbol that approached the prominence of the damaged headquarters: the U.S. Military Academy at West Point. It was a perfect target for terrorists, for in a single strike determined attackers could destroy an emblem of American power as well as hundreds, perhaps thousands, of the very officers that the Army would send to avenge September 11. The 82nd Airborne could be at West Point within hours. They could lock down the place tighter than Fort Knox, over-watch the main gate with crew-served machine guns, patrol the Hudson Highlands with light infantrymen, and scour the darkened parade field with night-vision goggles. Then again, the 82nd Airborne might also be of more value in Afghanistan. In fact, most of the Big Army seemed to have more pressing priorities than to guard a military college. But somebody had to.

In the years since the Berlin Wall came down, the Army had reduced its security to nominal levels at its bases across the United States. A majority of Army posts were "open," so much so that any schmuck could drive onto them and take pictures of tanks or troops or whatever. But the situation after 9/11 had changed. The Army needed to tighten security at their camps around the world, but there simply weren't enough troops anymore to handle the task. Since 1991 the Army had shrunk in size from eighteen active-duty divisions to just ten, had eliminated more than six hundred thousand military and civilian positions, and had closed nearly seven hundred installations. The Army was the smallest it had been since it last called the Fighting 69th to Federal duty in 1940. Moreover, the president had just launched a war in Afghanistan and, by some accounts, was already thinking about an action in Iraq. The Army simply had no regular forces to spare to secure its infrastructure, including its high-profile bastion on the Hudson. That left only one viable option.

"Hey, sir," a planner says as he holds up a picture of the Alpha Company Roughnecks in his newspaper, "what about these guys? They look pretty squared away. And they're from New York, too. I bet they could be at West Point in no time. We'd have to get them some guns, of course, but they haven't made asses of themselves at Ground Zero. What do you think?"

The case for deploying the National Guard in order to bolster se-curity at places like West Point was a slam dunk, as far as the Big Army was concerned. But nobody asked the opinion of regular old citizen-soldiers like Jay Olmo. The twenty-six-year-old contractor had three employees working for him in his kitchen-remodeling business. As a general rule, if Olmo didn't work, neither did they. Two of the men had wives and children. The third was a nineteen-year-old kid who liked to bend the elbow. Of the three, only the kid had a driver's license. But Olmo didn't trust him with his van. What if he got drunk and forgot to pick up the other guys? What if he got drunk and ran someone over? It was tough enough to get liability insurance; Olmo didn't need a DWI incident to make it harder. Further, Olmo was the guy who got new business leads, who wrote up the contracts, and who answered to the clients. If the 69th was called for any extensive duty, he knew that his business and his employees and their families were fucked. Although the United States does have laws designed to pro-tect the jobs of National Guardsmen who are involuntarily called up for Federal duty, they don't extend to independent contractors or their employees.

Olmo wasn't opposed to active-duty service; he had originally joined the Guard to get into the regular Army. But as he settled in to the Fighting 69th, it became apparent that his unit would never be called upon for anything substantial—*and God help it if it was.* So when he started his own business in 1998, he did so with the general understanding that his Guard duty would consist of one weekend a month and two weeks every summer, just like the advertisements on television promised. He believed—like most others in the 69th—that the unit would otherwise get summoned only for a week or so to sup-port a response to a hurricane or ice storm or other natural disaster. Olmo could manage that type of contingency and then get back to work. If the 69th would ever be asked to do more, he believed—like most others in the 69th—that it would be as the result of doomsday.

In that event, his employees would likely be drafted for duty as well, provided they hadn't already been killed in a nuclear detonation.

So when Acevedo notified Olmo that Alpha Company would be mobilized for Federal duty to stand guard at West Point for one year, Olmo replied that he was sorry, but as much as he'd like to go and watch over the pimply-faced, spoiled rich kids up the river, he wouldn't be able to make it.

Olmo wasn't alone in such feelings. The Fighting 69th claimed more than five hundred soldiers on its rolls, yet when the call came to send troops to West Point, the number who seemed willing and able was considerably smaller. Acevedo couldn't even track down all of his men; it seemed that when Uncle Sam called, a handful of soldiers dropped off the face of the earth. Phones were disconnected. Medical conditions were discovered. Parents claimed not to have seen their children in years. Dozens of soldiers in the 69th had something better to do. When Colonel Slack called the Bravo Company commander, Lieutenant Cliff Mason, and asked him if he would lead his company at the academy, the officer said he'd rather not. Mason had been asked by the leadership of the NYPD to help refine their tactical response to terrorist incidents, and the lieutenant believed he could make a bigger impact on the war in that capacity. Other soldiers had similar emotions. Having witnessed the devastation of New York, they wanted to kill terrorists and guard against another attack, not baby-sit cadets.

Mason was fortunate to have that opportunity; his fellow police officer and 69th commander, Mike Drew, had no such luck. He was a rank-and-file patrolman whose duties seemed to have no connection to the war. Lieutenant Drew told Slack he would be pleased to lead Mason's company at West Point. In Drew's opinion, the men of the Fighting 69th would be playing an essential role in the war, however unsexy the task. If the National Guard picked up all the low-intensity missions, it would free up more regular Army units for terrorist hunting. Drew knew that not all Army service was glamorous. His dad had served in the Fighting 69th and had been mobilized to deliver the mail during the 1970 postal strike—somebody had to do it. So Drew asked himself, If the Fighting 69th didn't step up to secure West Point, who would? Slack liked that kind of thinking. He told Mason he'd leave him with the cops and gave Drew the command. The lieutenant dropped his orders off at the NYPD military leave desk and traded his service pistol for an Army M9 Beretta.

The 69th completed its second rotation at Ground Zero on October 26. As he had in the week after the attack, Slack felt immeasurably proud of his men and their performance in Lower Manhattan. But as he watched his soldiers scramble around the armory in preparation for the mission at West Point, the commander also felt dejected. It was the Fighting 69th's first wartime mobilization since World War II, but the Army hadn't called for the entire battalion, just two hundred soldiers evenly divided between Alpha Company and Bravo Company. Slack had called his headquarters and pleaded that the entire battalion be mobilized—if not the entire unit, at least the headquarters. After all, somebody had to be in charge of the 69th men while they were mobilized! But the Army had its logic, and Slack didn't figure into it.

Daniels, who would also stay in the rear, looked over at Slack as the two rifle companies marched out of the armory early on October 29. The commander had been separated from half his battalion and looked it. Worse, Slack thought West Point was as likely a target as any for a terrorist strike in the U.S., and he wouldn't be there to lead his men when the bullets started to fly. It pained the commander deeply. Daniels turned to one of his NCOs and asked half-jokingly if he thought they should put Slack on a suicide watch.

4: PREEMPTION

PARKING LOT HEROES

In an interview with New York's military newspaper, the commander of the 42nd Infantry Division said, "The National Guard leadership could not have picked a better unit than the soldiers of the 69th Infantry" to deploy to West Point. Neither Geoff Slack nor his men were quite that confident. While he believed a terrorist attack against West Point was feasible, Slack spent far more time worrying about how his unit of independent-minded, wiseass, and street-smart troops would mix with the bastion of military etiquette on the Hudson. Soldiers had been known to flee Alpha Company because they didn't want to shine their boots or get their hair cut; now they were going to guard the most spit-and-polish military installation in the world. One officer called it a recipe for disaster. Another soldier likened it to a time bomb waiting to go off. Slack had spent his first year in battalion command stressing the importance of customs and courtesies and professional behavior. But the lessons were slow to sink in for many of the soldiers, especially those who had been in the Guard for a long time.

To stave off any incident that would embarrass the State and shame the history of the Fighting 69th, Slack's only hope was to send the very best soldiers his struggling unit could muster. So even though the Federal order called for troops from just Alpha Company and Bravo Company, the two hundred soldiers who went to West Point came from every quarter of the battalion. Acevedo's Alpha Company captured the best soldiers from all the city units, while Mike Drew's Bravo Company culled the best men from Long Island.

Despite numerous cases of missing or unfit individuals, Slack was able to fill every enlisted soldier slot with acceptable troops without too much difficulty. But when it came to selecting his officers, he struggled. He needed ten officers in all—two commanders, two executive officers, and six platoon leaders—an assignment that would have been a snap for a regular Army unit, but not for the resource-starved Fighting 69th. The battalion should have had a pool of ten captains and more than twenty-five lieutenants to choose from, but, in fact, it had barely half that number. Before the mission, Alpha Company had only one officer, its commander, and he was relieved during the unit's tour at Ground Zero. Bravo Company was little better; it had one platoon leader and a company commander who had already begged off the mission. Further, the Army required all the officers who mobilized for Federal duty to be graduates of the Infantry Officer Basic Course at Fort Benning. Half the 69th's lieutenants didn't qualify under those terms. Slack wanted to send the best men to West Point, but when it came to school-trained officers, he was ultimately forced to send the good, the bad, the ugly, and even Lieutenant Leonard London.

At first glance London seemed the ideal junior officer. He was physically fit. He knew Army doctrine. And he had spent time leading a platoon in the Big Army. But for all his strengths, the lieutenant believed his rank entitled him to the privileges normally reserved for a banana republic dictator. London first caused concern when he was observed waving down off-duty soldiers on their way home from training and then ordering them to chauffeur him around or to throw out his garbage. Later, at the home of a fellow officer for the first time, London brushed passed his colleague's wife without acknowledging her, trudged into the kitchen, opened the fridge, and then complained about the lack of leftovers. In perhaps his most pronounced demonstration of poor judgment, the soldier had accepted, albeit begrudgingly, payment for letting a civilian into his apartment inside the restricted zone near Ground Zero.

Chris Daniels, who served as the officer's commander at Ground Zero, had been shocked when he learned about London's antics there and began contemplating methods to drop the soldier from his rolls. But London was one of the few lieutenants who had been to the infantry school, and therefore made the cut for the West Point assignment. Daniels pleaded with Slack to have the soldier pulled from the mission, but Slack's hands were tied: This wasn't like the Big Army, where a lieutenant could be fired and a replacement found the next day. If Slack got rid of London, he'd have nobody. "London goes," Slack told Daniels. "If he's as bad you say, he'll cut his own throat at West Point."

Slack was so short of officers that he ultimately had to renege on his promise to allow Lieutenant Mason to remain with the NYPD's anti-terrorism squad. But instead of mobilizing as the Bravo Company commander, Mason would now serve as the executive officer or second in command over at Acevedo's Alpha Company. Mason was miffed about the assignment. Not only was he ordered against his will to active duty, but he had to take a demotion and work for Acevedo's and Alpha Company's latest commander, a former Air Force Officer—a zoomie—who had joined the Army National Guard to hike in the mountains one weekend a month. Though both were lieutenants, Mason had been in command longer—and had never been in the damn Air Force! He asked Slack to bump the flyboy down, but Slack wouldn't consider it. In his mind, Mason was a fair-weather officer who had been given his chance at company command and had blown it by opting to stay with the NYPD. The nation was now at war, and despite what Mason believed, service in the Army trumped anything the cop could do with the police. *You don't serve for yourself, you serve where the Army needs you!* So Mason, along with the ethically challenged London, would work for the zoomie in Alpha Company. First Sergeant Acevedo looked over the officers and worried for his Roughnecks.

But not all the brass was tarnished. Amid the ROTC graduates, State-trained lieutenants, and direct-commissioned officers whom the 69th would send to West Point, there was a bona fide ring-knocker: Lieutenant Joe Whaley, Drew's executive officer. Nobody in the Fighting 69th knew West Point better than the former Black Knight lacrosse stand-out. Tall, dark, and lean, the twenty-seven-year-old officer looked like a Fortune 500 vice president and an esteemed member of the academy's alumni club. The problem for Whaley, however, was that nobody knew his civilian business like he did. The officer ran his family's massive chocolate company, and a tour of duty back at the academy would threaten the future of the enterprise. Further, the business was planning to expand operations to Asia that year, and the lieutenant was the linchpin for success. He appealed to Slack for a bye but it was useless. "I don't give a shit about your cookie factory," Slack told him. *Don't these kids realize we're at war!*

Many enlisted soldiers faced the same attitude. When Specialist Olmo told Acevedo he wanted to sit out the West Point mission due to business concerns, the first sergeant said, "Too bad." It seemed the officers and sergeants in the Fighting 69th didn't care about what happened to a guy's livelihood once Uncle Sam called. It didn't matter how much money Olmo would lose or how many people he would have to lay off. Like it or not, the citizen-soldier was going to West Point to protect the corps of cadets. Olmo called everyone he knew in the trades to line up jobs for his employees, but there seemed little employment for contractors in post–September 11 New York. *Happy fuckin' Thanksgiving, guys.*

Not that it was any consolation, but Jay Olmo wasn't alone. More than thirty thousand National Guardsmen and reservists were called to active duty in September and October 2001.

Although Slack had told his men the mission was to defend the base, there were a handful among the Fighting 69th who thought the deployment to West Point was merely a ruse for public consumption. The real plan, they insisted, was to train for a special mission in Afghanistan. As improbable as it sounded, some of the soldiers believed they were at the center of an elaborate information operation. Who better to get even with the terrorists than a unit from New York that had suffered casualties at Ground Zero? The city would be avenged, and America could have a sense of closure. Rumors of raids on Taliban strongholds rippled through the charter buses that brought the two hundred soldiers from New York to Fort Dix, New Jersey, where the alleged high-speed training would be conducted.

But instead of aggressive preparation for combat, the soldiers were rushed through a two-week block of instruction that seemed to revolve primarily around how to properly search a car for a machine gun shoved into the glove box, how to use handcuffs, and how to cope with a bomb threat. Jay Olmo called it parking lot training and wasn't impressed in the least. The men would set up cones to replicate the front gate at West Point and then practice the correct methods to check an identification card. During one iteration Olmo was so disgusted that he just let the car drive through without searching it.

"What the fuck are you doing?" Acevedo shouted.

Olmo looked at him, confused, as if to say, *Did I mess up?*

"You guys don't know what the hell you're doing, do you?" Acevedo asked.

"Nope," Olmo replied. Checking an ID card was not in the infantry manual, and Olmo and many of the soldiers were put off by the simpleton training. "If I wanted to check ID cards, I would have become an MP."

Acevedo laughed. "That's funny, because you'll be working for the MPs at West Point."

Many of the gung ho troops were disheartened; except for shooting on the rifle range, there was little they were learning that was at all relevant to the infantry. More than anything else, the two-week period served as a reindoctrination into the sights and sounds of the Big Army: This is how to march. This is how to shine your boots. This is how not to piss off a West Point officer.

The fact is, by mid-November 2001, a 69th soldier could have pissed on a West Point colonel's lawn and still have been invited inside the officer's home for dinner with his daughter. Since September 11 every soldier (except the cadets) at the military academy had been required to augment the military police presence at the gates, with colonels standing guard alongside privates, and by now everyone needed a break. So instead of cringing when the Fighting 69th's gypsy caravan of banged-up cars blaring salsa and hip hop arrived at Thayer Gate on November 13, 2001, the academy officers cheered.

SAINT PATRICK'S DAY 2002

Olmo fought to keep his eyes open. Although he had drunk only one wine cooler from his canteen, when the alcohol mixed with the steady hum and warm embrace of the space heater, the soldier nodded off, then caught himself. He rose from the stool inside the telephone booth–sized guard shack and looked around for his battle buddy. *Where the fuck are you motherfucker!* The two soldiers had an agreement: One guy was supposed to grab a thirty-minute nap in the bathroom while the other stood guard in the shack. If any brass came by, the soldier on guard would vouch for the other. "He's out conducting a foot patrol of the area, sir." But Olmo's partner had been gone for more than an hour.

Olmo had already been busted for dozing. A few weeks earlier he woke to find an officer staring back at him. "Did you get enough sleep?" the officer asked. "Yeah, don't worry," he answered. "I just caught like five minutes." Olmo's platoon sergeant ripped him apart the next day. And now his partner had disappeared, and Olmo was at risk of falling asleep again. Olmo cursed his partner's name for a solid ten minutes before sitting down again. It was around 3:00 a.m. and very dark and quiet and comfortable in the little guard shack. Olmo stared out at the long gray line of stone buildings through his sagging eyelids. He might as well have been counting sheep.

He nodded awake again a few minutes later when he heard a girl mumbling. Olmo looked out of his shell and saw that about ten feet away, a young, attractive blond cadet in civilian clothes was struggling to walk. He recognized the stammer; the girl wasn't just drunk, she was smashed. *Would you look at this fuckin' shit! This is some governor's daughter!* The girl stumbled past his shack and giggled softly before falling heavily into a row of bushes.

Without moving, Olmo gazed around the area looking for other cadets, but there were none to be found. He glanced over at the girl and waited for her to pull herself together and move along, but she didn't budge. *Motherfucker!* Olmo finally stood up, grabbed his rifle, and walked out into the cool March air. By now, the cadet had thrown up on herself, and he nudged her with his boot. "Hey, wake up. You're not at home." The girl rolled over and asked for help. Olmo bent down and started to pick her up but then realized the implications of what he was doing. *White girl in the bushes + little brown guy = rape charges.* He let the girl fall back into her vomit.

The batteries in Olmo's radio were dead, so he called his squad leader on his cell phone. "Listen, you need to come down here and get a drunk white girl out of the bushes."

"What the hell are you talking about?"

"She fell in the bushes. She's drunk."

"I ain't touchin' her. Leave her there."

"But it's cold out."

"Fuck it, leave her there."

Olmo continued to nudge her to no avail. A smattering of male cadets eventually came by.

"Listen, you need to come grab this girl and take her up to her room," Olmo told the cadets.

"Hell no, we'll get in big trouble for that. That's your job."

"*My* job? Fuck you! I ain't touchin' her."

The cadets took off, leaving the soldier with his charge.

Up until then Olmo thought nothing could be worse than Saint Patrick's Day with the Fighting 69th. But March 17 at a guard shack at the U.S. Military Academy was worse. He should have been out getting drunk himself, not baby-sitting the future officers of America. Nothing about the deployment to West Point made sense to the soldier. *Why the fuck do we need to guard a bunch of rich guys' kids? The cadets should guard themselves. There were four thousand of them, and they had the same weapons training as the Guardsmen—probably more. If not the cadets, how about two hundred welfare bums from New York? Let them earn their goddamn money. Teach them how to shoot and send them to West Point. But don't call me. I've got a job. I own my own business. I have people who rely on me. If I don't work, they don't work. If you want to send me someplace and ruin my business, at least send me to Afghanistan so I can kill some fucking terrorists.*

The West Point mission turned out to be far worse than even Olmo had imagined. The soldiers spent their days standing like hall monitors among throngs of cadets. They searched squadrons of soccer mom minivans. They parked cars for the *Blue's Clues* children's concert at the base theater. And they put up with mounds of petty chickenshit. The goodwill shown the Guardsmen when they first arrived had been short-lived. By Christmas, officers' wives were yelling at the soldiers for failing to salute the blue windshield stickers that proclaimed their status. Big Army sergeants were yelling at them for wearing their uniforms incorrectly. Retired generals were yelling at them when they tried to search their cars. The situation had become so bad that Olmo and some of the other men had decided to blow off the stupid rules completely in hopes that the National Guard would be thrown off the base. They saluted delivery men instead of officers. They wore wool caps instead of berets. And they took long breaks in the middle of searching the cars of retired officers.

The Big Army officer responsible for the 69th men tried to keep the Roughnecks focused on the importance of the job. Lieutenant Colonel James Rice, a loud infantry officer with a barrel chest and a shaved head, told his charges that there were plenty of sons of bitches who would love to do harm to West Point. He'd point up in the sky and remind the soldiers that the planes that slammed into the World Trade Center had flown directly overhead on their way to Manhattan. "Right over our heads!" He'd quote the latest terror plot news he'd heard from the *Today* show. "Katie Couric says there are new threats against the United States; we can't let our guard down." Prior to a home football game, Rice sought to get one formation of Guardsmen really fired up. "Today there is no more Mr. Nice Guy. I don't want any son of a bitch getting in here that doesn't belong here. There are bastards that want to do harm to the United States of America. Search bags three and four times. Break down anyone that looks like they're up to no good. I don't want anyone getting shot, but I wouldn't mind if they got butt-stroked. Just call me first so I can watch. Hoo-ah!" Rice believed an attack against West Point could kill future four-star generals, captains of industry, and perhaps even a future president of the United States.

Maybe so, but even Lieutenant Drew began doubting the mission's validity. On the very first day of duty at West Point, Drew watched his men toss the contents of a car driven by a group of senior citizens who had come to the academy for Thanksgiving Day brunch. The commander was all about helping the Army, but wondered what possible good could come from searching a late-model geriatric Cadillac.

The monotony and apparent uselessness of the mission drove the men even crazier when they began to see video of *real* U.S. troops slugging it out in Afghanistan. They wanted to be there with them, but it seemed that security for the basewide yard sale at the academy was the priority. The frustration bubbled to the surface on a regular basis. Soldiers began fighting on and off duty. In one incident at the main gate during rush hour, a 69th soldier disarmed a West Point MP and began clobbering his teammate with the baton. When they weren't fighting, many of the soldiers began drinking excessively. The Fighting 69th essentially took over two bars just outside the academy, the South Gate Tavern and the Fireside Hotel, where the Roughnecks were involved in several alcohol-fueled brawls with locals and garrison soldiers. In the worst such incident, one of Bravo Company's platoon sergeants drank a case of beer off post, put on a disguise, and then stumbled with a shotgun toward his own men's security position at the front gate, intent on conducting an ad hoc readiness exercise. The NCO was lucky that not *all* the men on duty were cops in the civilian world, and that instead of pumping him full of holes, the soldiers patiently convinced him to drop his weapon and lie down.

To his credit Colonel Rice recognized the motivation for all the misbehavior and, with the exception of the drunken platoon sergeant, generally left any disciplinary matters up to the company commanders. "Hell, you're infantrymen. If you weren't drinking and fighting in garrison, I'd wonder what was wrong with you, Hoo-ah!" But like Slack, Rice wouldn't tolerate a soldier whose values ran counter to the Army's. A sergeant who had taken unauthorized leave was court-martialed. A non-commissioned officer who fell asleep and abandoned his men at their post lost two stripes. And the questionable Lieutenant London, whom Slack suspected would run aground, was relieved. The Alpha Company platoon leader was charged with kicking a soldier, barring his men from speaking their native Spanish in the platoon areas, and calling one troop's girlfriend "easy." Though an investigation cleared London of any criminal charges, Rice found his behavior reprehensible and an embarrassment to the officer corps. He told the lieutenant to pack his bags and ordered him to be sent back to the New York Army National Guard.

While the relief of Lieutenant London was a high-visibility action in Colonel Rice's battalion, it was the exception for the Fighting 69th, as the New Yorkers faced far fewer disciplinary actions than the regular Army units assigned to West Point. One might infer from this that the 69th men were better behaved, but that was almost certainly not the case. Rather, the two companies of the 69th began to deal with infractions at the lowest level possible. If a soldier was late for his shift, his squad leader applied the appropriate penalties, which consisted of everything from extra duty and denial of a pass to good old-fashioned push-ups. In most cases managing infractions did not rise above the sergeant level unless they became a chronic problem. And when they did reach an officer, the lieutenant usually sent them back to the sergeant to deal with, saying, "This is NCO business."

This represented a breakthrough for the new Fighting 69th, for it demonstrated that it had rebounded enough to field an effective group of leaders for at least two companies. In addition to cleaning up their teams, the sergeants were also in charge of their operations. Every duty position at West Point was designed to be garrisoned by a nine-man rifle squad, led by a staff sergeant, who quickly learned to sink or swim. Finally, the West Point mission gave the NCO corps an opportunity to retrain their soldiers as infantrymen. The 69th was able to dedicate ten days out of every thirty at the academy to training, all of it led by platoon sergeants. The NCO corps has traditionally been the backbone of the infantry, and for the first time in years the 69th started to develop a spine. Sergeants who had no previous leadership experience now got valuable time in charge of men and a mission. Those who failed were sidelined. Those who stepped up were promoted and would ultimately become the top sergeants across the Fighting 69th.

Similar growth took place among the officer corps. Of the ten lieutenants sent to guard West Point, only the academy alumnus, Lieutenant Whaley, had had significant active-duty Army experience. The platoon chiefs were now learning how to manage the outfitting, training, and employment of thirty soldiers. As with the sergeants, some of the men proved to be great leaders, while others revealed their weaknesses. Mike Drew, who was promoted to captain at West Point, honed his leadership style on a company of more than one hundred soldiers. He was a soldier's officer and the epitome of selfless service, willing to go wherever the Army sent him and to work with his platoon leaders and NCOs to do whatever the Army asked. He was not a braggart or a yeller—just a soldier who happened to be the guy in charge. His men grew to love him for it, and Drew would emerge from West Point as one of the top officers in the 69th.

In the end, the academy became a proving ground for all the soldiers assigned there. As the months went by, each one was tested in competence, dedication, and reliability. This was especially true among the junior soldiers. In Alpha Company, the men spent the days standing a post together and the nights back at their own mini–El Barrio at the barracks, drinking beer, splashing around in a baby pool, and grilling burgers. They learned about where their comrades had grown up, the life experiences that made them who they were, and the degree of their willingness to fight for a friend. As they watched the war in Afghanistan progress, the soldiers assessed one another and passed silent judgment. *If we ever have to go there, I will fight next to this guy, but I'll run like hell from that one.* Though he bitched about his teammates on a regular basis, Olmo had come to respect his peers as both soldiers and friends. More important, he believed he was now honor-bound to stick by their sides. No matter what was going on in their civilian and personal lives, Olmo and many of the other soldiers had become blood brothers, who knew that if one trooper got called to deploy, they would all have to go and watch his back.

Olmo, however, felt no such loyalties to the drunken white cadet. She fell asleep where she lay, and Olmo returned to his guard shack, keeping an eye on her from an appropriate distance. The military police ultimately arrived to pick up the woman. But as the MPs took her away, Olmo second-guessed his hands-off approach. Had he carried the blonde to her room, perhaps he would have been accused of rape and, if his luck held out, sent home immediately.

THE BRIDGE-AND-TUNNEL GROUP

Though Slack had lost two companies of his best troops to the Federal deployment, he still claimed more than three hundred soldiers on his rolls. Convinced that the rest of the Fighting 69th could contribute to the war effort, he called his headquarters and lobbied for another mission. The Guard still maintained a large force in New York City in late 2001, with about three hundred soldiers from the 101st Cavalry Regiment securing dozens of posts throughout Manhattan and Brooklyn. Slack told the State of New York that the 69th was ready to relieve the cavalrymen for a three-month tour beginning in early 2002.

Daniels suggested that the colonel was volunteering the 69th for duty because he felt guilty that two of its companies were serving at West Point while the rest of the battalion had gone back to their civilian lives. If the Fighting 69th was going to serve, they would sacrifice together—or at least at the same time. It seemed a noble idea, but Daniels and others were concerned, given that the State Active Duty (SAD) system was full of holes, and any long-term deployments could threaten the livelihoods of the citizen-soldiers. Because the men who deployed to West Point were on Federal duty, they received all the benefits an active-duty Army soldier would. In addition, the men's civilian jobs were protected by the Uniformed Services Employment and Reemployment Rights Act. Few of those benefits or protections extended to SAD. The men were not given tax-free housing or subsistence allowances, like active-duty soldiers were, and they did not earn any points toward their military retirement. Their families did not receive health insurance. The Department of Veterans Affairs would not cover any disabilities incurred while on duty. It was a raw deal, and Daniels argued the issue up the chain of command. Slack understood his concerns and passed them up the flagpole as well, but nothing ever came back down.

Raw deal or not, Daniels was still a soldier. He'd go where his commander told him and expected his men to do the same. Slack told Daniels and the other senior leaders in the battalion to put on their "best war face" and get their men ready. Daniels accordingly evoked patriotism, fear, and JFK in his next two newsletters to his soldiers.

"State Active Duty starting on February 1, 2002 is still a very strong possibility," he wrote in December 2001.

> Do what you need to do now to prepare yourself mentally [and] financially and make those plans to ensure that your family will be taken care of. If called, it will be mandatory. Your options are show up for duty or be prosecuted to [the] fullest extent of the law. What does that mean? [You will be charged for] any bonus money or college money you have received. You will receive a less than honorable discharge. You will be charged for all uniforms. Basically,

unless you are homeless and never apply for a job or any kind of loan, your life will be ruined. I do not want to threaten anyone, but your country is calling you and now is the time to step up to the plate to serve and protect the freedom that we all cherish but take for granted.

We can all look back at September 11th and take pride that when our country called, the Fighting 69th delivered and then some. We were prepared and we exceeded our mission requirements. But it is not over. Watch the news and you will see that there are still terrorists packing C-4 [explosives] in their shoes. It is only a matter of time before they start shoving the stuff up their rear ends with a fuse hanging out. Thank your lucky stars that you are not on airport duty searching for that.

"Don't even think about going AWOL," Daniels added in January.

Everyone must participate or you will be picked up by the MPs and I will be in no rush to bail your useless body out of jail. Your country needs you. Most of you will not be held for active duty, so do not be a fool. Show up and be a patriot, your country has been attacked and is at war. Think back to WWII and how this country responded to the attack on Pearl Harbor, this is the same thing only worse because civilians were attacked. Now stand up like a man/woman and show this country that you are [a] true soldier and patriot. Now is the time for every soldier in the 69th to ask not what their country can do for them, but what they can do for their country.

Some of the sergeants in the 69th had heard the spiel before—the original one, back in January 1961. With his young troops up at West Point, Slack had to turn to the old guard of the Fighting 69th. First Sergeant Paul Raimondi, First Sergeant Lee Ortiz, Master Sergeant Bill Gerke, and Master Sergeant Bill Cooke were all Vietnam veterans. They had three Purple Hearts between them, two Combat Infantryman Badges, a Marine Combat Action Ribbon, and two Silver Stars.

All the men had seen real war in Vietnam, had earned their veteran status, and then had cooled off in the Army National Guard for the next thirty years. Each had threatened to retire dozens of times, yet none could quite let go. When the towers came down they thanked God they had stuck around. Slack rejoiced, too, for without them, his bridge-and-tunnel team would have been in serious trouble. Intelligence officer Mike Dunn served as acting executive officer for the team, which he described as a "photo-negative" of the force that was at West Point. For every thin, twentysomething developing soldier at the academy, there was a fat, fiftysomething career private at Grand Central Station. But that didn't necessarily mean they were poor soldiers, and Slack believed in his heart that, with effective leadership, even his worst-looking soldier could play a vital role.

Twenty years earlier, when Slack was on active duty with the Big Army, he met his first National Guardsman at a training event, and concluded the Guard were stupid and couldn't be trusted. But he had since come to love his part-timers for what they were: true citizen-soldiers, as described in the U.S. Constitution. When the founding fathers designed the American government, they conceived of a national defense based on a well-organized militia. For most of the nation's history it was these citizen-soldiers of the militia and later of the National Guard who actually fought the wars. The equation changed during the cold war and fully manifested itself in Vietnam, when the United States went to war largely without its National Guard. But with the end of the cold war, the National Guard began returning to its roots.

Slack's troops looked like, acted like, and lived the same lives as the masses of civilians who lined the subway stops in Harlem, the Bronx, Brooklyn, and Queens. But they were something more, too, and it was that something that set them apart from their neighbors. On one weekend a month, six weeks at Ground Zero, or three months standing guard at Penn Station, they became soldiers in the United States Army. The public embraced them. The governor and the mayor trusted them. All Slack needed to do was to give them a mission and

competent leadership, and he was certain they could move mountains.

The remainder of the 69th Infantry officially relieved the 101st
Cavalry on February 1, 2002, at sites around New York City, including the Brooklyn-Battery and Queens Midtown tunnels; the Brooklyn,
Manhattan, and Williamsburg bridges; and Grand Central and Penn-
sylvania rail stations. Slack shifted his command post from the Lexington Avenue Armory to Fort Hamilton, in Bay Ridge, Brooklyn.
Two weeks into the mission one of Slack's junior soldiers, who had
been a homeless vagabond on the fringe of society just a few days earlier, was patrolling the Brooklyn Bridge. He noticed a suspicious package on the span and ordered the police department to shut the six-lane
artery down and clear the object with a bomb squad. If that soldier
had been wearing his dirty civilian clothes, the PD would have laughed
at the order. But as a soldier, he was deferred to by the NYPD. The
cops closed the bridge for the better part of a day until the object was
clear. For some of the soldiers, it was as if they had put on their Super-
man costumes.

The bridge-and-tunnel mission was slated to last three months, but
Slack was intent on keeping the battalion on duty until the troops that
had deployed to West Point came home. Three months turned to six,
then to nine, and by then the majority of the men in the battalion had
begun full-time military duty on September 11, 2001, and had been
serving into October 2002 in the city or at the academy with very
few breaks. A year after the terrorist attacks the soldiers were exhausted and eager to return to their homes and civilian lives. "War is
over!!! Mission accomplished, terrorism defeated," Drew wrote in an
e-mail to a fellow commander on October 5, 2002, when he left West
Point.

Within weeks of being back in New York, though, Drew was ready
for another mission, as the West Point duty hadn't cleansed the demons of September 11. Other soldiers felt similarly, especially those
who had spent a year at the military academy. By the end of their tour,
the soldiers had gone from a pure base defense force to a ceremonial

guard whose responsibilities involved little more than parking cars and taking part in funeral details and parades. They would spend six days of the week locking down the post, only to open the gates wide again for college football Saturday. Lieutenant Mason, who had served as Alpha Company's executive officer, summed up the perceived uselessness of the mission in a mock award citation: "With total disregard for his personal safety, and without any discernible trepidation, 1LT Mason did command A Co. 1/69 during the first post-wide yard sale since the Tragic Events of September 11th. His actions allowed the families of West Point to sell second-hand wares to the public without fear of reprisal from Al Qaida, and in doing so reflected great credit upon himself, his unit, and the United States Army."

Daniels's Scout Platoon, which served with Acevedo's Roughnecks at West Point, likewise believed the duty was a waste of time. Daniels tried to put the mission into perspective for his soldiers when they returned home.

You should be proud. Your country called and you answered. Some of you have expressed displeasure with your assignment. You have stated that you felt that this mission was not important. But let's think back to WWII. Some men landed on Normandy while others loaded underwear in Bayonne, New Jersey. Which job was more important? Both were equally important. The men in the theater would not be able to fight without those soldiers in the rear. Compare that to West Point. When you deployed the threat was and still is real. How do we know that terrorists have not driven to West Point to kill cadets but instead of completing their mission saw the gates heavily guarded and turned around? Imagine the horror if you were not there to guard this institution and one crazy terrorist came on those grounds and just starting killing people? Can you remember the damage done by two crazy students at Columbine? Your mission was damn important and you should all hold your head [high] that you were the first National Guard troops to deploy fighting terrorism. You went from the horrors of Ground Zero to defend the flag waving on the Hudson in less than two weeks. Pretty damn impressive, and we are all proud it was 69th soldiers who answered the call when your country asked.

Slack was also characteristically proud of his soldiers but didn't belabor the point, figuring the men would get a medal and then the Army would soon enough be asking, "What have you done for the flag today?" "We're in the middle of a war," he wrote October 30 in a newsletter to his men. "We participated in a campaign. Our side lost some and won some. You played your part with honor but the fight goes on. Let's get over any lingering feelings of self-pity and understand that we're an integral part of the National Defense; there's no time for any 'me first' sentiment."

Before September 11, Slack's comments would have been out of place. But after a year of duty in New York City and at West Point, Slack's belief in the need for a ready and relevant National Guard was being validated. In June 2002, President Bush further reinforced the changing nature of national defense when he delivered the commencement address to West Point's graduating class. As Specialist Olmo and other 69th soldiers patrolled the wooded hilltops around West Point's Michie Stadium searching for any would-be snipers, the president warned that if the nation waited for terrorist threats to fully materalize, it would be too late to defend against them. "We must take the battle to the enemy, disrupt his plans, and confront the worst threats before they emerge," Bush proclaimed in his first enunciation of his strategy of preemption. "In the world we have entered, the only path to safety is the path of action, and this nation will act."

Slack had heard about the shift in policy on the news and knew the proclamation would impact the National Guard. With the end of the West Point mission, the commander turned his attention toward the readiness of his battalion. The men had done well at Ground Zero and on two security missions, but they were nowhere near the level of proficiency needed for a true combat infantry mission. "Some of you will not make it. Some are too fat, too unfit, too incapable of accepting the new facts of life, too bound with job or family problems, or just too self centered," he wrote. But he also believed the attacks of 9/11 had sparked a new level of patriotism in his Guardsmen. When Slack first joined the Fighting 69th, most of the soldiers served for college money or for some other personal gain. Now they served for their families, their city, and their country. "Freedom ain't free and most of you saw, firsthand, that the enemy intends to kill you and your family in their home or workplace. Let the sick, lame and lazy fall out. I honor them for their past service but for some it's just time to go. For the 'Sun Shine Patriot,' we don't need you. For the real American Soldiers in our ranks, ruck up!"

5: THE END OF THE WHIP

THE STORM BEFORE THE HURRICANE

Cliff Mason, the 69th officer who had tried to avoid duty at West Point only to deploy there in a lower position, received Colonel Slack's October newsletter via e-mail. Mason was a short, bookish soldier whose head seemed to sink into his shoulders as he typed away at a computer. He cringed as he read Slack's call to arms, judging that the commander sounded like a flag-waving maniac. But the newsletter was just the latest in what he viewed as Slack's broken-record repertoire of patriotic guilt trips. Mason had heard the pitch every month since he joined the unit in early 2001. The rhetoric picked up after 9/11 and had grown into a fevered pitch a year later. What bothered Mason most, however, was not the wartime drumbeat, but the simple fact that Slack apparently believed every bit of it. And because he did believe in it so passionately, Mason feared that the colonel could not be trusted to look out for the best interests of his men and the long-term health of the unit. He worried that Slack would lie to the soldiers, deceive them, and blow smoke up their asses to fill the ranks for whatever mission he had most recently volunteered the 69th Infantry. Mason, who was a highly intelligent Ivy Leaguer, thought Slack should have told his bosses, "Barring disaster, leave my men alone for all scheduled deployments until at least 2005. The 69th has done enough and needs to recover so it can at least look like a semblance of a cohesive unit." Instead, Mason suspected that the commander wanted to pull all his soldiers back onto active duty because, for the life of him, Slack simply couldn't understand why a person might have something better to do than serve in the Army on nonsense missions like parking cars at West Point, standing guard on the Brooklyn Bridge, or sitting in the Sinai desert to monitor the contested border between Israel and Egypt.

The Sinai duty—officially, "the Multinational Force and Observers (MFO) mission"—was to be the next big event in the life of the post-9/11 Fighting 69th. Mason, who had been promoted to captain and reinstated as commander of Bravo Company following the West Point mission, thought the MFO sounded like a laughable posting for an infantry battalion. In twenty-five years there had been no action in the Sinai; it was a place to send soldiers to keep them out of trouble elsewhere. The Americans spent most of their time watching boats transit the Suez Canal or scuba diving at Egypt's Sharm al-Sheikh resort town. Mason figured the mission would be mindless, meaningless, impossible to do poorly, virtually non-infantry related, and unknown to the public. In that regard, perhaps, it was perfect for the Fighting 69th.

Mason still felt jilted by the West Point experience and increasingly frustrated by the realities of working in an underfunded FAD-IV National Guard unit that struggled to outfit, pay, and train its soldiers. The lieutenant had come to the 69th fresh from another Guard unit that was considered highly competent and regularly trained alongside the elite paratroopers of the Southern European Task Force. Mason wanted to transform his new charges from a group of weekend warriors into a professional infantry company that could rival the best in the National Guard. He set high standards for the unit, told the older soldiers they could keep up or get out, and forbade the use of the company's World War I–era canvas pup tents in the field, as he believed that infantrymen should sleep under the stars, or at most under a poncho suspended between trees. It was, after all, standard in the Big Army. Yet some of Mason's men alleged he was abusing them by depriving them of their right to shelter. The soldiers concluded that

Mason was an arrogant jerk to think he could just come in and make whatever changes he wished. Mason didn't know how to react to non-commissioned officers who boldly igored what he considered the basics of discipline and tactics. They didn't support him, and his command foundered; instead of strengthening the unit, the captain broke it apart.

Although he ultimately enjoyed himself at West Point, Mason was bitter after the mission. With the Army at war, he did not believe a deployment to a low-stress affair in the Hudson River valley was appropriate. He vented in e-mails and conversations to the other company commanders, railing against the 69th and its soldiers. The unit had allowed too many old, out-of-shape, and drug-using men in its ranks, making whatever accommodations were necessary to keep a soldier on the rolls. The regiment rested too much on its proud history instead of trying to improve itself in the present. And by being relegated to useless homeland security missions it was allowing itself to be used as cheap labor. By October 2002 he had come to despise the Fighting 69th, and the Sinai mission only provided him even more reasons to do so, as it was an acknowledgment that the Big Army didn't have enough faith in it for a combat-oriented mission.

The 69th was slated to mobilize for nine months beginning in May 2004, but Captain Mason thought the job was too much for the unit to handle, came too soon after West Point, and was not in keeping with the National Guard's origins as a homeland defense force. In addition, Mason believed the training plan to prepare for the mission was bogus. The 42nd Infantry "Rainbow" Division had directed all units to abandon collective training in order to focus on individual tasks, such as how to don a protective mask. The new division commander, Brigadier General Joe Taluto, called the training plan the "Rainbow Ready" program, a designation Mason thought sounded more suited to a throng of gays ready to have an orgy. He would have preferred training for urban warfare, which would be more in keeping with the 69th's home base in New York. But in light of a pending deployment, Slack saw sense in the Rainbow Ready program and called it the best training plan he had seen since he left the 1st Infantry Division in 1982. Slack then told Mason and the other commanders and staff that they should expect to pull more State Active Duty security missions as they readied for the Sinai. That was the last straw for Mason. He decided to start looking for a new unit.

As word of the Sinai mission spread around the battalion, other soldiers considered packing their bags. After a year of full-time duty, many wanted to spend time at home. Others requested transfers to the Big Army, since it seemed they were destined for near full-time service anyway. For them the National Guard's unofficial motto— "One Weekend a Month and Two Weeks Every Summer"—had become a bad joke. Captain Daniels, meanwhile, pushed his men to make a decision about their future in the Guard. He, for one, thought the Sinai would be a great mission; after all, when was the last time New York Guardsmen had the chance to stand in front of the pyramids? But whatever their answer, he wanted the troops either to commit or to file their transfers or resignations. "No shame on those that leave," he told his men. "You are being given a seventeen-month notice to get your affairs in order." That might sound like a long time, but seventeen months is little more than fifty days of training in the National Guard, and Daniels sought to stabilize his deployment roster as early as possible. While this was important for a successful train-up for the Sinai, the HHC commander believed a war with Iraq could very well change the plans for the 69th. In fact, Daniels felt fairly certain that the 69th would never get as far as the Sinai. "I believe that the war with Iraq will start soon, very soon," he wrote in his November 2002 newsletter.

> This is not classified, only my opinion. If the war starts sooner than later, I believe that we will be called up to partake in some other mission. Whether it be guarding the [demilitarized zone] in Korea from the communist hoard to standing watch over the front gates of a US base in Holland, we will be called. Each soldier needs to make the decision now and stand by it. Either you are in or get

out. If you want to leave and join active duty, let's get it done now. If you want to move to Canada because you joined the Guard for the free uniforms and cheap cigarettes then process out now. I just want to look at my formation and see committed soldiers. If you cannot commit to the long fight, then step out.

Daniels anticipated that about 20 percent of his soldiers would leave on their own, and expected to have to toss out another 10 percent for failure to meet basic soldier standards, such as weight and physical fitness. Those numbers represented junior soldiers, for the most part. But Daniels and Colonel Slack were both shocked when they discovered how many senior leaders had either decided to cash in their chips or failed to meet the necessary requirements. Three platoon sergeants with a wealth of active-duty experience bolted; two requested transfers, while the third, a soldier who had earned the Silver Star while in the Special Forces, was a single father and left the Guard to tend to his daughter. A first sergeant pissed hot for drug use. The zoomie who commanded Alpha Company at West Point resigned to move to Martha's Vineyard. Lieutenant Whaley, the West Point ring-knocker and New York chocolate mogul, resigned to finally spend more time with his business. The battalion personnel officer, a captain who had formerly commanded a company of the 82nd Airborne Division, moved to North Carolina to attend business school. The Delta Company commander, a former active-duty artillery officer who had once served in the Balkans, told Slack his job came first, and he wouldn't have time for a deployment. The Charlie Company commander, the longest-serving officer in the battalion, was forced to retire after he failed to meet the Army's education requirements. The Echo Company commander, a DEA agent who had used his credentials to help purge the 69th of soldiers with criminal records, requested a transfer to the 42nd Infantry Division headquarters, which was planning a deployment to Bosnia. The intelligence officer, Mike Dunn, who had been a fixture in the 69th's staff for years, left for a company command at the 258th Field Artillery.

In the two-month period after the Sinai announcement, Captain Mason lost 10 percent of his soldiers in Bravo Company; another 10 percent announced they would leave the 69th when their enlistments were up. Mason concluded that the only men looking forward to the deployment were the young kids who wanted to travel and the older troops who couldn't get a job elsewhere. The rest were simply disillusioned. They had joined the 69th to defend the nation in times of true crisis and instead were going to guard a line in the sand, when the only real risks to America were being defended by police officers at home. In Mason's opinion the 69th was becoming more of a joke every day; the unit was incompetent and not dedicated to the craft of the infantry. He believed the good soldiers who were leaving the 69th had realized there was no place in the unit for serious soldiers who wanted to make a meaningful contribution to the Army. At the rate the battalion was losing men, Mason was sure the unit would fold—and good riddance. He himself submitted a request to transfer to the staff of the United States Army Mountain Warfare School in Vermont.

On a personal level, Slack was hurt by the departure of so many senior leaders. He loved the 69th more than anything else save his family, and in his view, when the officers and senior NCOs walked out on the 69th, they were walking out on Geoff Slack, destroying a bit of the work he had put into the battalion. Slack's disappointment soon enough turned to anger, and in mid-January 2003 the colonel convened what was left of his command and staff and told them that the soldiers who were leaving the battalion were not true patriots and didn't have it in them to withstand the immense selfless sacrifices that life in the New York Army National Guard entailed. They were too selfish and too self-involved to realize it, but they were just not up to the finest traditions of the Fighting 69th. Slack almost seemed to be directing his comments directly to Mason, who had come to represent all the officers and soldiers who fled the 69th. It enraged Slack to be near soldiers like Mason, men who did not love the Army or the Fighting 69th as fiercely as Slack did, men who would bail on the country when the going got tough.

Slack had encountered plenty of Masons in his decade with the 69th—men who he thought were nefarious lollapaloozas. He had soldiers who lied and cheated and stole to feather their own caps. He was accustomed to officers who moved to their own agenda at the expense of their commands or the unit. Slack stood on the right side of honor, and he would rather work with an honorable moron who didn't know the business end of a rifle than a smart Mason who had dishonored himself, first by attempting to avoid the West Point mission, then by resigning from the 69th during wartime for a job in which he would not be deployed overseas.

Mason, for his part, believed that Slack was the one who was selfish. He privately accused the commander of believing that he had been entrusted with a mission direct from God to get the 69th onto duty, and in that Mason wasn't entirely wrong. Slack was not simply standing by waiting to execute the Army's grand plan; he was willfully seeking a deployment. Just as he took it upon himself to lead the 69th to Ground Zero, Slack was taking it upon himself to lobby for whatever missions were on the table. He knew the 69th had been placed on the planet for one purpose: to fight. A couple of battalions in New York had backed away from accepting any future deployments; they wanted to give their men and their families and employers a break. Slack was cognizant of all their concerns, but he persisted nonetheless. He told his brigade and division commander that the Fighting 69th was ripe for the next job.

Slack always sought to do what was right for the Army, but the consequences of his actions often hit him late at night after a staff meeting as he was driving the seventy miles back to his home on Long Island. The commander had a habit of engaging his mouth before his brain, which didn't catch up until the solitude of the commute. He reflected on his words and his decisions, having made so many mistakes and said or done the wrong thing more often than he cared to admit. He wished he could take back many, but volunteering the Fighting 69th for duty during a time of war was not one of them. He believed the regiment's history demanded they participate in every fight they could. The unit's motto—"Who Never Retreated from the Clash of Spears"—echoed true in Slack's mind. Although he knew many soldiers and virtually all their families would hate him for offering up the 69th for another mission, he just wasn't interested in their personal problems. Half the U.S. Army was either fighting in Afghanistan or suffering in the desert, preparing to go to war in Iraq. And what were the soldiers of the Fighting 69th doing? Drinking wine and squeezing their women back at home. Slack was ashamed and believed that in their hearts most of his soldiers were ashamed, too. The 69th must get into the fight.

Mason could only laugh at the colonel's romantic reference to the history of a long-ago era when the National Guard was at the forefront of America's wars. Those days were passed. The 69th hadn't participated in any conflict in six decades, and Mason was certain that barring some terrible, unplanned accident, they weren't about to anytime soon. In that case, he believed the 69th would be immediately replaced with some other unit. He thought Slack had lost sight of the simple fact that duty in the National Guard was a part-time job. The soldiers had volunteered for times of emergency, events like 9/11 or a second Korean War, and not to be a continuous, open-ended augmentation for the Big Army. For any sustained conflict, the Army needed to grow in size, not call upon the National Guard year after year. While Mason certainly didn't think that standing at airports, in front of monuments, or in the Sinai was what being an infantryman was all about, the 69th apparently didn't merit anything better. The captain pushed his transfer.

SAINT PATRICK'S DAY 2003

"All the decades of deceit and cruelty have now reached an end," President George W. Bush told the nation in a television address on Saint Patrick's Day 2003. "Saddam Hussein and his sons must leave Iraq within forty-eight hours. Their refusal to do so will result in military conflict, commenced at a time of our choosing. For their own safety, all foreign nationals—including journalists and inspectors—should leave Iraq immediately."

The looming war would be the first major test of the preemption doctrine the president announced at West Point in 2002. But the soldiers of the Fighting 69th who marched up Fifth Avenue on March 17, 2003, had far more pedestrian concerns than the success of the administration's policy. Scheduled to deploy to Egypt on a peacekeeping assignment, several soldiers wondered how a war with Iraq would impact their mission. Media reports indicated the Arab world was not onboard with the Bush Junior administration the same way they had been with Senior's in 1991. For all the 69th men knew, the peacekeeping mission to the Sinai could well devolve into a shooting war.

More immediate, however, was how the initiation of a war might tax the 69th in New York. Media reports indicated that the NYPD was already stepping up its security measures. Slack knew those efforts could well result in a tasking for his battalion. The Fighting 69th had been on the tail end of a very long whip since 9/11. Even a hint of terrorist activity could result in a citywide deployment of Guardsmen to screen cars at bridges and tunnels, or walk like a beat cop at Grand Central or Penn Station. Slack told his officers to be prepared.

On Long Island, Lieutenant Joe Minning was having none of it. The freshly minted butter bar skipped the 69th's Saint Patrick's Day celebration out of sheer frustration with the Army National Guard— an organization he was doing everything he could to distance himself from. Minning had transferred into the 69th as a sergeant from the 82nd Airborne Division the week before 9/11 and then went on to earn his commission through Hofstra University's ROTC program. Minning's entire male lineage had served in the U.S. or German militaries as far back as he could trace, and the officer looked every bit the product of the warrior class. He stood more than six feet tall and was built like a solid keg of beer. He wore a high-and-tight buzz cut that bordered on a Mohawk, and he had a perpetual bulge in his lower lip where a wad of tobacco had seemingly taken root. When National

Guard videographers documenting the Army's response to September 11 hurried to Manhattan, they immediately zeroed in on the martially endowed Minning. Even when compared to his experiences with the 82nd Airborne Division, the soldier reported that the 69th had done a great job at Ground Zero.

But the luster had worn off significantly in the year and a half since. As an ROTC cadet Minning had not been able to deploy to West Point or participate in the long-term bridge-and-tunnel mission in New York, and instead reported for weekend drill with the handful of other soldiers left behind. He was shocked at the unit's poor state of readiness. There were soldiers in the unit who looked as if they could have been his grandfather. There were soldiers who seemed to have no proficiency at even the most basic tasks. On one drill weekend he found a trooper trying to load his bullets into his rifle magazine backward. Junior privates showed no respect for senior NCOs, calling them by their first names and not hesitating to tell them where to shove it. As for training—forget about it. The 82nd Airborne was like a group of race cars all going in the same direction at top speed down a highway. The 69th was a traffic jam of jalopies trying to go any which way but forward. The situation hadn't improved when the soldiers returned from West Point and State Active Duty in late 2002. In general, it meant only more gridlock. On top of that Captain Mason seemed so uninterested and negative that a pall of despair settled over the unit's armory at Bay Shore, Long Island. Once the strongest and healthiest 69th unit on the island, Bravo Company had dwindled to some 25 soldiers out of 111 authorized. Minning was frustrated. Like Slack, he wanted to get into the fight in Afghanistan or Iraq. But with so few troops, the mustang couldn't imagine any sort of wartime duty for the hobbled regiment. Even the peaceful Sinai mission seemed a stretch. After two of the more competent NCOs put in requests to transfer out of the unit, Lieutenant Minning started looking for a way back to the Big Army and the 82nd Airborne Division and Fort Bragg, his favorite home away from home.

A former linebacker at Hofstra, Minning had dropped out of college to join the Army in the mid-1990s. The broad-shouldered athlete yearned for something more in life, dreading the prospect of becoming another Long Island automaton who commuted in and out of the city every day like a cow on the way to slaughter. He found his passion in the 82nd Airborne. He loved the physical training, the thrill of airborne operations, and the élan and camaraderie of an elite unit. In just three years he had made sergeant and had an exceptionally bright future as an NCO with the Army. But instead of taking a promotion to staff sergeant, Minning opted to apply for ROTC. He was frustrated at some of the inept leaders he occasionally worked with in the 82nd and believed he could make a bigger difference for his men as an officer. While he was assigned to the Fighting 69th during his time as an officer candidate, he had every expectation of returning to the 82nd or to another of the Army's elite infantry units upon earning his commission. His wife, however, had other ideas and pushed him to stay in the National Guard. Minning relented and gave up his Big Army contract. Shortly after, though, he and his wife split. Minning, burned, called the infantry-career branch managers in the Army and begged for an active assignment. But fate was playing in favor of the Fighting 69th. The Big Army had all the lieutenants it needed; Minning would have to stay in the Guard.

As Chris Daniels had predicted, the winds blowing the 69th through the Global War on Terror shifted when the Army invaded Iraq two days after the officer led his company up Fifth Avenue. The MFO mission was canceled, and New York's Own were ordered to head to Bosnia in April 2004 instead. Minning was surprised at the posting. Though Bosnia had been quiet for years, it was still an operational mission with the threat of enemy contact. Perhaps staying with the Fighting 69th wouldn't be so bad, after all. That said, he thought the Bosnia mission was beyond the scope of the 69th, as currently configured, as there just weren't enough deployable troops in the battalion. The 69th had struggled to assemble enough competent leadership to oversee two hundred men on the West Point mission.

The battalion needed 163 more soldiers and leaders for the Bosnia rotation, officially designated as Stabilization Force (SFOR) 16. Minning didn't think it possible.

Slack had his doubts as well. By the summer of 2003, soldiers were abandoning the 69th Infantry in droves, leaving him with less than 550 of the 750 troops he was supposed to have, and he knew that a large number of those would not pass the required medical and physical screening to deploy. Another percentage could be guaranteed to refuse to reenlist or go AWOL. By Daniels's calculations, the battalion faced the loss of 30 percent of its soldiers, which would bring the Fighting 69th to a barely capable force of just 385 men. Slack couldn't do much about his soldiers with medical conditions, but he wanted a hammer that he could use to force soldier attendance. Slack asked his chain of command to implore Governor George Pataki to push for a law that would lead to the prosecution of New York National Guard deserters. The State Headquarters told Slack it wasn't an option they planned to pursue and scolded the commander for using the word "deserter" when describing the soldiers who were AWOL for an extended period of time. They told him it sent the wrong message to the absent GI, making it less likely he would return. The frustrated Slack wished he could figure out the magic solution that would keep his soldiers in the ranks, but there seemed to be no such thing. The nature of National Guard service had changed, and many soldiers were protesting with their feet.

Slack believed that the greatest influence on retention was his junior officers. Only a savvy captain or lieutenant could keep a competent National Guardsman in uniform. Commanders who had regular personal interaction with their men and understood the dynamics of their civilian and military careers were usually the most successful. Daniels was great at that. After taking command of the HHC, he learned that most of the unit's soldiers weren't in the military jobs they had hoped for. Accordingly he retrained them into what they wanted to do, and the men stuck around. From a low of one hundred soldiers when he joined the HHC, Daniels now commanded around three hundred. On the other hand, commanders who failed to take the time to know every man in their unit and to work to solve their problems were prone to fail, as Captain Mason had. He misread the needs of his men, and they left his company the moment they had the chance.

In addition to retaining quality soldiers, the 69th needed to get smart and healthy new recruits into its ranks. Though the soldiers despised recruiting duty, the units in the 69th once again joined in the effort, harkening back to the 69th's World War I recruiting slogan—"Go to the Front with Your Friends." Minning and the other leaders told their soldiers to look at their thin ranks. Did the men want to deploy with a ragtag group of backfills provided by the State? If they didn't, they needed to encourage their experienced comrades to stay in boots and then recruit their neighbors, their high school classmates, their drinking buddies. If a soldier wanted to deploy overseas with the 69th, he needed to enlist and ship off to basic training by February 2004.

The pitch had worked well for the Old Fighting 69th in 1917. While the regiment had its problems recruiting during peacetime, the 69th's revered chaplain, Father Duffy, said the unit managed to gather fifteen hundred soldiers for the war in Europe in just weeks. They had so many volunteers, in fact, that they were able to cull the best from among them. "Nobody was taken who fell below the standard in age, height, weight, sight or chest measurement—or who had liquor aboard or who had not a clean skin," Duffy wrote in his 1919 memoir, *Father Duffy's Story.*

In 1917 the 69th was turning away three hundred recruits a week, most of whom had no trouble at all getting into other units. But in 2003 that was hardly the case, for after all, why would a civilian choose to join the National Guard? Doing so for the college money wasn't a plausible reason anymore, because the would-be student would be deployed and not able to attend school. Joining to avoid the draft didn't make sense, either, as there was no serious talk of instituting mandatory service. Joining for beer money or an extra car payment made no sense at all. If a New Yorker needed a few extra bucks, there were scores of employment options in the metro area that didn't entail the possibility of driving over a land mine outside Sarajevo. The U.S. military may have been fighting in Iraq and Afghanistan, but the rest of the United States—even the people of New York—did not seem to be at war. There were no fuel rations. People did not practice air raid defense. Sons were not receiving draft notices in the mail. Of course, nobody wanted to suffer another terrorist attack, but any National Guard or regular Army recruiter would tell you that America's desire to avoid another 9/11 did not necessarily equate to committing its children to uniform. This is not to say the American people did not support their soldiers. On the contrary, the population cheered its GIs at airports, mailed them cookies overseas, donated money, and affixed yellow "We Support Our Troops" ribbons to their cars, but stopped short of driving those cars to the Army recruiting station.

There were exceptions, certainly. The most famous were the Tillman brothers, who after 9/11 set aside their promising and lucrative athletic careers to enlist with the Big Army. Kevin Tillman, a baseball player with the Los Angeles Angels, and Pat Tillman, a safety with the Arizona Cardinals, joined the U.S. Army Rangers in May 2002. Both brothers served in Iraq. Corporal Pat Tillman, who passed on a $3.6 million contract with the Cardinals, was later killed in Afghanistan.

While no investment bankers fled Wall Street for the Lexington Avenue Armory and none of the Yankees ditched their pinstripes for fatigues, a handful of New Yorkers did take their place in the Fighting 69th to support the war effort. Francis C. Obaji, a seventeen-year-old Nigerian immigrant studying to become a doctor, watched the World Trade Center attack unfold as he stood at the Staten Island Ferry terminal across the harbor from Manhattan. He had been in the country for only five years and believed he owed everything to America. As he watched the towers fall, he pledged to join the Army National Guard to defend his adopted home.

Pat Callahan was just beginning work on his doctorate in psychology at New York University on September 11. When he saw on his television the National Guard working at Ground Zero, he decided without much deliberation that he would serve, too. He had never undertaken anything truly selfless but thought joining the National Guard was a way to give back and do something for the country.

Sam Cila, a muscle-bound corrections officer on Long Island, enlisted with the 69th a week after September 11. An avid Harley-Davidson rider, Cila believed all able American men should have joined the service in some form or another. The country was now at war, and it was time to pick up a rifle and defend the United States.

Unlike the thousands of men who had joined the National Guard in the decades prior to 9/11, Obaji, Callahan, and Cila enlisted with the full expectation and hope of being called up to serve on Federal duty. But they were all realistic about what type of Federal service they could expect. Callahan thought some sort of homeland defense duty was in the cards. That belief was reinforced at basic training when the Big Army drill instructors belittled the National Guard recruits by referring to them collectively as "airport security."

But, in actuality, airport security duty was yesterday's news for America's Citizen Soldiers. At the National Guard Bureau Headquarters (NGB) in Arlington, Virginia, officers were hard at work finding and training units to backfill the Big Army for combat duty in Iraq. Before the war had even started, the Pentagon was dipping into its "Strategic Reserve." Florida's 53rd Infantry Brigade was called for duty in advance of the invasion, and scores of other units followed.

Major Charles "Chuck" Crosby, a New York Army National Guardsman on loan to the NGB, worked as a deployment officer in the bureau's SCIF, or Sensitive Compartmented Information Facility, a room where classified information was spread out on desktops like a scattered deck of cards. So many National Guard units had been called up in the days preceding the war that the once-quiet work center now looked like an overturned anthill. Soldiers hurried reports from one cubicle to another. They offered advice to alerted units over the phone. And they mused with one another at the water cooler about how years of neglect by the Big Army resulted in short-notice or no-notice deployments of Guard units with horrendous readiness ratings.

Though he was an Army brat, Crosby claimed Oklahoma as home and looked as though he had just come in from the fall harvest. He was a tall, fair-skinned, baseball-and-apple-pie officer who could have played Richie Cunningham on *Happy Days* if he was a little older. Instead he served in the role cast for him before his birth: West Point graduate and career Army officer. Crosby graduated from the academy in '85. His dad graduated in '60; his granddad in '24; his great-granddad in 1893; and his great-great-granddad in 1822. The major had served in the 10th Mountain Division before joining the New York Guard, and loved the Army, just as he was supposed to. But at the same time he was upset with his parent organization. The Big Army seemed to have broken all the rules in going to war in Iraq. Units that were supposed to be given ninety days for training were given thirty. Units that had only half the soldiers they were supposed to have were called for duty. Units that didn't have the equipment they rated were being alerted for frontline service. In one instance, the Army told the Guard to deploy two combat support units that didn't even exist. When the Guard responded that it did not have the heavy petroleum companies the Army wanted, the Pentagon directed the Guard to hurry up and build the units from disparate pieces and then alert them for Iraq immediately.

Soldiers in the Fighting 69th and units like them might have been concerned about their strength and equipment, but a lack of soldiers and radios didn't seem to be slowing the war effort. Units were being called and shipped overseas whether they were ready or not. In Crosby's opinion, the Army had failed to include the Guard as a full partner in the defense of the United States. At best, the National Guard was the Big Army's bastard stepchild. Yet now they were being asked to play alongside the first string. But Crosby and others were concerned many units did not know the snap count.

By the fall of 2003, months after the end of "major combat

operations," the excitement surrounding the opening days of the war had subsided. The Army seemed to be catching its wind and requesting and deploying units at a more rational pace. The pace in the deployment cell at the NGB slowed down, and Crosby was reassigned elsewhere in the building. But the job he really wanted was back in New York. The Army had finally gotten around to calling a combat unit from New York, the 2nd battalion, 108th Infantry Regiment of the 27th Enhanced Infantry Brigade. Crosby had served as the unit's operations officer before moving to the NGB in March 2003 and immediately longed to get back to his old headquarters in Utica. But all the field-grade officer billets were filled. Crosby, who was the only adult male in his military family who had not been in combat, was crushed. He had trained for the big game since 1984 but was no longer on the squad. Worse than that, the major thought it likely the war would be over before he ever found a new team. He sank into depression.

New York's 108th Infantry might not have needed a major, but they were short every other rank. To make the mission, the brigade had to pull men from its other two infantry battalions, including troops from Bravo Company of the 105th Infantry, a unit that shared the 69th Infantry Regiment Armory. The 105th counted dozens of former 69th men in its ranks, as well as friends and family of many of Slack's soldiers. As the unit packed to train for Iraq, some of the 69th men wondered if their own Bosnia mission would ultimately become a Baghdad mission. In communications with his company commanders, even Slack entertained the thought. "We may be in Iraq yet," he mused in an e-mail in September 2003.

But publicly, at least, Slack was still focused on Bosnia. As he had done for the West Point mission, his plan was to fold the three understrength rifle companies on Long Island (B, C, and D) together under the Bravo Company flag. He called the ad hoc unit Company Team Bravo. In the city he would combine elements of his anti-tank company, HHC, and rifle company under the Alpha Company flag, a conglomerate he named Company Team Alpha. The rest of the soldiers would fall under the HHC. If the 69th mobilized the way it had been designed, it would have included an HHC, four line companies, and an anti-tank company. But the best Slack could offer was a diminished HHC and two line companies—less than half the soldiers and combat power he was supposed to have. The commander had asked his higher headquarters to transfer soldiers from other units into the 69th's ranks, but the 42nd Infantry Division already had its hands full. In addition to the Bosnia deployment, the 42nd was sourcing units for the Sinai, Kosovo, Guantánamo Bay, and multiple locations in Europe. In addition, the 42nd was still supplying soldiers for security missions in the New York City area.

Because so many of his soldiers had been performing full-time duty since 9/11, Slack had hoped to take only volunteers to Bosnia. But as the war widened in scope and the division and State took on more missions, it seemed likely that Slack would have to take every swinging Richard he had. In his September 2003 newsletter, he told his men that unless he got a large injection of forces from outside the unit, everyone in the 69th should plan on packing his bags for the Balkans the next summer.

"Men, I'm deeply sensitive to how much turmoil has attended your lives these last two years and how much your lives, and those of the people who love you, will be touched by what we're getting ready to do over the next twenty months," he wrote.

> I'm not deaf, dumb, or blind and I see and hear just about everything you guys are saying. It may take a couple of months to get to me but I eventually hear it all. I know some of you don't wish to go to Bosnia. Well gents, the battalion needs you. Hell, this stinks and I know it! You have every right to be angry on not getting a straight word in order to set your lives in the right direction. I'll tell you this though, I can't find anyone to blame except the God damned terrorists.

In acknowledgment of the dual mission of the National Guard— support for state emergencies *and* a reserve for the Big Army—Slack added a warning order. "One last word, we're now in hurricane season. If a hurricane hits, take care of your family first then make your way to your armory. Come in prepared to stay for a week. If the phones and power are out you can be sure the Guard will be called. Be ready!"

Between the year of Federal and State duty the men had served and the prospect for more of both, Slack knew the battalion was close to its breaking point. He asked his men to bring patience, a determination to get the job done, and goodwill to each drill. "If this was easy and did not require sacrifice our nation wouldn't need an Army. *Stay frosty!*"

Shortly after issuing his newsletter, Slack received another change of mission. After studying up on the Sinai and Bosnia for the past year, the Fighting 69th would now deploy to Kosovo instead.

WHEN PIGS FLY

In the fall of 2003, Major Mike McNutt, who had replaced Joe Obregon as the second in command of the Fighting 69th, left the battalion. The major had been working as the full-time administrative officer in the city, leaving his family alone in upstate New York. When a family crisis arose, McNutt requested transfer back upstate. Slack approved the request. He frequently recalled his own decision to leave the Big Army to save his marriage and reflected often on the toll military duty took on families. "Cling to the wreckage," he counseled several of his soldiers. In addition, Slack believed that a soldier with a problem at home would not be effective in the field. As the Fighting 69th struggled to get ready for Kosovo, Slack couldn't afford to have a distracted executive officer. He named Captain Daniels his temporary executive officer (XO).

Daniels was the perfect guy for the job. Not only was he a master organizer and consummate realist—both traits required for the position—but he was now working at the 69th full-time to prepare the unit for deployment. In the spring of 2003 the accountant had been fired by Fimat. Officially, the French firm had sacked him for an e-mail he had sent to a coworker that contained a joke with a foul phrase, but Daniels was certain that that was just an excuse to shed a highly paid employee who seemed to be spending more time as a soldier than as a loyal employee. His civilian boss had been openly critical on that account, so Daniels wasn't surprised when he got the axe. Though the Army salary was only one-third his civilian pay, the captain came aboard the 69th eagerly and began to bring Slack's visions for the battalion to life.

With Daniels in place as the HHC commander and acting XO, Slack's "wartime" team of senior leaders began to take shape. George "Up the Rebels!" Brett, an Irish American throwback to the Old 69th, took over as command sergeant major. Captain Drew, who had commanded Bravo Company at West Point, took command of Company Team Alpha with First Sergeant Acevedo in the city. The Air Force zoomie who had moved to Martha's Vineyard had asked to come back to the 69th, and Slack placed him in command of Company Team Bravo with long-serving First Sergeant Jorge "George" Vasquez on Long Island. All but one of these key soldiers had served in command or staff positions at Ground Zero and at West Point, or on the extended bridge-and-tunnel security mission in and around Manhattan. More important, they had all worked together since 2000 and functioned exceptionally well as a team. The lone newcomer was Sergeant Major Brett, who was universally accepted after he clobbered some British reservists for making disparaging comments about the Irish at the 69th's Officers Club. *Up the Rebels!*

While Acevedo was the only one of the leaders with significant Big Army experience, Slack's leadership team was fairly seasoned from a National Guard perspective. With a stable command, the 69th began to stem the number of its soldiers going AWOL and to get a handle on its retention issues. The unit hit its low-water mark for strength at 513 in November 2003 and slowly started to rebound thereafter.

Slack's confidence grew. Finally, the Army announced a personnel policy that seemed to lock, once and for all, the 69th into a specific mission.

That policy declared that no member of a reserve component who had been called to active duty in support of the Global War on Terror (including the deployment to West Point) could serve on active duty in excess of twenty-four cumulative months. For the 69th that meant that the soldiers who had spent a year at the academy or supporting other Federal deployments could not deploy to Iraq, Afghanistan, Guantánamo Bay, or Europe, because those deployments generally lasted up to eighteen months, which would put a West Point veteran six months over the cap. The new rule affected so many of his soldiers that Slack believed the Fighting 69th could deploy only to Kosovo, which called for a ten-month mobilization.

That logic made sense to Daniels, too, who in football terms had always viewed the National Guard as the deep bench, with the Fighting 69th closer to the fifth string or injured reserve list. New York's weekend warriors were like Vinny Testaverde, a quarterback who was well past his National Football League prime but who could still manage a season or two in the Canadian league. When the Big Army went to war, the Guard was the perfect option for backfilling necessary but menial missions such as base security and low-intensity peacekeeping. While he thought Kosovo was a perfect fit for the 69th, Daniels was surprised that it had even been called for the mission, which was technically a peace-enforcement operation, as violence in the fractured state still flared up from time to time. Former NATO commander and then–presidential candidate General Wesley Clark referred to Kosovo as the "Wild West," and before the wars in Afghanistan and Iraq, it was the sexiest conventional infantry mission in the U.S. Army. The fact that the lowly 69th was getting the nod for the posting only underscored the strain the Global War on Terror was placing on the post–cold war Army. In fact, Daniels and the other leaders of the Fighting 69th truly had no idea how precarious the state of the U.S. Army had become. The Pentagon was well past the need to commit

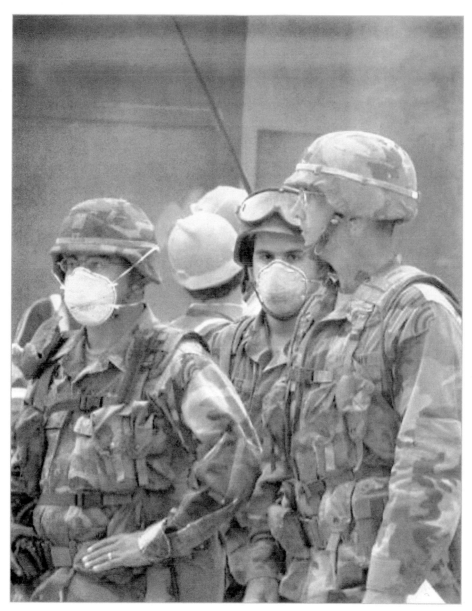

Lieutenant Colonel Geoff Slack *(right)*, commander of the Fighting 69th, and Major Joe Obregon *(far left)* scan their security perimeter at Ground Zero on September 12, 2001. Slack joined the 69th in 1991 when the regiment was in such poor shape that its only role in the Persian Gulf War was to hand out hot dogs to the regular Army soldiers marching in the Welcome Home ticker tape parade in New York. He poured his heart and soul into the unit for ten years, but it was still struggling when terrorists attacked on September 11. *(Photo by Specialist Gurpreet Singh)*

Specialist Jay Olmo, a second-generation Hispanic soldier from Queens, takes time out from security duty at Ground Zero on October 12, 2001 to raise the 69th Regiment Colors in Battery Park to mark the regiment's 150th anniversary. Founded by Irish immigrants, the 69th has long been at the center of Irish American culture in New York. However, by 2001 the regiment was no more Celtic than the Notre Dame football team. *(Photo by Sean Michael Flynn)*

Sergeant First Class Michael Howley from the 101st Cavalry Regiment helps firefighters hoist a flag at Ground Zero on September 12, 2001. National Guard units like the 101st Cavalry and the 69th Infantry were underfunded, underequipped, understaffed, and had been all but written off by the Pentagon. Yet when terrorists attacked New York, National Guardsmen were the first to fight. *(Photo by Specialist Gurpreet Singh)*

Though based in the heart of Gotham, the Fighting 69th never trained to fight there. With no large-scale maps of downtown Manhattan, officers posted their maneuver graphics on tourist kiosks. *(Photo by Lieutenant Dave Friedner)*

The 69th Regiment Armory was turned into the Family Bereavement Center by city officials. After working all day in the horrors downtown, soldiers returned to the armory at night only to find grieving families and friends desperate for information. The armory walls were papered with pictures of the missing. *(Photo by Lieutenant Dave Friedner)*

Many soldiers joined the National Guard for college tuition or an extra paycheck. Few thought they would ever mobilize for war, but 9/11 changed the nature of Guard service. After nearly six weeks of security and recovery duty in and around Ground Zero, two hundred soldiers from the 69th were called to active duty for a year-long security mission at the U.S. Military Academy at West Point. It was the first wartime mobilization for the Fighting 69th since World War II. Here soldiers depart the armory for the security mission on October 29, 2001. *(Provided by the New York State Division of Military and Naval Affairs)*

Specialist Alan Colombani *(right)* screens traffic alongside a Military Policeman at West Point in November 2001. While eager to help the war effort, the soldiers wanted to avenge their own losses by fighting in Afghanistan, not babysitting Army cadets. They would get their wish to fight. *(Provided by the New York State Division of Military and Naval Affairs)*

Lieutenant Colonel Geoff Slack stands in front of Joe Brady (regimental piper), Lieutenant Adam Headrick (adjutant), Captain Alec Lange (assistant operations officer), and the Fighting 69th at Camp Smith in New York on May 17, 2004, before leading his battalion to Iraq. Slack believed the only purpose of an infantry unit, whether in the regular Army or in the National Guard, was to move toward combat, but he wondered if the 69th was truly up to the task. *(Provided by the 69th Infantry Regiment)*

Soldiers wait to board a plane in Newburgh, New York, on May 18, 2004. Before going to Iraq, the Fighting 69th would spend four months training and fleshing out their team. The state of New York needed to pull soldiers from five other battalions just to bring the 69th up to wartime strength. *(Provided by the New York State Division of Military and Naval Affairs)*

Returning to active duty was a seamless process for veterans like First Sergeant Richard Acevedo of Assassin Company, who served in the regular Army in the late 1980s. But many 69th soldiers found the transition from citizen to soldier difficult. *(Provided by the 69th Infantry Regiment)*

Soldiers from the battalion Scout Platoon take a break from training at Fort Hood, Texas. From left to right: Specialist Azhar Ali, Specialist Wai Lwin, Staff Sergeant Henry Irizarry, Specialist Jay Olmo, Corporal Christian Reardon. *(Provided by the 69th Infantry Regiment)*

When the 69th arrived in Kuwait on October 5, 2004 for their final preparations, they expected to find a "Golden Connex" container full of all the combat equipment they had been promised. But the mythical connex never materialized and soldiers scoured junkyards for the gear the men wanted for the drive north. When later challenged on the issue, Secretary of Defense Donald Rumsfeld told it like it was. "You go to war with the Army you have. Not the Army you want." Here, a five-ton truck from Assassin Company outfitted with "Hillbilly Armor" for the road march to Baghdad. *(Provided by the 69th Infantry Regiment)*

The 69th's first mission in Iraq was to patrol around the Taji region to suppress indirect fire against Camp Cooke, twenty-five miles north of Baghdad. The area had not been patrolled regularly for the previous six months, and when the 69th hit the streets, the mortar fire ceased. Here a Blacksheep Company Bradley Fighting Vehicle patrols the village of Awad al Hussein. *(Provided by the 69th Infantry Regiment)*

Many 69th soldiers believed they were helping to improve Iraq. But it didn't always seem like the locals in places like Taji wanted the help. Here children give 69th soldiers a "thumbs down." *(Provided by the 69th Infantry Regiment)*

A destroyed Humvee. With no regular U.S. presence in the area, the insurgents operating in Taji were able to bury massive improvised explosive devices (IEDs) under the roadbeds. The 69th had some initial successes in Taji, but then the insurgents struck back, crushing this armored Humvee and dealing the regiment its first combat deaths since the Battle of Okinawa. *(Provided by the 69th Infantry Regiment)*

The bagpipes were standard fare for the 69th's annual march up Fifth Avenue at the head of the Saint Patrick's Day parade. In Iraq, however, they were most often heard at memorial ceremonies, where Lieutenant Brian Rathburn, Banshee Company executive officer, played "Amazing Grace" following the 21-gun salute and taps. *(Photo by Staff Sergeant Sean Gilday)*

There was no such thing as a day off in Taji. In order to keep the enemy from lobbing mortars and rockets against U.S. bases, the Fighting 69th had to keep its units in sector for as long as possible. Here soldiers from Assassin Company (Sergeant Andrew Neason, left, and Specialist Reynoso in gun) patrol on a rainy Christmas Day in 2004. *(Provided by the 69th Infantry Regiment)*

After some early mistakes, the 69th started to get a handle on the insurgent network of Taji. While they rarely engaged in sustained firefights with the enemy, the unit captured more than a hundred insurgents in only a few months. Here the Salem family sits among a large weapons cache that 69th soldiers uncovered in Taji on December 27, 2004. *(Provided by the 69th Infantry Regiment)*

In February 2005, the Army brought the 69th back to Baghdad to secure the city's Airport Road—or Route Irish, as it was dubbed in the initial invasion. The media called Irish the "most dangerous road in the world," and on it the 69th faced a new threat: Vehicle Borne Improvised Explosive Devices (VBIEDs). Captain Mike Kazmierzak, commander of the Blacksheep, found the first VBIED for the battalion just before Saint Patrick's Day. *(Photo by Michael Kazmierzak)*

VBIEDs seemed to blow up on Route Irish every day in the spring of 2005, and often killed innocent bystanders, such as American social worker Marla Ruzicka. Captain Mike Drew, commander of Assassin Company, sends a radio report on April 16, 2005, following the VBIED attack against a defense contractor that also killed Ruzicka and her driver. *(Provided by the 69th Infantry Regiment)*

Captain Chris Daniels, commander of Horrible Company, pays tribute to one of his fallen soldiers in a Buddhist memorial ceremony in March 2005. The 69th men had seen so many of their friends killed and wounded that many resigned themselves to the same fate, which allowed the soldiers to overcome their fear and continue to fight aggressively. *(Provided by the 69th Infantry Regiment)*

Lieutenant Joe Minning's Banshee Company had been held back in Baghdad for a base security mission while the main body of the battalion was in Taji. When the 69th returned to Baghdad to take on Route Irish, Minning, seen here with Staff Sergeant Hendrik Soelhout, and the Banshees came back, bringing the 69th back up to full strength. *(Provided by the 69th Infantry Regiment)*

The 69th saturated Route Irish with soldiers, making it a dangerous place for insurgents who might want to conduct a sustained attack. When two Iraqis launched mortars on Irish for too long, the Assassins maneuvered on them, killing them in their vehicle. *(Provided by the 69th Infantry Regiment)*

Fighting was only one technique used by the 69th soldiers to secure Route Irish. Community relations was often more effective when dealing with neighborhoods around Route Irish. Here Major Charles Crosby, 69th Infantry executive officer, meets with an Iraqi sheik in the Jihad neighborhood of Baghdad. *(Provided by the 69th Infantry Regiment)*

Lieutenant Colonel Geoff Slack patrolled the streets of Iraq for hours daily and appeared to have no fear when it came to facing the enemy or even walking up to possible bombs. His moxie endeared him to the soldiers. *(Provided by the 69th Infantry Regiment)*

By August 2005 the Fighting 69th got the upper hand on Route Irish and had garnered lauds from higher commands and the soldiers and civilians who transited the highway daily. In recognition of his efforts, Captain Chris Daniels *(left)*, who had served as a company commander for seven years, mugs for the camera alongside his brother Lieutenant Rob Daniels *(right)* after receiving the Bronze Star Medal. *(Provided by the 69th Infantry Regiment)*

Nineteen 69th men made the ultimate sacrifice in Iraq; another eighty-six were wounded. Here Specialist Fernando Trujillo clutches the dog tags of his fallen comrades at a memorial service on August 18, 2005. *(Provided by the New York State Division of Military and Naval Affairs)*

Staff Sergeant Timothy O'Brien hoists the unofficial Green Colors of the 69th Infantry Regiment in Iraq. Though the Fighting 69th is largely Hispanic and Black, thirteen percent of the soldiers still claim Irish roots. *(Provided by the New York State Division of Military and Naval Affairs)*

the second or third string; all four quarterbacks were hurt and it was time to bring Vinny Testaverde back to prime time.

Slack's first hint of the Army's truly desperate condition came in 2004 as he worked, smoked Camels, and drank coffee late on a cold February night in his office in the Lexington Avenue Armory. Daniels had given the commander the final roster for the Kosovo mission, and Slack was looking it over, name by name. He had known many of the soldiers for years, since his earliest days in the National Guard. Some of the men were standouts, and Slack expected they would shoulder much of the weight of the Kosovo mission. Others had spotty records and would need a great deal of supervision. Many of the junior troops were unknown commodities. It wasn't a dream team by any stretch, but they were the only 360 viable names the Fighting 69th could put in the field, and they were probably good enough for a low-intensity mission such as Kosovo. Slack was required to submit the roster to his division headquarters that week, just ahead of a statewide conference for all New York National Guard officers and senior NCOs in Albany. He blessed off on the roster and leaned back in his chair to sort out his next moves when the phone rang. It was Lieutenant Colonel Mario Costagliola, the former commander of the 101st Cavalry, with whom Slack had responded at Ground Zero.

Costagliola was now the operations officer for the 42nd Infantry Division and had just returned from a "sourcing" conference at the NGB, a meeting at which operations planners from the State and NGB matched Big Army requests for augmentation with specific Guard units. The division had attended dozens of these gatherings with State officers in the past year. In one recent session, the Rainbow had lobbied successfully to deploy its headquarters to Iraq, where it would become the first Guard division to command troops in combat since the Korean War. The 69th was not part of that deployment, but at the most recent sourcing conference, Costagliola had learned that the Army and NGB were looking for one infantry battalion to round out an enhanced Guard brigade from Louisiana that was scheduled to deploy to Iraq. The Fighting 69th was mentioned as a possibility.

Costagliola was ultimately directed to nominate the New Yorkers and then called Slack.

"Do you remember seeing the desert-pattern Rainbow patch?" he asked Slack. Since January, the division had been showing off the patch it would wear to Iraq. "Expect dramatic news when you get to Albany."

Slack laughed off what he dismissed as a tongue-in-cheek comment. He finished the phone call and lit another cigarette. The desert? What a bizarre thing to say. By now he had been given so many changes of mission and so much confusing and contradictory instruction from his chain of command that he took everything with a grain of salt. Besides, per the current Army policy, soldiers who had already pulled a year of Federal duty at West Point would not be eligible to deploy to Iraq or Afghanistan unless they volunteered. With such a small force already, it seemed unlikely anyone could rely on the 69th to muster enough troops for a mission to southwest Asia.

But wouldn't it be something if the 69th did go? Slack stood from his desk and began to pace around his ornate office. With its twenty-foot ceilings and mahogany paneling, the room was more a museum than a workplace. A fireplace dominated one wall, and above it hung five of the 69th's seven Medals of Honor. Other walls featured portraits of the unit's wartime leaders and paintings depicting the regiment in combat. A massive glass-topped conference table stood in the middle of the floor. Under the glass rested the twenty-three battle streamers the Fighting 69th had earned since the Civil War. Slack looked down at the table. Would the Fighting 69th actually have the chance to add another streamer? Was there room under the glass? Or were the regiment's glorious days of active warfare over? The commander's heartbeat quickened. The prospect of taking his battalion to combat was electrifying, the fulfillment of a lifetime of preparation. Slack had served in the Army for more than twenty years but had hardly come off the bench. He had loitered in the Fulda Gap and responded to six natural disasters and the 9/11 attacks. But a combat command, the graduate-level education of any professional officer, had eluded him. Could it be possible? Would he get the chance to avenge the carnage the Islamic extremists had wrought on his home?

The more he considered it, however, the less Slack thought a deployment to Iraq or Afghanistan likely. Who could conceive of sending the 69th off to combat? Slack thought back to the Kosovo battle roster. His battalion, despite his best efforts and those of his key leaders, looked more like the Bad News Bears than the Big Red One.

Soldiers died horrible deaths in battle, and even the best units in the Army were suffering casualties in Iraq. What would happen to an unprepared unit? If it were given proper augmentation and some additional training, Slack thought the Fighting 69th would prove to be a fine unit for the Balkans. But actual, active combat? It didn't seem possible or appropriate, given the stakes and the readiness of his battalion.

Rumors of a mission change had picked up pace when Slack arrived in Albany on Friday, February 27, 2004. The next morning, Major General Thomas Maguire, the adjutant general of New York, made it official. "Guess what? You're not going to Kosovo, you're going to Iraq."

That night the senior officers and non-comms from the 69th and the Rainbow Division met for a pre-deployment pep rally at the Albany Pump Station, a microbrewery and restaurant in an old industrial building near the Hudson River waterfront. The beer flowed, and the men passed cigars, with Slack the unofficial guest of honor. Fellow officers patted him on the back and congratulated him on getting the nod for a combat deployment, the first for New York's Fighting 69th in sixty years. The men shared stories of the National Guard antics they had witnessed over the years and in the next breath boasted about kicking Iraqi ass New York style.

First Sergeant Acevedo sat apart from the main group of celebrants, watching the officers glad-handing and wondering why the men were so confident and the mood so festive. The NCO had received news of the deployment like a punch in the stomach. He had trained with infantry units that stood on the front lines in Germany during the cold war and knew the level of preparation needed for a war-traced unit. It would be a very long and hard road for the 69th, and the first sergeant was truly afraid for the battalion. He looked around at the faces of the other leaders he would go to war with—Colonel Slack, Sergeant Major Brett, Captains Daniels and Drew, First Sergeant Vasquez, a dozen others. Acevedo drained his pint of beer. He didn't think any of them would ever be the same.

BOOK II

OPERATION IRAQI FREEDOM

MARCH 2004–SEPTEMBER 2005

6: WHEN THE 69TH COMES BACK

SAINT PATRICK'S DAY 2004

Specialist Jay Olmo had wanted nothing to do with the West Point mission in 2001 and 2002. He thought the assignment was ridiculous to begin with and only got dumber every day. He didn't want an assignment like that ever again, and after the academy deployment pledged to himself to do whatever he could to avoid the next bullshit mobilization. But there was no grousing when word about the Iraq mission came down. Instead of running for the door, Olmo was among the first to step forward. "When do I get to shoot someone?"

The soldier had been watching the shock and awe of the American blitzkrieg unfold every night on television for the past year. He reveled with every big bomb blast and loved video of U.S. soldiers unleashing entire magazines of ammunition into enemy positions. The day the Americans yanked down the statue of Saddam in Baghdad was second only to the day Americans pulled the former dictator out of a hole in Tikrit. That was what Olmo had joined the Army to do. Whether the enemy was the Taliban, Iraqi, or Afghani, the grappler wanted to kick his ass and come home with a fistful of medals. He just needed someone to tell him which way to point his rifle. As an added bonus, Olmo was now surrounded by a group of like-minded soldiers who viewed news of the Iraq deployment as a belated Christmas present.

Gone were the days when Olmo shuddered at the thought of going to war with his comrades in the Fighting 69th, for the specialist had found his own little Dirty Dozen within the regiment. Olmo was now in the battalion Scout Platoon, a unit that had become the reservoir for all the 69th's discipline problems. Whenever a soldier ran aground in a line company, he was traded into the Scouts without any quid pro quo. In most cases the units were simply happy to be rid of the problems. Olmo had requested transfer into the Scouts after the West Point mission, having spent the last few months at the academy running afoul with First Sergeant Acevedo for a series of petty violations. When he heard about the Scout Platoon from Specialist Emil Makish, he jumped at the chance. Nobody in Alpha attempted to stop the transfer.

Makish and Olmo had served together in Alpha at West Point. Though Makish was a white soldier with an open admiration for the World War II–era German army, he and Olmo hit it off. They lived only a few blocks from each other in Queens and both bucked authority at every opportunity. Makish, a wiry soldier with the physique of a meerkat, did so through sarcasm—always greeting the former Air Force officer who had led Alpha at West Point with the zoomie recruiting slogan "Aim High!" Olmo was more blunt, telling senior NCOs and officers to go fuck their mothers. Neither tactic endeared the soldiers to their chain of command. Makish, who had served in the Big Army's 101st Airborne Division, knew all infantry battalions had a Scout Platoon that was traditionally the home of the best soldiers in the unit. Such platoons operated and trained separately from the larger line companies and enjoyed a great deal of independence and élan. He requested a transfer to the Scouts, and soon Olmo and other Alpha Company soldiers hoping to flee the wrath of Acevedo did the same, including Corporal Adrian Melendez, another Big Army and West Point veteran, and Specialist Kelvi Batiste, a soldier with a hair-trigger temper who had been busted at the academy for socking an NCO.

One of six specialty platoons under Captain Daniels's HHC, the Scouts were essentially nonexistent when Daniels took command in late 2000. By March 2004, however, the commander had built them into one of his strongest (albeit unruly) platoons. Daniels first had his full-time technician, a Chinese American with heavily accented English named Corporal Qiyu Luo, ensure that the recruiters were driving new soldiers into the Scouts instead of the line companies. The Scout Platoon then deployed to West Point as a part of Alpha Company, which gave the platoon's non-commissioned officers a year of leadership experience. The academy deployment also resulted in a shuffle of the platoon's management. When Lieutenant Leonard London was relieved for cause, he was replaced as platoon leader by Lieutenant Rakesh "Darryl" Ramnarine, then Alpha Company's top lieutenant. The Scouts' platoon sergeant was also sidelined after he demonstrated that he could not control some of the more miscreant of his soldiers. He, in turn, was replaced by a former Big Army NCO who had served in the Special Forces. Finally, the Scout Platoon benefited from the transfers of soldiers like Olmo, Makish, Melendez, and Batiste who were eager to be part of an elite unit—so eager that they would punch their way in, if necessary.

All were jazzed when they looked around at the platoon with whom they would go to war. They thought they were heads and shoulders above any other unit in the 69th. The Scout Platoon's ranks included physical training studs, great shooters, computer geniuses, and guys like Olmo who just liked to fight. Some were quiet. Some were so loud they were known across the battalion. All had aggressive attitudes. They didn't hesitate to take on a tough task or to tell a stupid leader where to go. Olmo considered his group to be a bunch of infantry maniacs spoiling for a fight.

But not all the battalion's leadership was so confident that the Scouts were up to the task. While they recognized there were many strong soldiers in the platoon, they also identified another dozen men who had proven records as problem children. Daniels thought the platoon had great potential, but knew he would have to keep a close eye on them, especially when the 69th got into Iraq. While there was clearly a low-grade insurgency taking place in March 2004, it looked to Daniels as if the war was winding down. He believed the main focus of the 69th's rotation would be peacekeeping and nation building. Even if there were some hot areas, the commander didn't think that the 69th, as a fourth-string National Guard unit, would be anywhere near the trouble spots. Daniels figured the 69th would only be sent to an area where the Iraqis and Americans were all singing "Kumbaya," and he didn't want his Scouts going into such a peaceful mix eager to "get the first kill," as some of the Scouts were already contemplating. That sort of thing might upset the apple cart. The other New York infantry battalion, the 108th Infantry, was already in Iraq and hadn't gotten into any major scrapes, even in the so-called Sunni Triangle, which led Daniels to wonder if the 69th's infantrymen would even get the chance to earn the coveted Combat Infantryman Badge (CIB), the award given to infantry soldiers who have engaged in combat. But while Daniels had his doubts about the nature of the fight, he didn't share them with the Scouts or other platoons. He wanted his men focused on training, to be razor sharp. If the Scouts thought they were going to some Iraqi version of the West Point mission to do nothing, they would be even more difficult to keep in line.

Colonel Slack likewise doubted that the 69th would get a significant mission. Given the state of the battalion's personnel and equipment, he believed they would be lucky to make it to Iraq at all. Rather, he suspected the Fighting 69th would be relegated to guarding an equipment depot in Kuwait, far away from any potential for action. Still, he realized that a deployment to a combat theater was far more complex than what he was planning for Kosovo. In the days after the Albany conference, Slack contemplated the mechanics of mobilizing for war. It was already March. How much time would the unit have to train? The 69th's equipment was crap from top to bottom. What would the unit take overseas? Slack was certain the first two questions would be answered in short order. But his most vexing concern was personnel. What men would fill out the sparse ranks of the battalion?

On March 17, 2004, Slack sat at the reviewing stand inside the armory for the annual Saint Patrick's Day pass-in-review. As he looked out over the crowd before him, he saw a whole bunch of soldiers he didn't think could deploy. Even some of the troops who would have been fine for the Kosovo mission were not fit for a deployment to the desert, including certain members of his own staff. Slack glanced to his left and right at some of the senior and retired National Guard officers who had come down from Albany to watch the 69th on parade. He believed some were responsible for the problems he faced. Others were simply victims. Strength in the New York Army National Guard had been down for such a long time that the State had evolved a culture of keeping every sick, lame, and lazy human being in the ranks. Now Slack was saddled with scores of coyote-ugly soldiers who shouldn't have been in the National Guard, let alone in an infantry battalion with an alert order for Iraq. It was absurd, and it made the colonel smirk an "I told you so" grin. The time had come for the chickens to come home to roost, he thought.

Slack and Daniels had struggled to build a 360-man roster for the Kosovo deployment. They learned in late March that the Iraq mission called for more than double that number—760 soldiers, in total. When the company commanders looked at the numbers, they concluded either that the National Guard had lost its collective mind or that the Army was in truly desperate shape. Each commander was required to submit a Unit Status Report every quarter. That classified document was sent to the Guard Bureau and the Army so that top planners could both allocate funds and prepare contingency plans in the event of war. When the Fighting 69th got the call for Iraq, the brass in Arlington, Virginia, knew full well that the 69th was in no way able to meet the mission requirements. Yet the New Yorkers got the nod anyway. In his April 2004 newsletter, Slack acknowledged the *Twilight Zone* nature of the unit's alert for Iraq. "By now, you guys have got to be wondering what the Hell happened to the sanity of the National Guard! The truth is that in war all normalcy goes out the window. Like the old adage says . . . a plan is only good until the first contact."

That adage had never been more appropriate than it was in Iraq. The Department of Defense plan assumed token resistance on the initial invasion of the country, but some Iraqis decided instead to fight like hell. The plan assumed American soldiers would be treated like liberators, but the honeymoon was brief. The plan assumed the lowliest of National Guard units would be needed only for a peacekeeping mission in a sleepy area of the globe, but the Fighting 69th was going to the Middle East. The more the commanders examined current events, the more they realized the National Guard may have been crazy, but the war was indeed taking a tough toll on the Big Army and its all-volunteer force. Within a year more than half the combat forces in Iraq would come from the Army's stepchildren from the National Guard. The Army would have to find someone else to pass out hot dogs at the welcome-home ticker-tape parade.

Slack finally got word that the 69th would mobilize in May 2004, training from May through September in the States and then shipping to the Iraq area of operations in October. Once in theater the 69th would serve with boots on the ground (BOG) for one year. As Slack had feared, the length of the tour meant all soldiers who served at West Point or on other Federal homeland security deployments now had to volunteer for service in Iraq, because the mission would put them over twenty-four months of cumulative service. The rule affected more than 150 of Slack's remaining soldiers, and the commander worried that many of them would bail out due to the amount of time already spent away from home. When insurgents launched their first major offensive in Iraq on Easter Sunday, Slack was even more concerned. A soldier from New York's 108th Infantry was killed north of Baghdad, bringing home the possibility of death. Fear is a strong motivator, and several troops did opt out, including three experienced NCOs from Bravo Company. The commander was incensed, refusing to accept that parking cars at West Point counted as legitimate wartime service. Anyone who was abandoning him now was a disgrace to the uniform. "Eventually, you'll hate yourselves for your cowardice, but by then it will be too late," Slack told them. "You'll have to live with yourselves."

Fortunately for the Fighting 69th, only a small number of soldiers chose that road: nearly 80 percent of the men who could have opted out of the mission volunteered to deploy with the 69th to Iraq. Others, including chocolate magnate Lieutenant Joe Whaley, even returned to the battalion. The number of volunteers proved to be among the highest in the National Guard and reaffirmed Slack's belief that old-fashioned patriotism was rippling through his ranks. The 69th had lived through Ground Zero; most lost friends or family. If they could prevent another attack in their own backyards, they would do whatever it took to make that happen. If the commander in chief said Iraq was the place to do it, then the men would go to Iraq. The politics of the war rarely played a significant role in troopers' decisions to volunteer. Their lot was to do their job as soldiers and as comrades.

A second significant factor was loyalty to their friends. Most of the men in the Fighting 69th had served together for years, and they didn't want to let their mates down. In the case of Whaley, he didn't want to let his brother-in-law down. At West Point Whaley had introduced Captain Drew to his sister Ellen. It was a good match, and the couple rushed their wedding plans forward when the Iraq mission was announced. Both officers then prepared for Iraq with strict instructions to bring the other home in one piece.

Captain Daniels was also given instructions to watch out for family. The officer had encouraged his younger brother Robert to join the 69th. Now both were going, and Ma Daniels all but threatened Chris to bring Rob—her baby—home safely.

But even with the volunteers, Slack was still drastically short of troops. Since the start of the war in Iraq, National Guard planners had learned that it generally took three battalions to make two healthy ones. In some instances it took two battalions to make just one. But in the case of the alerted 69th Infantry, the State Headquarters in Albany had to break four other battalions to bring the New York City unit up to wartime strength—a shocking five-to-one ratio. When the 69th Infantry mustered on May 16, 2004, at Camp Smith, in Peeks-kill, New York, for its first mobilization to a combat zone in more than sixty years, the battalion included an entire company from the Staten Island–based 101st Cavalry Regiment, two New York City–based pla-toons from the 105th Infantry Regiment, and more than one hundred soldiers from the 152nd Engineer and the 127th Armor Battalions out of Buffalo. Another score came as volunteers out of disparate units from as far away as California. A full half of the Fighting 69th's men were strangers to the battalion. In Alpha Company, now authorized 139 men, the number of outsiders topped one hundred soldiers. Drew and Acevedo were essentially putting their team together from scratch. And while there were some standouts among the newcomers across the battalion, there seemed an unsettling number of citizen-soldiers who needed remedial training. Most were not infantrymen. When Jay Olmo and the other Scouts looked at the grab bag of soldiers who were sent to backfill the battalion, they were even more convinced they were the best platoon in the 69th. The Scouts were all New York originals and exceptionally proud of it.

Slack's commanders and primary staff officers and NCOs were also largely organic. With only a few exceptions, the colonel had worked with every key leader for years. He knew their strengths and weaknesses. And for their part, they were among the few people in the world who knew how to interpret Slack's intent.

One notable new arrival was Slack's executive officer and second in command. Daniels had been the acting XO for months and hoped to get the job and a promotion permanently. His hopes were dashed, however, when the State sent down a major to fill the slot. Daniels, too busy to hold a grudge, welcomed the new major into the battalion and reviewed with him a ten-inch-tall stack of personnel and equip-ment paperwork that needed to be completed before the deployment. The new major thanked Daniels, picked up the stack of paperwork, and dropped it into the trash bin. "Now we're ready to get started," he said. Daniels was puzzled, then washed his hands of the matter. Obviously, the State Headquarters knew best or wouldn't have sent the new officer. But Daniels and others couldn't help but conclude the 69th's new second in command was overwhelmed—not unlike *Catch-22*'s Major Major incarnate. While he was working in the armory it wasn't so bad, as the windows in the XO's office had bars on them, so the major wasn't able to jump out and disappear whenever he needed to make a decision. The men worried there would be no such barriers at Fort Hood, Texas, though, where the 69th would conduct the bulk of its training for Iraq.

CHECKING THE BOX

Brigadier General John Basilica squinted through the dazzling Texas sun to get a better look at the vehicles that sat atop the line of flatbed railcars. The 69th's heavy equipment had just arrived at Fort Hood's rail head, and the commander of the 256th Brigade Combat Team, the Louisiana Tiger Brigade, wanted to see his new battalion's kit for himself. The word on the street was that the Yankees' trucks and armored vehicles looked more like redneck lawn decorations than warfighting chariots. Basilica scanned the lines of railcars searching for the 69th's gear, but all he could see was a column of old vehicles, probably on their way to a scrap yard. Before he could ask for clarification, a soldier climbed inside one of the old trucks, an M35 Deuce and a Half, and took a seat behind the steering wheel as another group of men pushed the vehicle off the car and into the parking lot. *Now, that can't be right,* Basilica thought. *Not even the National Guard uses deuces anymore.* But the soldiers pushing the truck wore the Rainbow patch of the 42nd Infantry Division, which could mean only one thing. The general turned to his new battalion commander, Lieutenant Colonel Slack.

"Geoffrey, are those your vehicles? Is this the status of the 69th's equipment?"

Slack cringed. The truck Basilica was pointing to didn't have an engine, its fenders were rusted completely off, and shrubs were growing out of the bed. The next vehicle in line had to be towed off the train because it had flat tires.

"No, sir. Only a small piece of it's mine," Slack said. "The rest is equipment from across New York State."

Basilica had expected that the 69th, as a fourth-string unit, would have equipment issues and wouldn't be outfitted like the 256th, which was a well-funded, enhanced heavy brigade with Bradley Fighting Vehicles for armored personnel carriers and M1 Abrams tanks for heavy hitting. In his first conversation with Slack, the New Yorker had informed Basilica that the 69th had long been ignored by New York. But Basilica didn't appreciate how much of a bastard the 69th was and certainly didn't expect to see antiquated trucks without engines. The general marched forward and called to the troops. "Stop it. Stop right there. Do not unload those vehicles. Get that truck back on the train and send it back to New York."

Slack was as embarrassed as he had ever been. He had hoped to make a strong impression on his new boss and the Tiger Brigade. When the 69th arrived at Fort Hood, Slack had his men marching in formation. He urged them to execute proper customs and courtesies. And he threatened his commanders with violence should anyone in their units disgrace the regiment. But there was only so much lipstick he could put on his pig.

Sensing Slack's shame, the general, who was several inches shorter, put his hand paternally on the lieutenant colonel's shoulder. He spoke in a quiet yet immensely confident voice. "Geoffrey, don't worry about it. I wouldn't have cared if you came here in your underwear. We'll take care of it. You're on my team now and you'll get the same as everyone else in the Tiger Brigade. Do the best with what you have, and we'll cross-level the rest from my other battalions."

Although Slack took comfort in Basilica's words, at the same time his temper flared. He was sure there were people in New York trying their level best to help his battalion, but he also suspected that some of the bureaucrats at State Headquarters were up to their old tricks. At his first chance Slack called New York and accused the State of negligence. He was rude and confrontational to the officers who were supposedly supporting the mobilization, telling them that they were failing the Fighting 69th.

Slack gave Basilica the same message, and the general relayed his concerns to his boss. The State Headquarters assured Louisiana brass that they were doing everything they could for the 69th. The New York Headquarters was almost certainly cordial with the Cajuns, but they were furious with Slack for causing a stink. One bureaucrat phoned Slack.

"You need to cease and desist," he ordered, thinking Slack was so far out of line in his accusations against New York that the battalion commander should be relieved. Slack, never one to be intimidated, made it clear to the officer that he didn't have the authority to give anyone in the 69th an order.

"I'm no longer in the New York Army National Guard," Slack said. "I'm in the United States Army. I work for the Tiger Brigade. The only thing you are is a resource. New York State is a resource, and all I expect out of you is equipment and personnel, and that's all." Slack slammed down the phone.

Slack assumed his outburst would mark the end of his career after the Iraq deployment, and, in fact, he almost didn't make it to Iraq. The New York State Headquarters sent word to Louisiana officials that the Tiger Brigade shouldn't hesitate a minute to relieve any problematic 69th soldier, including the battalion commander. Slack had told Basilica about his rocky history with New York brass, and the Tiger Brigade commander might have wondered if the call was an extension of that relationship, perhaps even a veiled effort to professionally embarrass Slack. But Basilica didn't overanalyze the green light to sack 69th men. As the brigade commander, he didn't believe he needed anyone's permission to relieve a soldier. Further, the general had already made up his mind about the rogue New Yorker in their first few meetings. Basilica had encountered a lot of fakes in his life and could tell pretty quickly if someone was blowing smoke. Slack, he knew, was the real deal. He discerned in the blue-collar officer an

honest, candid, and passionate man who was committed to his soldiers, proud of his unit, and eager to do a good job. Basilica was confident that he could trust Slack and that he would be a great fit for the
Tiger Brigade.

Perhaps as a result of Slack's prodding the floodgates open, so
much equipment arrived on the 69th's loading docks every day that
the battalion struggled to keep track of it. New rifles, machine guns,
and night-vision goggles poured in from New York. Even more equipment came from the Army, whose "rapid fielding initiative" ensured
that every soldier bound for Iraq had the latest body armor and weapons accessories. A bundle of cash from NGB also found its way to the
69th and into the hands of Joe Whaley. The West Pointer had been
promoted to captain upon his return to the battalion, but rank was
the last thing he needed; as the new battalion logistics officer, Whaley
relied most on his business acumen. The officer tossed out every
Army rule about how to acquire new gear and set forth as if the 69th
was his latest venture. He issued contracts, made deals, wrote checks,
and bartered with anyone who had something of value. Complement-
ing his efforts was Lieutenant Steve Kitchen. Whatever Whaley
couldn't get his hands on, the HHC executive officer and a carefully
selected team of soldiers who knew "how to get stuff" acquired from
Big Army units at Fort Hood, who may or may not have known they
were helping the Fighting 69th get ready for war. The unit arrived at
Fort Hood with nothing, but with Whaley in charge of logistics and a
handful of strategic acquisitions, the 69th soon wanted for nothing.
In short order, New York's Own had more gear than the rest of the
Tiger Brigade.

The only thing Whaley and Kitchen couldn't get were vehicles.
Those had to come from the Louisianans, and they weren't always
happy about it. The Tiger Brigade commanders were a tight bunch
who had grown up together in the Louisiana Guard. Most of the senior officers and NCOs in the brigade had been with the 256th when
it was called for Desert Storm. They had trained for four months for
the first Gulf War, and then trained again and again for rotations at

the National Training Center (NTC) at Fort Irwin, California. An NTC rotation was the most grueling preparation for any mechanized unit in the Big Army or the Guard, and the Tiger Brigade had earned a strong reputation there. Basilica would tell you the 256th was one of the few units who defeated the heavily favored opposing force at the NTC. Consequently, the Louisianans took great pride in their readiness and their equipment, and were not eager to share their kit with some broken-down and thieving Yankee battalion that could control itself only by marching everywhere it went. Truth told, the Tigers didn't even think they needed the 69th for the Iraq mission. The New Yorkers were sent by the National Guard Bureau because the NGB planners weren't convinced that the Tigers had enough forces to deploy one of its battalions. So instead of its own 3rd Battalion, the Tiger Brigade had to suffer the carpetbagging 69th Infantry—the same damn unit the Louisiana Tigers had fought against in the War of Northern Aggression. A handful of the 256th men had long memories and weren't predisposed to cooperate with what some viewed as a Northern, inner-city, hip-hop gang of thugs who represented all that was wrong with America.

But Basilica forced them to play nicely, reminding his commanders and staff about the Fighting 69th's long road since September 11. For his part, Basilica considered it an honor to command the same unit and the same men who had responded to Ground Zero. Those attacks and the New Yorkers in the Old 69th were what the war was all about. While some of the Tigers continued to complain privately, the overwhelming majority quickly got on point.

But sometimes it did seem as if the 69th was beyond help. When it came time to prepare training reports and equipment status reports and sensitive items inventories, the 69th came up woefully short. On more than one occasion, Slack showed up at brigade staff reviews without the data he was supposed to have. "I'm sorry, sir. My staff has let me down," he would report. The New York grunts seemed as solid in field training as any soldiers from Louisiana, but the senior 256th officers quickly concluded the 69th headquarters was broken.

That was hardly a revelation, for even Daniels and the other 69th company commanders scarcely had faith in their battalion staff. It seemed that one or two soldiers in each section did all the work while eight others sat around on their thumbs. The commanders placed the blame squarely on Major Major's desk; as the XO, he was the battalion's chief of staff. But he didn't seem to have his arms around the problem or its solution. They wondered why Slack was hanging on to the overwhelmed officer. Perhaps the XO had lewd pictures of Slack hidden away someplace.

Major Major's failings were further exacerbated by the lack of an operations officer. Major Pat Macklin, who had served in the Fighting 69th for fourteen years and was one of the longest-serving and most respected officers in the regiment, had been reassigned to the 42nd Infantry when the Rainbow Division was tapped for duty in Iraq. The move was the end of an era for the regiment. Macklin had commanded Bravo Company during that unit's best days, had held the post of battalion logistics officer for years, and loved the Fighting 69th as much as any man alive. One could practically hear the bagpipes playing the "Garryowen" regimental march anytime the good-natured Irish American cop walked into a room. But the pipes seemed to have faded, and Pat's seat was still empty when the 69th landed at Fort Hood.

When Chuck Crosby learned of the vacancy from his posting at the NGB, he lobbied State officials for the job. Though the major had already served two assignments as a battalion operations officer, he got the nod to replace Macklin and was eager to get started, albeit somewhat concerned. He had heard so many negative stories about the Fighting 69th that he expected to see the worst on his arrival. In that regard the 69th did not wholly disappoint. The major concurred with the Tiger Brigade's assessment: The battalion headquarters was absolutely broken. It was a joke, and had nothing that resembled a healthy battalion operation. While good people were on staff, some duds held key positions. In that category Crosby included Major

Major, who had effectively jumped out the office window, as Daniels had feared. But Crosby was confident; he knew every job in an infantry battalion and recognized that he had to fill the vacuum left by Major Major's incompetence if the battalion was ever to become healthy. Unbeknownst to Colonel Slack, Crosby began discreetly picking up many of the pieces that had been falling through the cracks.

If there was a bright side to the 69th, it was its three line companies, which surprised Crosby with their competence and functionality. While each 139-man company had a dozen or so hopeless cases, every unit has its share of them, and good leaders know how to get the most out of their men, even if it involves just having them make coffee or answer the phone. There was something for everybody to do in the Army. Daniels often noted that he had twenty-seven jobs for such cases in his headquarters unit, though there were fewer such duties in the infantry companies. But by and large the 42nd Division and the State seemed to have sent a competent, if not always solid, crop of troops to the line. Captain Drew and First Sergeant Acevedo had scored dozens of ringers in the two platoons they picked up from the 105th Infantry. Their new and improved company included a number of combat veterans who guided the rookies through the gates. Delta Company, the unit from the 101st Cavalry, had culled the best from their battalion. Their only significant weakness was constant complaining. Delta was an armor unit deploying to Iraq as infantrymen, yet they still begged Crosby and Slack for tanks at every opportunity.

In Bravo Company Lieutenant Joe Minning felt as if he won the lottery. The former paratrooper had just completed the Infantry Officer Basic Course at Fort Benning, Georgia, and arrived at Fort Hood late. When he had left for school in the spring, Bravo Company numbered less than 30 men; the company stood now at 139 soldiers, and Minning was in command of a full platoon that included a surprising number of NCOs with strong active-duty experience. Two of his squad leaders had served with the 10th Mountain Division, and another with the 82nd Airborne. Minning's only gripe concerned the training his men were getting at Fort Hood. It was nothing like what he had experienced in the 82nd Airborne, and the platoon leader was afraid it wasn't enough to get his boys ready for whatever they would be doing in Iraq.

Major Crosby felt much the same. The officer stayed up in his room late at night, sitting in his skivvies and poring over the training plan. It was all wrong. Instead of a carefully thought-out blueprint that would prepare the 69th for war, the plan seemed merely like a cookie-cutter response to congressional concerns that reserve-component units weren't getting the training they needed. He believed those concerns could all be traced back to Jessica Lynch, the Army reservist who was taken prisoner after her maintenance company was ambushed on its drive north to Baghdad during the initial invasion. Like many of the Guard units Crosby saw rushed to Iraq in 2003, the maintenance troops had never trained sufficiently for a direct engagement, and in their struggle to fight back, most were killed. To mitigate the chances of a similar tragedy, the Army instituted a training program for all citizen-soldiers that was generic enough to work for any type of Army unit, whether it consisted of mechanics or finance specialists. But the fact that it was generic enough for the lowest common denominator meant that it was not at all appropriate for an infantry battalion. Instead of training to find, fix, and kill the enemy, the 69th was being prepared on how best to react to a Jessica Lynch–style ambush. They would shoot at suspected insurgents from the back of a slow-moving truck, then quickly drive away before anyone was seriously hurt. The 69th wasn't even exposed to the basic building blocks of infantry training: live fire exercises. Big Army units were training for Iraq by maneuvering platoons, squads, and teams; by shooting live ammunition; and by calling in live mortar, artillery, or close air-support missions. The 69th rehearsed guarding a gate with blank rounds. Crosby shared his concerns on this score with the 256th Brigade, but it seemed there was little anyone could do to change the top-down-driven checklist of tasks the units had to complete in order to validate for service in Iraq. Realistic infantry training had been replaced by canned instruction that concluded with a box-checking ceremony.

The job of ensuring that the 69th was trained according to the Big Army program went to officers in the Training Support Battalions (TSBs), who generally recognized the same shortcomings Major Crosby had identified. Before the war, the primary role of the TSBs was to assist part-time soldiers in their training and to evaluate a unit's level of proficiency. The officers were passionate about their roles and believed their work could save lives. However, in the rush to get troops out the door, the TSB officers had often been reduced to mere conductors with the essential duty of keeping the troop train on schedule for a prompt arrival in a combat theater. Their measure of progress was not necessarily the quality and success of the formation, but rather the number of required tasks the unit had completed on schedule. The TSB officers complained about the system's effectiveness, and while senior officers were universally sympathetic, they could not change the reality of a stressed Army.

The line soldiers in the 69th found the training disheartening. Many had sworn to their loved ones that the Army would get them ready for the big fight, but their training often felt more like an exercise in accounting.

Everything the soldiers did had to be recorded on a roster. Lieutenants and sergeants stalked the training areas with clipboards, holding a list of some 100 tasks that needed to be accomplished before anyone could leave Fort Hood: Drivers training. Land navigation. Weapons qualification. The gas chamber. And God forbid someone missed a box. "Stop everything! Private Smith did not complete vehicle search training. This unit cannot deploy to Iraq until Smith learns to search a vehicle!" And the moment Smith did get the training and his platoon leader thought he could finally testify that his unit was fully checked off, the lieutenant received five replacement soldiers, and the entire process had to start again.

But while they struggled to complete their rosters, Daniels and the other commanders often believed it didn't really matter: the 69th would complete its training at Fort Hood in August 2004 whether all its soldiers had checked the boxes or not. In lieu of a check mark, the TSB at Fort Hood would simply ask the company commander to write a letter that acknowledged that while Private Smith had missed the field sanitation class, the commander was willing to accept that risk and pledged to get Smith the potty training at the first available opportunity. So instead of getting worked up over a missed training event, Daniels suggested the 69th simply run every soldier's name through his latest invention, The Box Checker 1000. "It's that easy. Step One: Enter the soldier's last four digits of his Social Security number. Step Two: Enter the name of the country you are deploying to. Step Three: Hit Enter. Step Four: Repeat as needed." No matter how honorable the intentions of the politicians or the Army brass— and nobody doubted those intentions—training at Fort Hood seemed to boil down to a giant CYA exercise. If the 69th suffered casualties, it wasn't the Army's fault. Soldiers were being taught how to spot a random cardboard box with an artillery shell on the shoulder of an otherwise pristine country road. If somebody got killed and his relatives wanted to push the issue, they could dig into the training records at First Army headquarters and see that Private Smith, God rest his soul, had in fact signed his name on the Improvised Explosive Device (IED) roster. He was trained.

The 69th commanders and senior NCOs thought the process was a waste of time and energy, and chewed Slack's ear off about it every night. "The training is useless. This is not what's happening in Iraq. There is no rhyme or reason here. We will not be ready for war." But there was no stopping the Fort Hood freight train. "What do you want me to do? Pull the plug on this whole thing and ship the battalion home to New York?" Slack responded. "We have to do this training."

THE BLACKSHEEP

The check-the-box training hardly fazed Captain Mike "Kaz" Kazmierzak, an officer so lean he resembled a skeleton—and could look as frightening when he wanted to. The commander of Louisiana's Charlie Company, 2nd Battalion, 156th Infantry Regiment, simply told his men to do the stupid stuff as fast as possible, check the damn box, and then get on with real infantry training. The former Big Army officer from the 101st Airborne didn't show up at Fort Hood expecting anyone to train him. Rather, he expected someone to provide him the resources he needed and then get the hell out of the way so he could train himself. He started each day by thanking the Fort Hood TSB staff for coming to the field. "We'll do whatever you need us to do so we meet your requirements," Kaz told them. "Then I need you to stick around to support my training. I don't care if you miss your dinner. We're going to Iraq, and you're here to support us."

Kaz was a smug, aggressive, and absolutely stubborn commander, hellbent on doing things his way, which happened to coincide with the Big Army way. His audacity shocked his soldiers when Kaz first took command of the company in Houma, a blue-collar town of oil-platform roughnecks on the southern tip of Louisiana. The citizen-soldiers there could not have been tighter. They had all grown up in the same backwater bayou. They had all gone to school together, worked together, hunted together, fished together. They had all joined the National Guard together. Then this tall, sinewy captain—a Yankee originally from Indiana—shows up with his badges and his Ranger tab and wants us to do things *his* way? Two of the platoon sergeants who had been running the company told Kaz they wouldn't do it. "Fat fucking chance, Captain America." Kaz fired them both the next month. "Does anyone else have any questions or concerns?"

Kaz took command the same weekend in the fall of 2003 when the unit's new first sergeant arrived. Cliff Ockman looked like Adam Sandler, and with his Cajun accent could have equaled the actor's performance in the film *The Waterboy*. But Ockman was no comedian, and none of the soldiers made the Waterboy comparison openly. The NCO had even more Big Army experience than Kaz and had earned the CIB with the 82nd Airborne in Panama. The company also installed its new executive officer, Lieutenant Daniel Fritts, that weekend.

Together the three leaders ordered the men of their mechanized infantry company to get their shit together. The Tiger Brigade was
scheduled for Iraq, and they had better be as prepared as any unit in
the Army.

The company hated Kaz at first, but by the time the unit landed at
Fort Hood they were grateful for his leadership. The sentiment was
not universally shared among the top brass of their battalion, however. Charlie Company had always been the bastard unit in the 2nd
of the 156th Infantry. Its armory was a three-hour drive from the battalion headquarters, and the boys from Houma always seemed to do
their own thing. And now their commander was an overly demanding prima donna who expected his unit to be treated like a Ranger
company. Their longtime unit nickname—"the Blacksheep"—had
never been more apropos. When word leaked out that General Basilica had directed the 2nd of the 156th to trade out one of its companies
of Bradley-mounted infantry for one of the 69th's more traditional
"leg" infantry companies, Kaz knew it would be his Blacksheep, and
quite frankly, he was thrilled at the prospect. Kaz felt that he and the
Blacksheep had been receiving the short end of the stick for so long
that any change would be good. Rather than wait for the order, Kaz
told his commander, Major Conrad Gavel, that he wanted to be traded.
His wish was granted.

Slack, not surprisingly, thought Gavel was trying to slip him a
Mickey, for the major had a knowing twinkle in his eye when he informed Slack that he was getting the Blacksheep, and even told him
that he should feel free to relieve Kaz of command at any time. Slack
had his staff poke around the Tiger Brigade to find out exactly what
was wrong with this unwelcome gift. The report that came back would
have sounded bleak to most Army commanders: Kaz was hotheaded,
short-tempered, and very demanding and aggressive. He acted on gut
instinct. His company was rebellious and didn't conform. It was all
music to Slack's ears. If the report proved correct, the Blacksheep
would fit right in with the Fighting 69th.

General Basilica was busy swapping any number of combat formations to balance the Tiger Brigade for its mission in Iraq. Basilica had learned the 256th Brigade Combat Team would not, as the 69th had widely assumed, be relegated to guarding an equipment depot in Kuwait or passing out chocolates in peaceful northern Iraq. The brigade and—as improbable as Slack and Daniels found it—the 69th were going into the heart of Baghdad. By the summer of 2004, the city had erupted in a full-scale rebellion against the American occupation. Both former Saddam loyalists and the Shias who were supposed to be benefiting from the war were attacking GIs all over the city. Whatever Daniels's concerns about not earning a CIB, the soldiers in the 69th now wondered if they'd avoid "earning" a Purple Heart, which was sometimes referred to in the ranks as an "Enemy Marksmanship Badge."

To prepare for combat in urban areas, Basilica had to "task organize" his units to ensure that each of his battalion task forces had a similar complement of equipment and was versatile enough to execute any mission in the area of operations. A battalion of all tanks wouldn't have enough soldiers. A battalion of all dismounted grunts wouldn't have enough armor protection. Basilica's 1st Battalion was a tank outfit armed with the M1A1 Abrams. His 2nd Battalion was a mechanized infantry unit armed with the Bradley. His 3rd Battalion, which the general wasn't supposed to deploy with but did anyway, was now an understrength infantry battalion that would maneuver in Humvees. The 69th didn't fit any of those molds. Although the New Yorkers were officially a mechanized infantry battalion, instead of the Bradley, they were outfitted with the Vietnam-era M113 Gavin armored personnel carrier, a vehicle so outdated that the Army had no real expectation the 69th would bring it to Iraq. Instead, the Army planned to outfit the battalion with armored Humvees—mythical vehicles that supposedly awaited the battalion in Kuwait.

Basilica balanced the force by trading Kaz's Blacksheep from 2nd Battalion for Slack's Delta Company "Demons," the unit comprised of former tankers from the 101st Cavalry. The move gave the 2nd Battalion a lighter and more mobile force, and the 69th a heavier punch.

Basilica also directed certain platoons be traded out to increase the number of light soldiers in his tank battalion. The 69th's Alpha and Bravo companies each gave up thirty-nine-man Humvee-mounted infantry platoons in exchange for smaller sixteen-man tank platoons. Drew loved the idea of getting tanks, but his pleasure was short lived: the tank platoons didn't have tanks but came instead with Humvees. Although Slack called them "light wheeled reconnaissance platoons," in reality they were just infantry units similar to those Drew had given up, but half their size and without infantry training. If the 69th captain felt he was the loser in that particular exchange, Bravo Company was even worse off. Their "recon platoon" was even smaller, lacked a leader, and was considered to be one of the worst Louisiana platoons at Fort Hood. The Louisiana officer who had made the assignment freely admitted that he had done so because they were his worst unit. Within weeks, the Bravo commander had to fire the platoon sergeant for incompetence and would struggle for months to get the platoon up to speed.

But the problems associated with the task organization were small when compared to the benefits of the move. In addition to the firepower Kaz supplied with his Bradleys, he also brought a high level of soldier skill. Major Crosby thought the Blacksheep were as professional and competent as any unit he had encountered on active duty. Their presence alone raised the bar for the other 69th units, whose New York ethos wouldn't permit them to be shown up. Whether the effort was conscious or unconscious, the organic 69th units got better after Kaz arrived.

In addition to the Blacksheep and recon platoons, Slack also received the standard complement of fire-support personnel from the Tiger's 1st Battalion, 141st Field Artillery. Known as the "Washington Artillery," the New Orleans–based unit had trained its guns on the 69th at every major East Coast engagement of the Civil War. Their new assignment was to call in fire *for* the 69th, an irony the soldiers enjoyed. But in truth, one could hardly tell the difference between the inner-city New Yorkers and men from the Ninth Ward of the Big Easy.

They came from the same socioeconomic backgrounds, listened to the same music, and even had similar accents. Over the radio, the Washington Artillery soldiers sounded like they were from Brooklyn.

By late July 2004 the wartime Fighting 69th was set. No longer the 1st Battalion, 69th Infantry Regiment, the Fighting 69th was officially flagged "Task Force Wolfhound," in honor of its shaggy-haired and foul-tempered mascot. Slack had his companies pick monikers that described their units as well, with his only criterion that the nicknames start with the same letter as the company's designation. Thus Alpha Company, which represented the tough side of New York, became "the Assassins." Bravo Company, the suburban 69th unit with a significant Irish American population, became "the Banshees" of Irish lore. And the three-hundred-man HHC, which claimed the bulk of the original 69th soldiers who had been with the unit since Ground Zero, became "Horrible Company"—perhaps the most fitting of the nicknames. As the unit's commander, Daniels was now "Hagar the Horrible." With the rebellious Blacksheep thrown into the mix, Slack's confidence in his ad hoc team grew stronger every day. They had trained for six weeks, received more new equipment than they could use, and vetted out many of the remaining broken soldiers. The companies were functioning at all levels, and even the battalion staff seemed to be improving, although at a much slower rate than Slack hoped. Task Force Wolfhound was coming together.

GENERAL ORDER NUMBER 1

The more the 69th grew as a team, the more Specialist Olmo and the rest of the Scouts wanted to distance themselves from it. They thought Slack's strict rules at Fort Hood were stupid, and they showed their disdain for the regiment by taking off their 42nd Infantry Division Rainbow patch. They didn't march from place to place, as directed. They went off the garrison to party and drink when they weren't supposed to. And they continued their irreverence for authority. When one senior NCO from another unit told one of the Scouts to blouse his trousers into his boots, as they were supposed to be worn, Olmo jumped all over the sergeant. "Go fuck your mother. And if you ever talk to one of my soldiers that way again, I'll fuckin' kick your fuckin' ass."

While they weren't the only soldiers in the 69th who blew off the rules and did their own thing, the Scouts were the only unit that did it as a platoon. If one soldier was going to bust General Order Number 1, Basilica's rule that banned drinking alcohol, they would all break the rule together. Their loyalty to one another did make the platoon an even stronger unit, but it also attracted a lot of unwanted attention. Whenever something illegal or inappropriate occurred in the Tiger Brigade, the brass immediately blamed the Scouts. The soldiers even caught flak from other 69th units, especially Alpha Company. When someone made off with the Assassin guidon, the sacrosanct flag each unit used to mark its headquarters, Acevedo immediately suspected the Scouts—Olmo and the other former Alpha soldiers, in particular. Daniels, too, didn't put such a prank past his guys and ordered a mini–witch hunt to toss the Scouts' barracks. In that particular guidon incident, the Scouts were not guilty. The standard had actually been swiped by one of Acevedo's own platoons—the unit the company had detached to serve in a Louisiana battalion.

Nonetheless, the false accusation widened the divide between the Scouts and the rest of the 69th. They acknowledged that they broke any rules worth breaking, but they resented any inference that they were the only ones doing so.

And they continued to break those rules with even greater bravado.

The Scout Platoon contained some of the biggest drinkers in the battalion, and they refused to let General Order Number 1 get in the way of their habit. The soldiers kept covert rental vehicles that they used to get off Fort Hood and then drove them to whatever local bars looked appealing. They'd tie a good buzz on, fight a bartender or two, then head back to the Army post with a few women in tow. If the men didn't have women, they had their own private happy time. The soldiers had all logged on to Internet porn sites for free trials, during which they downloaded as much material as allowed, then passed it on to one of the computer geeks, who archived it for the long year they were facing in Iraq. In most cases the late-night partying didn't slow the men down significantly for the next day of training. They were the youngest platoon in the battalion and had no problem waking up at 5:00 a.m. to conduct physical training after a full night of drinking and other activities.

The alcohol seemed to slow down only one of the Scouts. Corporal Christian Reardon, a team leader in Olmo's squad, was a solid infantryman with a strong Army background that included Ranger School and several operational deployments. But a recent divorce and other personal problems were weighing heavily on him, and instead of a few shots, Reardon was guzzling entire bottles of vodka to drown the pain. When it came time to train, the soldier was still drinking. The situation got worse every week, until two concerned soldiers who worked for Reardon, Specialists Wai Lwin and Azhar Ali, told Olmo and their squad leader, Staff Sergeant Henry "Izzy" Irizarry, that Reardon had a serious problem and needed help. The Scouts tried to intervene and retrieve Reardon from his alcoholic haze, but he was well beyond platoon love. The sergeant was pulled from the unit and directed to counseling.

The move caused a shuffling of duty positions. Olmo backfilled Reardon to become Lwin and Ali's new team leader. Sergeant Adrian Melendez, the Queens native who had served with Olmo in Alpha Company, joined the squad as the second team leader. When it was finally set, Izzy's element contained six soldiers. In Iraq, the men would operate in two Humvees. Izzy would command one truck, with Melendez on the gun and Specialist Todd Reed behind the wheel. Olmo commanded the second truck, with Lwin on the gun and Ali behind the wheel.

Olmo couldn't have asked for a better team. Lwin was a short and quiet Burmese American with characteristically Asian features. He was easily one of the most competent junior soldiers in the battalion.

Ali, who was a foot taller than his partner, hailed from Pakistan and had served with the 2nd Infantry Division in Korea, was much the same. Though he had been a chronic AWOL problem since duty at Ground Zero and wore his thick black hair as if he were still a civilian, the soldier returned excitedly to the Scouts when he learned the 69th was headed for Iraq. As their team leader, Olmo quickly realized he had no work to do. Though one was a Buddhist and the other a Muslim, his two soldiers were all but joined at the hip. They were always in the right place at the right time, ensured the vehicle's weapons were spotless, and were always ready to kick ass. Only one question truly remained: Who was going to get the first kill?

7: GREEN IN THE DESERT

RECONNAISSANCE

After completing its training at Fort Hood in mid-August, Task Force Wolfhound flew to the NTC in California for a three-week validation exercise. By the third week in September, with four months of training under their belts, many 69th soldiers believed, like Jay Olmo, that their sections were ready for a brawl in Iraq. Lieutenant Colonel Slack held no such illusions.

On September 28, 2004, nearly 150 days after leaving New York for training, Slack sat on patio furniture in his backyard on Long Island. The 69th was on a two-week block of leave before deployment to the Middle East. It was a dark night, and the steady ocean breeze blew the smoke from his cigarette away from the commander. An empty bottle of wine and a red-stained glass sat on a table next to him. Slack's wife of twenty-five years watched him from inside the house. Except for lighting another nonfiltered Camel every few minutes, the soldier hadn't moved for hours. It had been like that since the moment he got home. Instead of spending his last precious few days before shipping to Iraq with his wife and children, Slack sat alone in the yard, unable to connect with his family and unable to overcome the fear of pending disaster.

When he first announced the deployment to Iraq, Slack had promised his men that the Army would get the unit prepared for war. "You're going to spend one full month at the NTC outside of Death

Valley in the summer months. The sands of Iraq will feel like a vacation spot after that! Leave it to Uncle Sam . . . you'll be more than ready by the time you meet your first Iraqi. Trust me." But after several days in Baghdad on a pre-deployment reconnaissance with the 1st Cavalry Division, Slack was much less sanguine. What he saw happening on the ground in the capital of Iraq was far different from anything he had trained for his entire life. Instead of linear combat à la a cold war slog against the Russians, Slack saw an asymmetric battlefield where mortar rounds exploded without warning, where insurgents could lob rocket-propelled grenades (RPGs) into American base camps, where the staccato pop of gunfire seemed to echo in the distance at every turn, and where sergeants and lieutenants and captains were continually obliged to make snap judgments—shoot or don't shoot; raid the house or simply drive by; commit extra forces or let the boys sleep; risk getting blown up or give the insurgents free rein on the streets. Slack was absolutely impressed by the 1st Cavalry's professionalism and skill, but he was also sobered, because he didn't see anything like the same attributes in the Fighting 69th. In its final training event in California, Slack concluded that his battalion, however much it had improved, was barely functional in the field. Its ability to gain and maintain situational awareness was nil. It couldn't maintain good communications across the battlefield, and its ability to find the enemy—even a pretend enemy at a training center—was terrible. What would they do when they got into a real fight? Far from ensuring that his battalion was ready for war, the Army seemed to be shoving Slack to the airplane door without a parachute. The 69th, he saw now, had been woefully inadequate at every major juncture of the training process but allowed to move forward despite its shortcomings. The commander was baffled.

The answer lay with the TSB, however. Even if they reported a unit tactically deficient, the Army would send it forward, on time to its "latest arrival date," or LAD. The date was rigid. All the TSB could do was warn the combatant commander in Iraq that he was about to get a unit that was not yet ready for opening day.

At Fort Hood only about 75 percent of the battalion had checked all the mandated boxes, but the unit graduated to the NTC on the back of documents that were so flaky that Slack didn't think they would have flown at a traditional National Guard annual training. The pressure to push the 69th into combat and get the Tiger Brigade to Iraq was so great that the Army trainers themselves seemed to encourage use of Daniels's fictitious Box Checker 1000. It wasn't that anyone wanted to fudge the process, but they had all just run out of time. Soldiers had missed training for dozens of reasons—men had been sick, replacements arrived at the last minute, soldiers were home on emergency leave—and the battalion simply couldn't make up the lost time.

Besides, even if every soldier had completed the required events, a large portion of the instruction was useless. Slack thought the Army gave the 69th the best training it could, based on what it had seen on the battlefield at the time, but the situation in Iraq was changing so fast that the instruction back in Texas or California could scarcely accommodate it. In Slack's week on the ground in Baghdad, none of the combat units were doing things that the 69th was training to do back in the States. At Fort Hood, the trainers—none of whom had been to Iraq—instructed the 69th to drive their Humvees with their windows open and rifles sticking out: the more "bristly" the vehicle looked, the less likely they would be attacked by insurgents, the trainers explained. When Slack landed in Baghdad, he rolled down his window and shoved his rifle out, only to be yelled at by the specialist driving the vehicle. "What the fuck, sir? Are you trying to get us killed?" In country the 1st Cavalry Division never drove in their armored trucks with windows open but instead stayed buttoned up tight in the triple-digit heat, with their gunners sitting low in their turrets, down to their eyeballs. Their goal wasn't necessarily to see the enemy; he was invisible. The goal was simply to survive the first roadside bomb blast so they could continue the fight. "Let the truck do the fighting for you," the 1st Cavalry Division commander was preaching. Roadside bombs—officially, "improvised explosive devices" (IEDs)—

were the top killer of American soldiers in Iraq, yet the 69th had no experience with them at the NTC, as the war-fighting center was designed to train armor units in large tank versus tank fights.

At the end of their three-week exercise in the desert, the colonel who was evaluating the 69th pulled Slack aside and told him his soldiers looked good. They had a lot of spirit. But the battalion's systems were all screwed up; Slack's staff was not functioning properly under the leadership of Major Major. They didn't have the smoothness or the agility to control a battalion fight. Slack didn't need the evaluator to point out his weaknesses, for the commander knew just how ugly the 69th still was. He told the colonel that his unit should stand down from the deployment for a couple of months and really go back and fix the problems that were laid bare during the NTC rotation. The 69th needed to learn to operate its new high-tech equipment, which would enable them to gain and maintain a common operating picture with the Tiger Brigade. Likewise, Slack and his staff had to learn how to command and control a battalion. He told his evaluator bluntly that if the 69th walked out of the NTC and into a high-intensity conflict, a battle against a large and functional enemy, the men of Task Force Wolfhound would likely have their heads handed to them. The trainer seemed to nod in agreement, and then said that it wasn't in the cards. Short of a mass suicide, the Fighting 69th would make its LAD in Iraq.

Major Crosby was more upbeat. The 69th's operations officer had spent a relatively worry-free two weeks with his wife and two children at their home in Annapolis, Maryland. He believed the 69th was ready for Iraq—at least as ready as a green, un-combat-tested, cherry battalion could be, but a hell of a lot better than some of the struggling units the major had seen deploy while he was at the NGB. The 69th had four months of training, while others were lucky to get four weeks. Certainly the Fort Hood process had been woefully inadequate, and the battalion headquarters was completely dysfunctional, but Crosby was convinced that the NTC had been a major success for the task force. The 69th transformed itself from a collection of rifle companies doing their own thing to a battalion working toward a single objective. When the unit arrived in the Mojave it would have been lucky to manage to draft an operations order every other day. By the time it left the NTC, Crosby's team could generate a new order every two hours, if necessary. Granted, there were still dozens of short-comings, and the 69th could have gone back into a training mode to address its deficiencies. But by doing so Crosby feared the unit would be following the General George McClellan leadership style of the American Civil War—training for perfection but not for combat. While Slack stewed in his backyard, Crosby was eager to get going. The Fighting 69th was *adequate* to the task.

But Crosby hadn't been to Baghdad, and as he wasn't the task force commander, he wouldn't have to answer to a dead soldier's family. That job, if (and God forbid) it became necessary, belonged to Slack and his four company commanders. If the Army would have given the New Yorkers more time, Slack would have taken every second of it.

Debbie Slack finally tired of staring at her husband through the glass and popped her head outside, urging the colonel to come in. "Hey, listen, you're going to be gone for a long time. You need to set-tle down and spend some time with us," she said. But Slack was com-pletely overwhelmed by the problems that were circling in his mind. *Where will we get our armor from? How will my commanders move around the battlefield? How will we be able to generate orders on the fly? How do we get well? We're shipping out, and I don't have a solution for these things.*

He went back to his Camels to look again for the answers. But he wouldn't find them until his boots were firmly on the ground in the Middle East.

SHITHOUSE POETS

The guys didn't shut up until a good fifteen minutes into the flight. Then mercifully, as the plane topped off at thirty thousand feet, Olmo could close his eyes and get a solid nap. The GI was still recovering from his two-week leave. Instead of going back home like most soldiers in the 69th, Olmo and a fellow Scout had caught a flight to the Dominican Republic, where they drank and caroused and bedded prostitutes two at a time. If the two Scouts were going to get blown up by an IED in Iraq, they intended to die full of penicillin and without any regrets. The soldiers likewise had concluded they couldn't buy anything if they were dead, so they spent whatever savings they had and ran up as many charges as their credit card companies would allow. The two men had been back in the U.S. for a few days, but the alcohol was only now starting to leave their systems. As his no-regret hangover began to take hold, Olmo leaned his head back against the seat of the chartered commercial plane and slept—from northern Louisiana through stops in Newfoundland and Germany and on to the Middle East. He was sober by the time he landed in Kuwait, but was ready for another drink the moment he stepped out of the aircraft.

The desert air hit Olmo as if someone was blowing a hot hair dryer in his face. The light was so bright he moved quickly to put on his sunglasses, only to discover that he was already wearing them. The soldier stood for a moment at the top of the portable stairway, shuffled his rucksack and his two weapons—a stubby M4 carbine and an M14 rifle for long-range shots—and then slowly descended, straining to make out any sort of a landmark from his vantage point on the stairs. But there was little to see. The only other plane on the Kuwait airstrip was a massive U.S. Air Force C-5 Galaxy. A few sand-colored one-story buildings with cement landscaping bordered the runway. Everything else disappeared in a heat-rippled haze that extended straight to the horizon.

When Olmo reached the bottom of the ramp, he was directed with the rest of his platoon to a white shuttle bus. The men were thankful that the driver had the doors closed and the air conditioner on. But once inside, they all scrambled to the back to distance themselves from the man's body odor. Soldiers on other buses were going through the same drill. The drivers were not perfumed Kuwaitis, but rather low-wage imports from every third world port east of Arabia. That the men stunk was a good thing, just the spark that the Scouts needed to recover from the shock of the heat and their pending date with destiny in Baghdad. The soldiers began to joke around boisterously, perhaps to hide their anxiety.

The first bus took the Scouts to yet another bus before the men boarded a third one, which was quickly joined by a Kuwaiti security vehicle, a khaki Toyota pickup truck with a machine gun mounted in the rear. Their bus fell in behind the security vehicle, and the 69th was swept off the air base and into the vast desert no-man's-land that separated the wealthy, pro-American Arabs in Kuwait from the poor, anti-American ones in Iraq.

Blue curtains were drawn over every window of the bus, and Olmo wasn't sure if they were a security measure or if they were there to keep the heat out. Since the Kuwaiti security guard in the escort vehicle didn't appear to have any ammunition, Olmo concluded it was the latter. He parted the blinds to get a good look at the Middle East beyond the airport. There wasn't much to see. Except for Arabic writing on the road signs, the highway they drove on looked like any highway in the States. In some regards it was better, and so were the other cars on the road. Most Kuwaitis drove Mercedes rather than salt-rusted Toyotas or Fords. In the distance, never closer than five hundred meters away, were row after row of new concrete town houses that could have been in Queens, but for their pastel color schemes. As they drove on, the houses became more and more distant. Soon there was no sign of life save for the soldiers themselves and the annoying cacophony of Indian music the bus driver played to drown out the incoherent babble of the goofy Americans.

Several hours later, the vehicle pulled off the paved highway and made its way over a dirt-packed desert road. They followed the trail for another hour until they arrived at a glowing tent city that was truly in the middle of nowhere. The sign said CAMP BUEHRING, their home for the next three weeks. The men de-bused around midnight and were told to hit the mess hall, a series of prefab trailers that had been pushed together to make a cafeteria that was stars better than anything the soldiers had ever experienced in the field with the Army. It was their first glimpse of KBR living. KBR, formerly Kellogg Brown and Root, was one of the larger defense contractors supporting the war effort and allowing the U.S. to keep its numbers of boots on the ground low. They administered the mess halls, set up the soldiers' tents, maintained the air conditioning, and ran training areas. While KBR did just about everything, the soldiers' primary interaction with the contractor was at mealtime. There was a main serving line, a grill-to-order line, and no limit on the amount a soldier could eat. Steaks on Monday. Crab legs on Friday. Ice cream anytime.

After chow the men were guided to a tent where their ID cards were officially "swiped in" to theater. It was October 5, 2004. As of that day the men's salary was no longer taxable, and they received extra pay for being in a combat zone—which Kuwait wasn't, of course, but the men weren't complaining. After a few briefings, the Scouts were guided to their tents—if you could call them that. The hooches were more like blueblood hunting lodges, with wood floors and such powerful air conditioning that many of the soldiers needed to wear wool caps to keep warm.

The purpose of the 69th's stop in Kuwait was to generate combat power, a process that was more officially known as RSOI: reception, staging, and onward integration. Before the 69th left Fort Hood, they had packed up all their vehicles and a plethora of other equipment, which was then stuffed into shipping containers, or connexes, that were railed to Houston and from there loaded onto a ship for the Middle East. While the 69th trained at the NTC, their equipment sailed halfway around the globe to Kuwait, where it was further advanced to Camp Buehring. Within a week of their arrival, the men married up with their vehicles and connexes, and started preparing them for the drive north to Baghdad. The soldiers also used the time to sharpen their infantry skills, however their commanders saw fit. Most units spent their time shooting, rehearsing battle drills, and conducting physical training to speed their acclimation to the 120-degree temperatures.

But no matter how much training the units conducted, there was still a great deal of idle time in Kuwait for many soldiers—time they just couldn't help but use to speculate about the forthcoming drive to Baghdad and the increasing levels of Iraqi combat they watched on the TVs every day in the KBR mess hall. Some soldiers were giddy; some were morose; many were scared. Slack had felt the tension start to build back at the NTC, where his men were growing suspicious of the training they had received in Texas and California, and skeptical about their inexperienced leadership. From Slack down, virtually none of the senior officers and NCOs had been in combat, and the soldiers had begun expressing their dissatisfaction with commentary and lewd sketches on the walls of the Porta-Johns, first at the NTC and then in a frantic outburst in Kuwait. One soldier wrote that the 69th was fucked up and that the unit "better have a good supply of body bags." Another simply observed, "We're all gonna die." The comments and diagrams zeroed in on Slack, Command Sergeant Major Brett, First Sergeant Acevedo, and Daniels's Scout and Medic platoons. One salvo against Acevedo was so bad that he ordered his men to provide handwriting samples so he could identify the poet. But no amount of admonishment or sleuthing could keep the bathroom walls clean. As October waned the writing became more frequent and telling of the men's fears.

One factor that exacerbated the Porta-John complaints was the vulnerability of the vehicles. The men had heard they would get the latest armor and other equipment in Kuwait, the so-called land of the "Golden Connex," a mythical shipping container that had all the kit a soldier headed to combat needed—especially vehicle armor. But the connex was never found, leaving the men despondent. One soldier in a unit that followed the 69th in Kuwait would later even challenge Secretary of Defense Donald Rumsfeld over the matter. During a televised news conference he asked the secretary why the soldiers were being forced to scour junkyards to outfit their vehicles for the drive north. Rumsfeld was momentarily taken aback, but ultimately told it like it was: "You go to war with the Army you have. Not the Army you want." And the military was simply short of armored vehicles. They tried to put a Band-Aid on the issue at Buehring. One of the civilian contractors there ran a shop whose sole purpose was to add thick armor plating to the sides of trucks and Humvees. But with the entire Tiger Brigade staging for Baghdad and a Marine Expeditionary Unit waiting to go north to Fallujah, there weren't enough hours in the day to equip all the old vehicles. A group of soldiers from the Banshees tried to pitch in. Welders in the civilian world, they volunteered to beef up the staff at the armoring shop and also Dumpster-dove for extra steel at every camp in Kuwait. The men welded day and night, covering their soft-skinned trucks with what Slack called "hillbilly armor." GIs added solid plates to the doors, built cupolas for the gunners, and cut steel with tiny vision slits to cover the windshields of the five-ton trucks.

Major Crosby had never seen the task force work so hard. When the men ran out of metal, they started painting their vehicles. Most units featured shamrocks on their trucks, a tradition in the 69th. One platoon sergeant in the Assassins spray-painted his entire truck black. Before long the 69th's fleet of Humvees and cargo rigs looked like something out of *Mad Max*. But just as the soldiers started to show some confidence in their improvised armor, word got out that the extra steel plating was useless. Some of the Banshees had taken the armor out to a rifle range and fired various-caliber weapons into it to see what would happen. The steel didn't stop a thing, not even the smallest bullet. Word of the ballistics test tore through the battalion, and the men threw up their hands in resignation. They were going to Iraq and were going to die because they had no real armor—and it was all Slack's fault. (At least that's what an outhouse scribble claimed.)

The primary maneuver platform for the infantry in Iraq in 2004 was the M1114 up-armored Humvee. Ten days before the 69th was set to drive into combat, they still hadn't received a single 1114 (pronounced "eleven-fourteen" by the troops). About the sexiest things they had were six M1025 soft-skinned Humvees with an add-on-armor (AOA) kit. Compared to the hillbilly armor, the 1025s with AOA were practically tanks. But the real benefit of the 1025s was that they came with a Blue Force Tracker (BFT). The BFT was a system new to the War on Terror and looked like a beefed-up dashboard GPS that a soccer mom could use if she needed to get her kids to a match in Sadr City. At its most basic function, the machine allowed the vehicle commander to see where he and other BFT-equipped vehicles were on a map. BFT operators could also send messages to one another, such as, "Don't go this way, lots of big bombs." Finally, the BFT provided a common operating picture for all forces in theater. When the machines were turned on, commanders at all levels essentially knew who was at work in a given area.

Slack would never ask his men to do something he wouldn't do himself. As such, he wanted to drive north to Baghdad in the homeliest and least protected of the 69th's vehicles. But because he needed his command elements monitoring a BFT, all six of the armored vehicles went to him and his commanders or key staff members. Slack was never comfortable with the decision, but paid for it on the shithouse walls, anyway. The perception among the troops was that the brass was getting the best armor while the men would drive north in their birthday suits.

As if the morale wasn't bad enough, the task force took another hit. The men learned that Corporal Christian Reardon died in his Texas barracks. Daniels had pulled Reardon from the Scout Platoon back at Fort Hood and enrolled the soldier in an Army substance-abuse program. The Ranger remained in treatment while the 69th moved forward, but help came too late. Denied access to alcohol, the soldier drank cleaning chemicals. He was found dead two days later in his barracks. Olmo learned about Reardon's death from Izzy, and both men took the news hard. Reardon was one of the original six members of their squad. Good humored, generous, and professional, he never hesitated to teach his fellow soldiers a better way to do something. And he was a loyal friend. It seemed to Olmo a horrendous waste of a decent man and a talented soldier. If he had to die, Reardon should have died in Iraq alongside his mates, not alone in a cement-block room in Texas.

On October 23, 2004, Task Force Wolfhound gathered to remember their fallen comrade. The soldiers marched in formation behind Slack and their Catholic chaplain, whose assistant hoisted a blue guidon with a white crucifix. As the soldiers filed inside for the memorial service, they passed by the battalion bagpiper and Banshee XO, Lieutenant Brian Rathbun, who played "Amazing Grace." The officer was slightly rusty in his rendition, but then, it was only his first performance.

MACH JESUS

Christmas arrived the following night when twenty 1114s with the 69th's name on them rolled into Camp Buehring. Though it was late, men climbed out of their cots and ran to have a look at their new trucks. The vehicle seats were still wrapped in plastic, and the Hummers had that new-car smell. The soldiers practically drooled on the trucks. These were National Guardsmen who had never received a major new piece of high-tech Army equipment in their lives. When Alpha Company responded to the 9/11 attacks, the unit still had World War II–vintage M3 "grease guns" in its arms room. The men got even more worked up when they opened the trunk. The vehicles came complete with brand-new machine guns and radios as well. One of the lieutenants stepped out of an 1114 and asked where the hidden camera was, certain he was the victim of a cruel joke. Within moments the vehicles were parceled out to the companies. Both the Assassins and Banshees scored eight, with word that even more were on the way. The Blacksheep, which would maneuver primarily in Bradleys, didn't get any. The Scouts claimed four.

Olmo was not satisfied. His platoon would be the lead element of the 69th after it crossed the border into Iraq for the march north to Baghdad. Their job was to drive ahead of the task force to clear the path for the main body. Still, Olmo and the rest of the guys thought they should have more than four of the 1114s. Every Scout should be in one. What the hell did the line companies need them for? They would be far behind any major enemy contact.

But the distribution was appropriate, as far as Major Crosby was concerned. The mission of the Scouts was to find the enemy and then come back and report; it was the line companies—the Assassins, the Banshees, and the Blacksheep—who would then move forward to close with and kill any bad guys through fire and maneuver. The line doggies logically rated the heaviest armor. Accordingly, when the Tiger Brigade ordered the 69th to give up two of its brand-new 1114s for General Basilica's security detachment, Crosby—though he fought the request with the brigade—concluded he had to pull two trucks from the Scouts. It made perfect military sense. Of course the Scouts didn't see it that way, but rather as just another example of the battalion's shitting on them because they were the bad boys. With a dozen detention notices under their belts, one fallen comrade, and now a puny complement of armor, the Scouts began to develop a bit of a martyr's complex.

Olmo had figured such poor treatment would continue in Iraq. He told Lwin and Ali that the Scouts "weren't gonna do nothing." If anyone was gonna have some fun, it would be the line companies, because they were supposed to "find, fix, and kill" the enemy. The Scouts would probably get relegated to some bullshit security detail like Olmo pulled at West Point. But the military academy analogy didn't seem to hold much water when he and the other Scouts were called to the ammunition supply point to pick up their combat load. Four pallets of ammunition were piled high in the HHC area. Because there were only twenty-eight Scouts out of nearly three hundred soldiers in the HHC, Olmo calculated that they would get only a small allotment of munitions. When the HHC XO told the Scouts to take three of the four pallets, Olmo was speechless. *What the fuck do we need all this for?* The Scouts had crates of anti-tank rocket launchers, called AT-4s, boxes of hand grenades, and a lot more ammunition than one needed to guard a schoolhouse. As he prepped his gear for the march north, Olmo had a mix of 30 high-explosive and smoke grenades for the M203 grenade launcher that was attached to his M4. He had another 360 rounds for the carbine itself. And for his M14 long-range rifle, he carried 175 more. For the West Point mission, Olmo had carried ten bullets. TEN BULLETS! He was now a walking arsenal. *Let's go fucking get some!*

The Blacksheep were the first to head north. On October 25 they loaded their Bradleys onto flatbed trucks, crawled inside the beasts, and were towed to Baghdad. While the soldiers couldn't maneuver, they could certainly unleash some serious shock and awe from their turrets if necessary. The main body of the task force rolled out of Camp Buehring at 1:00 p.m. on October 29 with 123 of their own vehicles and another 90 support vehicles from the Tiger Brigade, which was traveling with the 69th (and its machine guns) for protection. With all its hillbilly armor and outdated New York equipment, Slack thought his task force was an altogether grotesque-looking beast that was not ready for battle. They were driving junk. *What a terrible way to go to war.* But they were past the point of making any more improvements. Ready or not, the Fighting 69th was finally headed for combat. Slack spelled out his intent in his operations order: "We will leave no element, vehicle or soldier behind and will finish as we started; with everyone and everything. We will pace ourselves off our weakest vehicle. We will protect every element of the convoy with fierce reaction to any enemy action, and we will act with complete professionalism to give the enemy second thoughts about attacking our convoy."

After stopping at the Kuwait border the first day, the unit crossed "over the berm" and into Iraq early on the 30th. The first element of the main task force to enter Iraq was a platoon from Louisiana that was assigned to the Banshees. Lieutenant Colin Smith and his light-wheeled reconnaissance platoon set out ahead of the 69th to mark a confusing road juncture near the Euphrates River. With their BFT the platoon found the intersection easily enough in the early morning darkness. As he and his men dismounted their 1114s, the local mosque sounded its morning call to prayer. Except for the time his commander had made him watch *The Message,* a 1976 film about the founding of Islam, it was the first time Smith heard the call. With a force of just four vehicles and sixteen soldiers, the lieutenant suddenly felt incredibly alone and nervous. He was sure the Arabic singing was sending out a message to the insurgents nearby: "The Americans are here, grab your RPGs, attack at will, Allah Akbar!" A bead of cold sweat dripped down his side underneath his body armor. Then, out of the darkness, a donkey with a driverless cart strapped to it started plodding toward him. Since getting the call for Iraq, Smith had heard any number of stories about IEDs and suicide bombers and ambushes. Dead dogs had bombs stuffed inside them. Women carried babies full of TNT. What about a donkey-borne IED—a DBIED? It had to be a tactic. Smith keyed his radio and told his platoon to stand by. "Watch that donkey cart," he said. As the ass continued to come closer, Smith's mind raced, searching for the Arabic word for "stop." Finally he shouted, *"Ogaf!"* But the cart kept coming. The lieutenant's heart pounded against his body armor. *Fuck! Fuck!*

"Take it out!" he called to his gunner over the radio. "Engage!"

But instead of shooting, the men only looked around at one another, wondering if the lieutenant was serious. "Did he say engage?" Smith's platoon had been chosen to go to the 69th because it was effectively broken. They had improved since joining Task Force Wolfhound, but they still had a way to go. If they had been better trained, they would have immediately blasted the donkey and the cart back to Babylon.

"Hold your fire! Hold your fire!" Smith then called. A second after he had given the initial order, Smith made out a boy sitting in the cart. The officer allowed the donkey to get closer. He made eye contact with the kid. He was about twelve years old.

"Mister, Mister," the boy called in awkward English. "Chocolate?

Mister? Chocolate?" The kid motioned his hand to his mouth. He wanted a piece of candy.

Smith caught his breath and his heart slowed. He didn't contemplate (yet) the fact that he had just given an order to blast a small boy, and instead relaxed. The sun had begun to rise, and Smith scanned the village at the crossroads. Men, women, and children were coming out of their houses to start their day. None of them seemed to have guns, and none of them, save the kid, paid any mind to the soldiers. It was just a normal town on a normal—if you could call a platoon of Humvees in your backyard normal—Saturday morning. In the distance he heard the first vehicles of the battalion main body approach. It was Olmo and the Scouts. They gave Smith's platoon a wave, shouted "Get some" a few times, and continued north.

Once inside Iraq, the Scouts sped ahead of the battalion to "clear" the route. They were Slack's early-warning system and could give the commander a heads-up if the roads were closed or if insurgents had lined the highway with "Go Home Yankee" signs. Per the battalion order, they were supposed to drive no faster than forty-five miles per hour and ensure that their weapons were in an "amber" status: magazines in rifles but no rounds in the chamber. It was a safe way to travel and minimized the risk of a vehicle accident or an accidental discharge of anyone's gun.

Fuck safe.

Olmo and the Scouts chambered their rounds and pressed the pedals to the floor, cruising through southern Iraq at mach Jesus. Speed was security. If they went fast enough the enemy would have a tough time hitting them with an IED. And if they did attack, the Scouts didn't have to worry about returning fire immediately. If they were engaged their plan was to reflexively lay down a hailstorm of lead in the most likely enemy hiding spots—in that depression, on top of that ridge, behind that house. Olmo took note of any possible enemy hiding place as they sped north and told his gunner, Ali, over the headset to "watch that fuckin' house over there." If anything went down, Olmo wanted to make sure nothing around them survived.

The night before the 69th crossed into Iraq was the most scared Slack had ever seen his soldiers. They had watched beheading videos and footage of burning vehicles for months. They had heard nightmarish accounts of the effectiveness of the enemy's IED program. But mostly they knew so little about where they were going and what they were going to do there that the fear of the unknown was nearly unbearable. But the anxiety had been all for naught: the march to Baghdad took four days, but the 69th was not involved in a single hostile incident. Nobody got the first kill.

The main body arrived on November 1 at the Baghdad International Airport (BIAP) military base cluster, collectively referred to as the Victory Base Cluster (VBC). The 69th reported to a small section of the VBC known as Camp Liberty, in the northeast portion of the cluster, where a large billboard proclaimed WELCOME TIGER BRIGADE! That sentiment wasn't just southern hospitality. The 256th would be relieving a brigade from the 1st Cavalry Division that had already lost some fifty soldiers. They were, to no one's surprise, thrilled to meet their replacements.

8: TAJI

TASK AND PURPOSE

The move to Baghdad behind them, the Tiger Brigade commanders prepared for their next assignments. The officers hadn't been given missions so much as they were given places. First Battalion gets the farmland west of the airport. Second Battalion gets the shithole north of the airport. Third Battalion gets the road in the east. And the 69th—you wonderful old Yankee Wolfhounds—you guys get way up north, across the Grand Canal. "Get" wasn't a doctrinal term in the Army, like "attack" or "seize" or "clear." But Slack knew pretty much what it meant: the 69th had to enforce security and demonstrate American goodwill over everything and everyone in the largest sector of the Tiger Brigade—Taji.

The commander struggled to assess his assigned area from the window of a Humvee as it bounced along dirt trails that were just a bit too narrow for the vehicle. The driver slowed to balance the 1114 as it crossed a crumbling earthen bridge. Slack, in the rear seat on the passenger's side, pressed in close to the window and looked down to where the road should have been but saw only the green water of the irrigation canal. Taji was crisscrossed by hundreds of the reed-lined waterways, and Slack wondered how Kaz's Bradleys could maneuver in such constricted terrain. As the truck turned carefully off the bridge, the commander gazed ahead down each side of the long canal. Walls of dirt and weeds that had been dredged by hand out of the canal for generations rose alongside the trail, sometimes higher than the top of the vehicle. While the berms made the Americans invisible to any insurgents who might have been looking from the opposite side, Slack wouldn't have been able to see them, either. And if the bad guys had grenades, they could easily lob them over the mound and into the gunner's turret. Slack didn't like it.

As the last of four trucks crossed the perilous bridge, the lead driver stepped on the gas and disappeared in a cloud of dust. Slack's vehicle was second in the order of march. He was riding with the current commander of the AO (area of operations), a lieutenant colonel from the 2nd Battalion, 7th Cavalry Regiment of George Custer fame. The officer told his driver to gun it, and the vehicle eventually overcame the weight of its armor and soared along the canal trail. If the Humvee had shocks, Slack didn't notice as he bounced up and slammed down like a ragdoll, his arms flailing about as he struggled to get his hands on any anchorage he could. "Hold on," the colonel in the front shouted over his shoulder. They were approaching an intersection with a paved road. Slack got one hand on the seat in front of him and pressed another onto the ceiling only a second before the two-thousand-pound Humvee launched off the lip of the asphalt, skittered over the road, then slammed back down into another dirt trail. "That's Route Red Legs," the colonel yelled back to Slack. He advised the New Yorker to avoid the road at all cost.

Slack was black and blue by the time the patrol returned to Camp Cooke, the U.S. base in Taji. The 69th commander had left the camp with his counterpart an hour earlier and had hoped to take stock of the land that Task Force Wolfhound would inherit in the coming days. But they had driven so fast he barely saw a thing.

"Is there some reason you guys drive like that?" Slack had asked.

"You didn't see enough?" the colonel replied. "You wanna go back out there? 'Cause if you do, my truck's right there. Feel free to take it whenever you need it. In fact, you can have the damned thing."

The colonel looked at Slack sternly, perhaps with a trace of madness.

"No. I'm okay."

"Alright then. How 'bout some chow?"

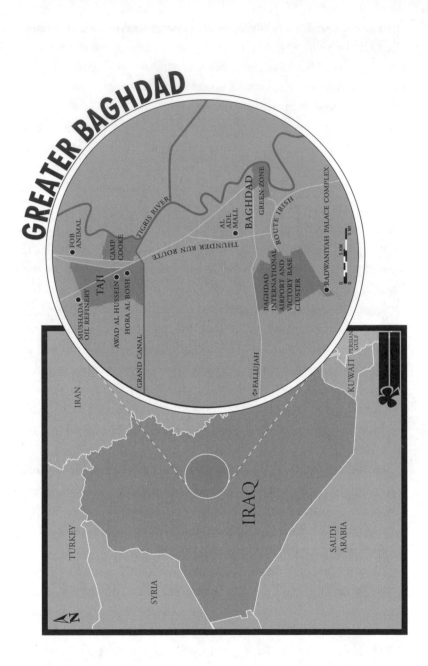

GREATER BAGHDAD

FOB ANIMAL

CAMP COOKE

TIGRIS RIVER

AL ADL MALL

BAGHDAD

GREEN ZONE

RADWANIYAH PALACE COMPLEX

THUNDER RUN ROUTE

ROUTE IRISH

MUSHADA OIL REFINERY

TAJI

AWAD AL HUSSEIN

HORA AL BOSH

BAGHDAD INTERNATIONAL AIRPORT AND VICTORY BASE CLUSTER

GRAND CANAL

FALLUJAH

5 KM

5 MI

KUWAIT

PERSIAN GULF

IRAN

IRAQ

TURKEY

SYRIA

SAUDI ARABIA

N

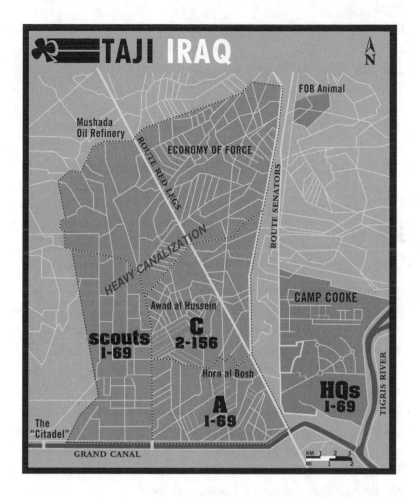

Before Slack could answer, one of the 7th Cavalry commander's soldiers ran out of the unit's headquarters toward the men. There had been a major mortar attack on Forward Operating Base (FOB) Animal, home to an Iraqi army company the cav troopers were training. There were casualties, lots of them.

"I guess we will take another ride after all," the cav commander said. He started walking toward his Humvee. "Let's go."

The soldiers rolled back off the base and turned right onto Route Senators, the main supply route between Baghdad and all points north. After twenty minutes the column of four Humvees pulled into a sandbagged and ramshackle mini-fortress that Slack thought looked

like Fort Apache. They dismounted near a crowd of angry Iraqi soldiers, the cav commander pushing past the gaggle and into the main
courtyard, where the mortars had exploded into a formation of troops.
Blood was three inches thick on the ground, and the walls of the surrounding buildings were splattered red. Bloody handprints smeared
the cement. Slack hadn't seen anything like it since September 11.
The colonels went inside an Iraqi barracks, where it looked like a
slaughterhouse. The floor was well marked with trails of blood that
led up a staircase the Iraqis used to drag up the wounded. The colonels were soon met by an American captain, who was soaked in blood
like everyone and everything else.

"Gentlemen, if you come to the command post I can give you an
update," the captain said.

Slack followed the cav soldiers into the CP and tried to listen to the
report, but he missed a lot of the words as he watched the officer who
was giving the briefing. His face was scarred, and his hands stained red-
dish brown from his efforts to treat casualties. More than twenty Iraqis
had been killed, he reported, and another sixty wounded during the attack. Yet the captain seemed unfazed. After he spoke, he leaned back
in his chair, picked up a sandwich, and ate as casually as if he were back
at a Denny's in Killeen, Texas. Slack was impressed. There was no hint
of fear in the captain, no emotion. It was the kind of cool detachment
Slack believed officers needed to function effectively in combat. He
wondered if his own men, if Daniels or Drew or Kaz, would react as
well. He wondered if he himself would have such composure.

Slack reflected on what he had seen in Taji on the forty-five-
minute drive back to Baghdad. The 69th commander was shocked
that the enemy had been able to rain that much carnage onto one unit.
An entire rifle company was decimated. Combined with the horror
stories he had heard from the 7th Cav commander about the area,
Slack was sobered and worried. *That's where we're going? He has the
capability of doing that to us?* Slack privately predicted the 69th would
take its first casualties by November 15.

The following morning the battalion commander described his trip to his captains and primary staff officers. The men sat outside one of hundreds of hastily built plywood-and-stud command posts that dotted the U.S. bases in Iraq. Being outdoors allowed Slack to smoke freely. He sat in a chair while the men leaned against or sat on the bottoms of eight-foot-tall concrete "Texas" barriers that were designed to deflect shrapnel from a mortar attack. The barriers ringed any building of import at Camp Liberty, but all the soldiers still wore their helmets and body armor. It was Ramadan, and the intelligence specialists had predicted the enemy would be more active against the infidels than usual. As the men talked a mortar or rocket slammed—*karumph*—into the camp about four hundred meters away, right in the middle of the 69th's motor pool. The soldiers had all heard explosions in training. But this first mortar round had a bit more impact: it was the first piece of enemy ordnance ever aimed at them. Most of the cherries flinched. Slack, a well-disciplined cherry, stoically lit another Camel.

"Might as well get used to it now," he told the men. "They hit Camp Cooke all day long up in Taji." Because the base had once been the home of the Iraqi artillery school, the insurgents who lived in the area knew how to get rounds on target and were causing casualities on a regular basis. Slack had been informed by the 2-7 Cav that one of the 69th's major missions in Taji would be to put a lid on all the indirect fire originating from the sector. In addition to dropping mortars on Camp Cooke and FOB Animal, insurgents in the Taji area were effectively launching rockets into both Camp Liberty and the Green Zone in downtown Baghdad. In Slack's opinion, there seemed only one possible way to suppress these fires: the 69th would have to get out into the countryside and spend so much time in the enemy's backyard that he would abandon the idea of deploying rockets or mortars. Slack and his operations officer, Major Crosby, had been contemplating for days how they would use their relatively small force to control such a massive area. The 69th's sector was 110 square miles, a land mass slightly greater than Brooklyn, and far too large to maintain a constant presence. Once Crosby subtracted the support troops, the 69th had

only about 350 combat troops, including their Scouts and mortar platoons, to cover down on an area with more than 50,000 residents and
an untold number of Iraqi insurgents. It didn't seem possible.

As Slack talked about his high-speed reconnaissance and reviewed
the tactical-employment options with his commanders, he received a
call from the Tiger Brigade and learned the 69th had to detach one
of its companies to conduct a base-security mission for the following
month, which meant the loss of another 120 men. Crosby was floored
when Slack relayed the news. The mission in Taji was a stretch for
three companies, let alone just two. As the operations guy, he felt as
though he'd just been raped.

If Crosby felt raped, Lieutenant Minning felt plain-old fucked. BO-
HICA! "Bend over, here it comes again," he told his platoon. When
Slack selected Minning's platoon and the rest of the Banshees for the
base-security mission, the platoon leader was livid. He wanted to head
north with his regiment and get into the fight. He was an infantryman and had trained for the job for eight years. The last thing he and
his men wanted to do was stand at some wall and watch the war go
by. Minning had seen some of the soldiers guarding the base when
he arrived. They looked far too casual, immensely bored, and altogether unprepared. Minning didn't want to be one of those guys.
When a car bomb struck one of Camp Liberty's main gates later that
day, Minning was even more certain that the base-security mission
was a bad thing. Not only were the Banshees sidelined from true combat, they would be posted in the middle of a big bull's-eye.

BABES IN THE WOODS

The Fighting 69th—less the Banshees, who remained in Baghdad to
pull base security—marched to Camp Cooke in Taji on November 8
in order to relieve the 2-7 Cav, which in truth had already left. The
battalion had been shifted west to participate in the main U.S. effort
at the time—a no-holds-barred assault on Fallujah, the notorious insurgent stronghold and alleged base of operations for Jordanian-born

bogeyman Abu Musab al-Zarqawi. When Slack's staff arrived at the former 2-7 headquarters, there were only enough cavalry troopers left to pass on a few computer files to the 69th. "Welcome to Taji. Here's everything we know about the place. Good luck."

That's not how it was supposed to work. When one American unit replaced another in Iraq, they were intended to conduct a formal battle handover or "left-seat, right-seat ride." This process is typically spread out over two weeks. During the first, the incoming unit rides along with the outgoing unit to watch how the salty veterans do the job. During the second week, the incoming unit takes more of a leadership role but remains under the command and watchful eye of the veterans. At the end of the process, the two units conduct a formal "transition of authority," and the new guys are large and in charge.

If the 69th had been able to conduct a proper battle handoff, it would have learned all sorts of useful information. Not only was Taji the home of the Iraqi artillery school before the war, it was also home to a Republican Guard tank division, an air base, several munitions factories, and a maintenance depot. Positioned strategically at the southern tip of the Sunni Triangle, Taji base and its surrounding lands were the final line of defense before the heart of Saddam Hussein's tribal stronghold. If the Americans made it to Baghdad, the Iraqi army planned to defend the heartland from the Taji area. And who better to fight the Americans than the people of Taji, 90 percent of whom were Sunnis? Further, Taji base was the primary employer for virtually every family in the area. Residents from senior Republican Guard generals to the newspaper boys depended on the base and Saddam Hussein's regime for their livelihood. If ever ordinary Iraqis had something to lose from the U.S. invasion, it was in the population centers around Taji.

Had the 69th soldiers been able to speak with the troopers who had worked in Taji, they would have learned that the people of the area were savagely anti-American. They had lost their dignity when the U.S. came to town, and they now struggled to feed their families. Some continued to farm. Some went to work in the black market that controlled the oil industry. Some took money from hardcore jihadist insurgents to continue low-level attacks against the Americans in order to degrade over time soldier morale and effectiveness as well as popular support for the war in the U.S. In the early days after the U.S. invasion, the disenfranchised Iraqis of Taji neatly folded their Republican Guard uniforms and stored them in the back of their closets. They quickly consolidated whatever military hardware they could get their hands on for their own use or for later sale and distribution on the black market to the jihadists. They dumped thousands of watertight artillery shells into the canals, they buried untold numbers of RPG launchers and ammunition, and they looted the massive Taji air base ammunition bunker—a mile-long repository of bombs that ranged from 250 to 2,000 pounds in size. Instead of dumping those in a canal, the Iraqis dug up entire roadbeds and plopped the bombs in with a homemade fuse sticking out. These were not the simple "roadside bombs" that were so popular throughout Iraq at the time, but rather Iraqi versions of the MOAB—the mother of all bombs. In some areas the Iraqis placed them under a road and then paved the road over so they could continue regular civilian traffic until a U.S. patrol happened by. Among the handful of documents the 69th did receive when it arrived at Camp Cooke was a photograph of an M1 Abrams main battle tank that had been hit by one of these devices. The hull of the tank was gored through the bottom, and the massive turret of the beast lay forty meters from the site of the blast. Although the Iraqis had not scored a "catastrophic kill" on American tanks in the first Gulf War or during the 2003 invasion, they were having surprising success doing so in the occupation.

The insurgents had been so successful in Taji, in fact, that the previous American units assigned to the area concluded that they should not enter the villages with anything smaller than a thickly armored Bradley Fighting Vehicle. Humvees, which accounted for 80 percent of the 69th's combat fleet, were definitely out of the question. The violence of the area was so severe and the size of American forces committed to the area had always been so small that the command-

ers who were given Taji before the 69th eventually stopped regular patrols. If they had a deliberate operation that was driven by intelligence,
such as a raid of a key insurgent figure, the Americans would blast into
Taji, grab whoever was at the target location, then blast the hell out before anything went boom. For the rest of the time, Taji belonged to the
insurgents, who leisurely buried more bombs and prepared for more
attacks to defend their countryside. "Route Red Legs," the road Slack
had rocketed over in a Humvee with the 2-7 Cav commander, had not
been cleared or regularly patrolled in the previous five months.

By the time the 69th rolled into Camp Cooke, the black market
and jihadist insurgents operating in Taji had developed a proven strategy for keeping the Yanks out of their business. Whenever a new unit
came to town—and one could identify them from the patches on the
infidels' sleeves—the insurgents would watch them for a couple of
weeks, determine the soldiers' favorite roads to drive on, then attach
a detonator to a previously planted bomb and lie in wait. When the
Americans rolled a tank, Bradley, or Humvee over the bomb, the insurgents triggered the detonator and watched the sparks fly. The key
was to use a particularly large bomb. It wasn't enough to simply damage a vehicle or kill one soldier; that would just piss the Americans
off, causing them to shoot up the place like a bunch of cowboys. The
insurgents sought instead to completely destroy a vehicle and shred
everyone aboard, breaking and scaring the Americans and almost certainly driving them to go somewhere else. The tactic had worked with
every unit that had ventured into Taji since 2003. After a couple of
catastrophic kills, the understrength Americans viewed the area as
too risky, leaving the black market insurgents alone to continue extortion
operations and weapons sales and distribution, and leaving the jihadist
insurgents alone to continue their regular mortar-and-rocket attacks
against the big U.S. bases and—perhaps more important—their chance
to rest, recover, and reconstitute insurgent forces for future operations in the Baghdad-Fallujah corridor.

Taji was a "rat line" between Baghdad and Fallujah, as all the
smart-sounding staff officers had told Slack. The Grand Canal north

of Baghdad ran straight as a die from the backwaters of Fallujah to the suburbs of the capital. With sparsely patrolled roads on each side, the canal was the perfect way to get from one area to the other without hitting any coalition checkpoints. If the 69th had conducted a proper relief in place, they would have learned that the few Americans working there believed that Taji was the area to which the enemy withdrew when the U.S. turned up the heat someplace else—specifically, Fallujah in November 2004. So while the New Yorkers and Cajuns were setting up their cots and their televisions at Camp Cooke, more insurgents were moving into their uncle Muttar's house just a few miles from the camp's gates. Muttar could tell his guests to relax and watch Al Jazeera in peace because, except for an occasional raid, the Americans had not been in Taji for months. And if the Yanks did come into town, they would have plenty of warning. Because of all the canals, there were only five places where American patrols could enter Taji. Muttar and his friends, all former Republican Guard officers, had devised primary and alternate signaling techniques that would alert them to a U.S. incursion. In most cases they just spread the word on mobile phones. If cell coverage was spotty, they could notify one another Paul Revere–style: by hopping into their Opels and warning each village and key farmhouse that the Americans were coming by land near the market. If all that failed, they could shoot up a flare, of which they had hundreds. Finally, if they ever suspected the Americans were around, they just listened for the dogs, who went berserk whenever they got a whiff of Ivory soap and cologne.

But the Fighting 69th got little if any of that information. Slack had been keeping a mental checklist of the weaknesses that hampered his battalion, and added blindness to the list. On top of that, the senior officer at Camp Cooke told Slack upon his arrival that the 69th now had to give up its ten Bradleys. General Ronald Chastain commanded the 39th Brigade Combat Team from the Arkansas National Guard—the Razorbacks. Chastain had been on the ground for seven months and would be patrolling the lands on the east side of Camp Cooke while the 69th hit the west side. In his opinion, the eastern area required a lot of armor. The problem was, Chastain didn't have any: every piece of heavy metal the brigade commander owned had been taken by the 1st Cavalry Division for use in the assault on Fallujah. The general was frustrated that he was responsible for such a volatile area and lacked the assets needed for the job. He wanted to replace his tanks with the 69th's Blacksheep. General Basilica ultimately told Slack he didn't have to give up his Bradleys to Chastain but pledged the 69th would help out the Razorbacks whenever appropriate. Chastain was disappointed but was glad for whatever assistance he could get. Taji was and always had been an "economy of force mission," as Chastain explained to Slack. "Economy of force" is one of nine principles of war adopted by the Army and can be defined as the use of limited military assets in an area where they will provide the most benefit. Strategic places like Fallujah and western Baghdad got most of the assets, while backwaters and secondary efforts like Taji, whom nobody in the States had heard of, got little.

If Taji was an economy of force mission, it seemed Iraq was an economy of force war. There was not a heck of a lot of military assets available for anyplace. Before the invasion, General Eric Shinseki, the senior officer in the U.S. Army, predicted he would need "several hundred thousand soldiers" to secure and rebuild postwar Iraq. Deputy Defense Secretary Paul Wolfowitz cavalierly dismissed the soldier's estimate as "wildly off the mark." But Shinseki's numbers were in keeping with recent operations, according to a 2006 Army study, *Boots on the Ground: Troop Density in Contingency Operations,* by John J. McGrath. When U.S. forces first entered Bosnia, they brought 15 soldiers for every 1,000 residents. When NATO entered Kosovo, they brought roughly 21 soldiers for every 1,000 residents. Using those numbers as a planning guideline, the U.S. and coalition planners could have reasonably projected a need for between 382,500 and 535,500 soldiers for Iraq, which, in fact, had always been the Army's plan for an Iraq war, according to Michael Gordon and General Bernard Trainor in *Cobra II: The Inside Story of the Invasion and Occupation of Iraq.* But the U.S. and its coalition partners never came close to that figure. When the 69th arrived in Iraq, there were roughly 160,000 U.S. and 24,500 coalition troops on the ground. Even with the addition of an estimated 78,000 contractors working in direct support of coalition operations, the total troop density was only 10 forces for every 1,000 residents. If one adds the nearly 125,000 "operational" Iraqi security forces, such as the unit Slack saw shredded at FOB Animal, the ratio of soldiers to residents becomes comparable to the ratio used when the U.S. entered Bosnia. But it would have been a great leap of faith to equate in this particular calculus an Iraqi soldier with questionable training, equipment, and loyalties to a U.S. soldier. Entire battalions of Iraqi soldiers had refused to fight alongside U.S. forces in 2004, and some intelligence officers estimated that between 10 and 20 percent of all Iraqi forces were sympathetic to insurgents or enemy fighters themselves.

Army Field Manual 3-24, *Counterinsurgency,* states that no fixed ratios of soldiers-to-residents or soldiers-to-insurgents exist. However, the manual does state that "counterinsurgency is manpower intensive because of the requirements to maintain widespread order and security." Whatever the optimum numbers of forces, by late 2004 it was generally accepted that there were not enough troops in Iraq. In late 2004 Major General Peter Chiarelli, the commander of the 1st Cavalry Division and the Baghdad area of operations, told the company commanders of the 69th and the Tiger Brigade during a question-and-answer dinner at Camp Liberty that he knew there weren't enough troops and that his repeated requests for more had been denied. So without adequate forces to do the job, General Chiarelli and commanders at every level needed to mass their troops in places where they would get the most bang for the buck.

General Chastain shared his frustrations with Slack, who understood the situation all too well. The 69th had lost their Banshees to a base-defense mission because security at the Victory Base Cluster was deemed more important than security in Taji, which was the economy of force mission within the Tiger Brigade. Moreover, one of the reasons Basilica had offered Chastain for not giving him Slack's Bradleys was that Basilica believed the 69th could be redeployed to Baghdad at any time. The moment the Tiger Brigade needed more forces to achieve their main effort mission downtown, they would pull the 69th out of Taji. The Tiger Brigade even told Slack he might be in Taji for only two weeks.

Since the invasion every unit that had been assigned to the Taji area was given the same warning order: they might be there for only a little while. And because in every instance the order proved accurate, some U.S. commanders were reluctant to risk taking major casualties there. Why suffer heavy losses when you could be pulled out of Taji the following week? Why attempt to make any inroads with the people, when any promise you make will effectively be broken the moment you leave town? If the Big Army didn't think Taji was that important, why should we? In that environment, staying out of Taji made perfect sense.

But that's not how Slack saw it. He was given a mission to suppress the mortars and rockets that were slamming into Camp Cooke, Camp Victory, and the Green Zone. It was clearly a dangerous job and seemed likely to be of short duration. But giving the effort anything less than 100 percent didn't resonate with Slack or most of his soldiers. Even if the mission lasted only a single week, the men knew that for a few days they could protect the soldiers on base who were getting killed or wounded by indirect fire. Further, the entire Fighting 69th had been spoiling for a fight since September 11, and all the anecdotal evidence they had picked up around Camp Cooke indicated they would get that fight in Taji.

Three days after the 69th arrived at Camp Cooke, General Chastain was back in Slack's operations center asking for his Bradleys again. This time, however, they were not for his Christmas wish list. Four Humvees from the 39th had been ambushed on Route Tampa north of the camp, and although Chastain had sent more trucks to fend off the enemy, many of those were hit, too. In total, eleven vehicles were disabled, and Chastain's troops were in sustained contact and taking casualties. "I need everything you got and I need it now," he announced to Slack, who was in the middle of a meeting with his commanders and staff. Slack thought for a moment, then told Kaz to get all ten of his Bradleys ready to roll while the task force sought approval from the Tiger Brigade. It was the first combat mission for the 69th in Iraq, and in typical fashion for New York's Own, it hadn't been planned, rehearsed, or even resourced. The men weren't even sure which gate to leave from. They didn't know where to line up their tracks. They were uncertain about how best to load their vehicles for combat. They had no polish. But when the Tiger Brigade gave the green light, Kaz headed north with his Bradleys on a mission to "destroy the enemy located in palm groves east and west of Route Tampa."

As the Blacksheep rolled out the gates, local residents fired flares into the air to warn the insurgents. As Kaz approached with his heavy metal, the enemy broke contact with the 39th and melted away into the countryside. It was all over by the time the Fighting 69th showed up. Nonetheless, the ordeal was another sobering moment for Colonel Slack. His small battalion had been on the ground in Taji for just three days. They hadn't done a proper battle handover and hardly knew how to get off the base. Yet despite the 69th's greenness, a seasoned brigade commander had come running to the Wolfhounds to ask for help. What kind of enemy can cause a general with 3,000 soldiers under his command to ask a rookie with a paltry 300 combat arms troops for assistance? The 69th was scheduled to formally assume control of Taji the next day. *Here come the babes in the woods,* Slack thought. He didn't know the worst of it.

NAPALM IN THE MORNING

Captain Kazmierzak's unscheduled relief mission marked a distinct upturn in the already steep learning curve the Fighting 69th had been experiencing for the past six months. While the battalion still had all the shortcomings Slack had seen at the NTC, he now had to try and fix them while mortars were literally landing all around him. If there was any good news for the Wolfhounds, it was that the enemy was shooting only relatively small 60-millimeter mortars at them. For days the rounds had all splashed harmlessly into the Grand Canal, to the merriment of the 69th soldiers, who cheered the 100-foot-high geysers that accompanied each impact.

On November 15, General Basilica had conducted his first brigade-level operation, an old-fashioned movement to contact as seen during the invasion. Basilica and his planners were keen to subdue a historic insurgent stronghold that straddled the Army and Marine Corps border northwest of Baghdad. During the operation, code named "Tiger Strike," the 256th would use the 69th to dislodge the enemy from his comfort zone while other brigade elements swooped in to pick them up. The mission all but screamed, "There's a new sheriff in town."

Kazmierzak had been alerted that there could be hundreds of insurgents waiting to greet him as he led the spearhead of the Fighting 69th's attack. The task force objective was a bridge over the Grand Canal, Objective Leyte, and a multistory building that looked out over the area, Objective Citadel. With his Bradleys rumbling along the canal toward the bridge, Apache attack helicopters flying overhead, and Air Force fighters stacked somewhere in the clouds, Kazmierzak was in pure infantry bliss. This is what it was all about. He was told to expect contact from the building and tensed with nervous excitement as his first unit approached. *Hell yeah. Bring it on!* Kaz felt invincible. The Blacksheep's first platoon secured the perimeter of the Citadel while his second platoon crossed the bridge and established security positions on its far side. Kaz stayed near the building and dismounted his Bradley with his infantrymen, who led the way inside, clearing every room in the place.

If there had ever been any enemy in the building—a girls' school, according to Kaz's interpreter—they were long gone, an anticlimactic outcome that the soldiers would come to understand as normal. Whenever U.S. forces showed up en masse, the gig was up. The insurgents hid their weapons and sipped a cup of tea as the Americans romped through their home or village.

It took just minutes for the Blacksheep to secure the battalion objective. They probably could have done it with just one platoon, save an entire battalion, but as they got their feet wet, the 69th took a lot of comfort in numbers. The trouble didn't begin until later that day. Slack had orders to remain in place at the bridge in order to block a known escape route from Fallujah into Baghdad. Sitting in one location didn't appeal to the infantryman, but he was pleased his 69th was doing its part in support of the Fallujah operations. He decided to keep one company at the bridge, leaving the other maneuver elements of the battalion to patrol the main routes in and out of the objective area and to screen the flanks of the unit sitting at the bridge. The Blacksheep would stay for the first twenty-four hours, then swap with the Assassins the following day. When the enemy learned that the U.S. troops were essentially sitting targets near the bridge, he decided to harass the Yanks with mortars. The men didn't hear the first round until it splashed with an explosion into the canal. At the initial impact some of the soldiers ran around wildly, looking for cover, while others stood fixed out of fear or indecision. All of them wondered, *Will another mortar come in?* A second explosion answered that question and sent the remainder of the men scrambling for the protection of an armored vehicle. Four rounds landed in the canal in that first salvo, with another two rounds following an hour later. In addition to the mortar fire, insurgents launched an RPG and sprayed inaccurate rifle fire at the 69th. With the Scouts screening the northern flanks, all the enemy activity seemed to be coming from the southern side of the canal, outside the 69th's area of responsibility. A captain at the 69th tactical operations center (TOC) called the brigade and asked the neighboring unit—Kaz's former battalion—to investigate the area where the fires originated. "Roger, they'll take a look." But when Kaz consulted his BFT, he saw that, instead of moving to the objective area, all the blue icons were driving *away* from the enemy, all the way back to Camp Liberty. *What the hell is that all about?* Kaz got on the radio and asked for permission to send his own tracks toward the suspected enemy positions, but it took nearly two hours for the Tiger

Brigade to give clearance. Any hope of finding the culprits was long gone.

The lack of a significant U.S. response to the mortars on the first day emboldened the enemy. On the second day, when the Assassins swapped with the Blacksheep on the bridge, insurgents fired another six mortars over the course of two hours. The men nervously laughed off all the attacks but also noticed a trend: The mortar teams seemed to be getting more accurate. Each impact struck a little closer, prompting Slack to send concrete bunkers out to the bridge for additional protection.

Activity picked up considerably on the third day. Mike Drew called in the first mortar attack before 9:00 a.m. and another five before 1:00 p.m. Jay Olmo and the Scouts were in pursuit of a suspected vehicle-borne improvised explosive device (VBIED) nearby. And the insurgents also targeted the 69th soldiers trying to keep the route to the bridge open, detonating their first IED against one of Kaz's Bradley Fighting Vehicles. No one was injured, but the blast was powerful enough to disable the track. When Drew and the Assassins heard about the attack, they couldn't help but think about what it would have done to a Humvee. But they had more immediate concerns, for another barrage of mortars had come in, the most accurate yet. Rounds had now impacted on all corners of the Assassins' position. It seemed only a matter of time before they hit the static soldiers.

The Blacksheep were back at the bridge on the fourth day when the enemy decided 60-millimeter mortars were too small. Slack was also present, discussing the apparently useless and dangerous mission with Kazmierzak. As the commander spoke, Kaz heard something *whoosh* through the air overhead. He knew it was incoming, but the fact that it was audible made him quickly conclude that it was bigger than normal. Before he could get cover, the round slammed into the ground less than 100 meters from their position. Kaz dove inside one of his Bradleys along with everyone else nearby until the track was packed like a clown car. Another round crashed in with a *KARUMPH,* and smoke and dust filled the air. Kaz looked out the

Bradley toward where he had been talking with Slack. The commander was still there, standing with his back to the track and hands on his hips as if he were Lieutenant Colonel Bill Kilgore, Robert Duvall's brash air cavalry commander from the film *Apocalypse Now*. Kaz shouted out to Slack, "Sir, there's mortars!"

"Yeah, I know," he replied over his shoulder.

Slack looked the picture of calm as he stood defiant in the cordite-filled air. But inside he was filled with a series of competing and contradictory emotions. His first reaction had been the same as Kaz's: he wanted to run for the protection of his armored Humvee and lock the door. While he had become accustomed to the 60-millimeter mortars, these rounds were either the 82-millimeter variety or rockets slamming into his position. Either way, they were a far greater order of magnitude. The commander wasn't physically frightened, but he did feel that he had everything to live for back in the States and wanted nothing to do with getting wounded or killed. At the same time he didn't want to hustle away and hide, because he was concerned that such an act would be a signal to his junior leaders that anytime they came under fire the only choice was to run. Though he would later reflect on his moxie as an act of lunacy, Slack screwed up his guts and stood his ground as the rounds slammed into his position.

The strongest emotion surging through Slack's veins was anger. It was the first time the enemy was shooting at him personally, and the commander's Irish American temper was flaring. He was pissed off, and his first reaction was to fight. He had been that way his entire life. Had an enemy showed his face at that particular moment, Slack would almost certainly have charged at him—with or without his rifle. Charging the enemy was the perfect reaction for a rifleman, perhaps even a platoon leader. But as a battalion commander, Slack believed his anger was a weakness. As a colonel, he knew full well that he needed to step back, keep himself healthy, and bring the rest of his assets to bear against the enemy. Instead, all he wanted to do was tangle.

Slack scanned the far side of the canal for any sign of insurgents but saw nothing. The enemy had too many palm groves and friendly backyards to shoot from. So in lieu of an enemy, Slack turned his anger toward the Tiger Brigade. The entire mission at the bridge seemed ass backward. There was never any enemy to engage at the target, yet the 69th was ordered to sit on that bridge while the rest of the brigade pulled out of the area. Now the Wolfhounds were getting pounded by mortars at the bridge and hit by IEDs on the road to it.

Another round whooshed over Slack's head, impacting on a mud-brick house some two hundred meters away. Slack had seen a family in the dwelling earlier and turned to Kazmierzak. "Get your medics."

The last round had leveled a good portion of the home. When the medics got on scene, they found a young boy and girl, both perhaps seven or eight years old. The girl had lacerations on her arms and legs; the boy had shrapnel in his head. The medics told Kaz and Slack that both needed to be evacuated immediately, or they would die. Slack called back to his command post and ordered a medevac helicopter for the children. But the family wasn't interested in American help, for as Kaz's interpreter told him, the family blamed them for the injuries. "If you weren't here, we wouldn't be getting mortars," the children's father said. However, Slack thought there might be something more to their refusal: if the man let the Americans evacuate the children, the insurgents would likely retaliate against the man for cooperating with the infidels. The family ultimately loaded the dying children into a beat-up car and drove elsewhere for help.

Kaz loved kids, and the incident shook him. He believed his soldiers were in Iraq to assist the Iraqis—help them rebuild, treat them with respect, give them medical aid. Now it seemed he needed to come to grips with a people that would rather risk their own children's lives than work with the Americans. From that day forward, the captain and many other soldiers began developing an emotional callus against the plight of the people of Iraq. The men grew colder with every incident.

9: THE ROUGE BOUQUET

FRAMEWORK OPERATIONS

Lieutenant Colonel Slack and Major Crosby faced significant challenges in developing a long-term maneuver plan for the 69th in Taji. They had little guidance from the Tiger Brigade, were not able to conduct a proper relief in place with another U.S. unit, and were moving the battalion into virgin territory. There were dozens of tasks the 69th needed to juggle during "stability operations," and they had been broken down into what the Army calls "logical lines of operations (LLOs)"—primarily security, governance, infrastructure, and economic development. But their own mission analysis indicated that stopping the indirect fire attacks against Camp Cooke was the essential task, or "glass ball" mission, for the Wolfhounds. If they dropped it, the 69th would fail in Taji.

The attacks were degrading the operations of two key 1st Cavalry Division assets based at Cooke, the Division Support Command and the 4th Aviation Brigade. Soldiers across the base wore their complete body armor anytime they were outside a bunkered area—at the chow hall, at the Post Exchange, even in the latrine. Nonetheless, people were getting hurt and equipment was being destroyed. Crosby believed the insurgents were conducting a deliberate "offense" by suppressing operations at Camp Cooke. And to date, no U.S. forces had made a concerted effort to check the enemy's actions. After their experience getting shelled daily at the bridge, the men of the Fighting 69th were eager to get after the indirect fire teams.

Slack and Crosby ultimately designed a mission statement that directed the 69th to suppress enemy indirect fires and air-defense artillery fires in Taji in order to provide force protection for Camp Cooke and for the aviators flying over the region, who had been taking small arms and RPG shots from the ground. In addition, the 69th would conduct limited civil-military operations to address the nonsecurity LLOs—governance, infrastructure, and economic development—in an effort to influence the local populace to support the new Iraqi government, which they also hoped would degrade civilian support for the insurgents.

The 69th employed generally accepted techniques currently in use in Iraq for accomplishing these tasks. Those methods were inspired by the series of "framework operations" developed by the British army in the 1980s to combat the terrorists of the Provisional Irish Republican Army in Northern Ireland. The Brits conducted vehicle check points, house searches, and area patrolling to reassure the public and deter insurgent activity, while also developing intelligence for targeted operations. Translating the approach to the doctrinal mission of the infantry—to find, fix, and destroy the enemy—the Wolfhounds would find the enemy by getting out into Taji to develop intelligence, they would fix the enemy through aggressive patrolling and random searches, and they would destroy the enemy by detaining or killing him.

The key to success was intelligence. The 69th had been given some information about their area, but it was largely dated and not overly specific. For example, while the 69th could tell you what tribes lived in what regions, they could not tell you what families among the tribes were running RPGs in and out of Baghdad or launching mortars onto Cooke. One of the greatest intelligence tools the U.S. had was Q36 radar, a system that could track short-range indirect fire and then template its point of origin (POO). By examining historic POOs in the Taji area, Crosby and his intelligence officer, Captain Dave Friedner, drew up mortar and rocket boxes, squares on the map that indicated places from which the bad guys liked to shoot. While the indirect fire assets were mobile, Crosby didn't think insurgents could move large stockpiles of ammunition quickly, so the mapping gave the men of the Fighting 69th a place to begin their framework operations.

Another factor that dictated where the 69th would operate was the population centers of Taji. In order to gain intelligence and address the civil-military requirements of the area, the Wolfhounds needed to develop relationships with the people of Taji. Crosby made an assumption that not all the locals were insurgents, but a significant number did support the insurgency out of fear—like the family that refused the 69th's help near the bridge. The locals were afraid that insurgents would see them cooperating with the Americans and then come to their homes in the middle of the night and start cutting heads off. Both Crosby's assumption and the civilian fear were well placed, for in late 2004 insurgents were delivering "night letters" to families across central Iraq. One missive recovered by U.S. troops near Baghdad roughly read (translated from Arabic):

> To enemy of Allah and Islam:
> No excuse for those who are warned. If you don't stop working with enemy, God will burn you and your family and we're guiltless from their blood. You're the criminal. In front of God we are responsible on our promise: we promise ourselves that we fight anyone who puts his hand with Americans, and we are working on it. You are the criminal. You are the cowardly chicken hearted.

A family gets a warning like that only once. On his next visit, the sender would bring his pistol. Yet Crosby believed a regular presence by U.S. forces would reassure the public that they were safe from insurgent reprisals. If he could mitigate the people's anxiety, he believed the civilians would give them intelligence. Crosby also knew that would be tough to accomplish, given the transient nature of U.S. forces in the area. The 69th had to overcome the perception among the civilians that the Rainbow patch was there one day and gone the next—even though all indications from the Tiger Brigade implied just that. To be successful, the soldiers of the 69th would avoid spending too much time in their barracks at Camp Cooke and go out in the town.

Most of the civilian population of Taji lived in three villages in the middle and southeastern portion of the 69th's area. That sector would be the focus of the task force's main effort and would be patrolled by the Assassins in Humvees and the Blacksheep in Bradleys. Another significant "rocket box" was identified in the far west, along the boundary that divided the Army in Baghdad and the Marines in Fallujah, from where insurgents had been effectively hitting the Green Zone and Camp Liberty. The location was also straddled by large roads—rat lines—that insurgents could use to move between Tikrit, Fallujah, and Baghdad. So even though the region was largely uninhabited, Slack and Crosby wanted to get forces there, designating this western sector an economy of force effort that would be patrolled by Jay Olmo and the rest of the Scouts. Without the Banshees, they couldn't even pretend to regularly patrol the rest of the AO, and so agreed to essentially ignore the northern third of their battle space unless they had specific intelligence about a target in the area.

Slack ran the concept by his company commanders, whom he collectively referred to as his "princes of the realm." Since they were the guys who would be executing the mission, the colonel would consider seriously any objections they had to the plan. After Drew, Kazmierzak, and Daniels recommended some tweaks, the unit was ready to execute. The 69th began limited framework operations—primarily zone reconnaissance—just before Operation Tiger Strike. They halted their efforts during the eight-day bridge mission, then dove into the Taji AO at full strength on November 23.

Major Crosby never got a chance to see the plan unfold as the operations officer, however. A few days before they started framework operations, Slack announced that his struggling executive officer, Major Major, had been reassigned—"disappeared" in *Catch-22* vernacular. Crosby was now second in command. The relief of Major Major didn't surprise anyone, for while the officer had his strengths, they didn't coincide with his duties as a wartime XO. Crosby had already filled much of the vacuum left by the officer's failings; the announcement simply made it official.

Captain Daniels, who had been passed over as both XO and operations officer before the Iraq mission, believed he was a shoo-in for the new vacancy, as no one else in the 69th approached his qualification for the major's job. But at that stage of his career, Daniels really should have expected to be screwed over again. The Tiger Brigade directed the job be filled instead with one of its own officers, Major Chris Cerniauskas, whom everybody in the 69th immediately assumed was a spy. On one of his first days on the job, several soldiers in the 69th command post swore they heard Cerniauskas call back to the Tiger Brigade to report that, "Yes, you were all correct, Colonel Slack is out of his mind."

But the change in senior management didn't slow the Wolfhounds. The Assassins, Blacksheep, and Scouts knew their mission and pressed on as if nothing had happened. Even Daniels shook off the affront, rolling into Taji with whatever element he could catch a ride with and not slowing down until he slammed into a telephone pole with his Humvee somewhere in the middle of the town. He reported that his men had been shaken up, and then got back on the job.

If ever someone could refer to the "good old days in Taji," they would be describing the 69th's first week of framework operations. So few Americans had recently been in the area that the insurgents had become careless in their fieldcraft. Everywhere the 69th patrolled they easily found caches of weapons and poorly concealed bombs. In their first few days on the job, the Assassins uncovered an RPG, blasting caps, grenades, some artillery shells, two cases of 127-millimeter rockets, a rocket launcher, and a couple of IEDs. The Blacksheep spotted a few more IEDs on the road and dug up two large caches of weapons, which included mortar tubes, dozens of mortar rounds, rocket launchers, RPGs, land mines, explosive cord, and artillery shells.

The local insurgents had to wonder what the heck was going on. Nobody had bothered them in months; now they had American vehicles all around them, and U.S. soldiers—the latest unit wearing the

Rainbow patch—were bagging their military supplies at every turn. The insurgents opted to lie low and wait to see what the soldiers would do next.

The change in enemy posture was exactly what the 69th had hoped for. The mortars, which had been hitting Camp Cooke at an unsettling rate, virtually ceased to be a problem. For the first time in many of the soldiers' tour in Iraq, the aviators and supporters back at the base were allowed to walk around without their helmets and body armor. Some of them were near euphoric with their newfound freedom. The Old Fighting 69th was on the job and it was making a difference. It was badass.

As the intelligence officer, Captain Friedner was responsible for putting on the enemy's hat and attempting to figure out what the bad guys would do next. So far it had all been playing out as he predicted. In his initial analysis, Friedner believed the insurgents would, in fact, slow their attacks against Camp Cooke. When the mortars stopped, he expected the insurgents would switch tactics, lying low and watching the 69th as it operated, learning what roads the Americans liked to use and when they were most likely to use them. Once they had a good template of the 69th's operation, they would do to the 69th what they had done to every other unit that had ventured into Taji—hit it hard with an IED, so hard that the Americans wouldn't come back.

THE FIRST KILL

In addition to framework operations, Task Force Wolfhound was also directed to conduct "surge" operations anytime dignitaries were to visit or other significant events were slated to occur in the Green Zone. The last thing anybody wanted was a U.S. diplomat or members of the fledgling Iraqi government to get smacked with a rocket while they were drinking tea. One of the first major surge operations for the battalion occurred between November 28 and 30. The operation called for the 69th to get every available pair of boots on the ground while the new Iraqi congress was in session. The first day of the surge was uneventful, and the second day was shaping up the same way.

Slack and Crosby stood alongside a canal in the middle of Taji, conducting an impromptu evaluation of the operation. They were both very pleased with its progress and discussed ideas on how to improve the next surge. As they spoke, a radio operator shouted over to the officers, "We got a contact," the general term for any engagement with the enemy.

Slack set off for the radio while Crosby ordered the vehicle commanders to get their rigs spun up and ready to move. He had no idea what was happening yet, but wanted to make sure the men were ready, especially the ambulances and recovery vehicles the major had in his formation. When Crosby got within earshot of the radio, he knew the contact was bad from the unmistakable tenor of the voice making the report—curt, halting, excited, scared. "We got a vehicle hit by an IED—out." The next voice on the radio, Captain Drew's, was more in control, but still shaken. "Roger, our trail vehicle was hit by an IED on Route Rams . . . We've got wounded, three urgent and two litter urgent . . . We've requested medevac . . . The site is marked with red smoke."

Both Slack and Crosby departed the area with their security detachments. In addition to Humvees, Crosby also had a tracked command vehicle, a wrecker, a tracked recovery vehicle, and an armored ambulance. He immediately set out for Drew's position in hopes he could get the ambulance to the company commander in time. But Drew's next radio call dashed Crosby's hopes of helping: "We've got three urgent and two KIA." The Fighting 69th had just suffered its first killed in action since the Battle of Okinawa.

It took Crosby about thirty minutes to reach the scene of the engagement. As he pulled up to the area, the medevac helicopter was lifting off with the wounded soldiers. The major had trouble getting close to the scene because the narrow road was utterly glutted with vehicles, with ten alone in the section that was engaged. It seemed everyone else in the battalion had since converged on the scene of the attack, presenting dozens of follow-on targets for the enemy if he was so inclined. Crosby judged it as a cherry reaction from a cherry battalion, but joined the traffic jam nonetheless, in an effort to get his ambulance to the scene of the attack. He was unprepared for what he found when he finally made it forward. As he stepped out of his vehicle, he was confronted by a few soldiers who were sobbing their eyes out. Not one of them had ever experienced casualties before, and Crosby tried to console them, hugging them while he encouraged them to drive on, to shake it off. But the same emotions started to fill the major's own throat. When he finally reached what was left of the Humvee, he was quite rattled. The M1114, the vehicle that the soldiers had celebrated as their armored guardian angel back in Kuwait, was now a jumble of twisted metal that left one wondering how anyone had survived the blast at all. Blood trails led away from the wreckage, with two 69th men lying still at the end of them. As Crosby looked over at the fallen soldiers, a sergeant handed him two sets of dogtags. Nobody had called in the men's battle roster numbers yet, so Crosby headed back for his radio with the tags and tried to do so, but he was too upset to get them right.

First Sergeant Acevedo was back at Camp Cooke when word of the engagement came over the radio. He ran out of his command post and headed to the battalion TOC, which was already abuzz with radio chatter and soldiers shouting instructions and updates. When the Assassin NCO walked into the room, all the noise ceased. Nobody could muster the strength to tell the first sergeant that he had just lost two of his men and that three more were severely wounded. They needn't have worried, for after a frozen moment, the radio chatter told Acevedo all he needed to know. The names of the dead hadn't come over the net yet. But Ace already knew in his gut who one of them was.

While the battalion was still back in Kuwait, one of Acevedo's top leaders had seemed depressed. Ace finally pulled him aside and asked him what was on his mind. Sergeant Christian Engeldrum had been out of the National Guard for a few years, but had re-enlisted when he heard that several of his old comrades from the 27th Brigade were going to backfill the 69th for duty in Iraq. He couldn't let his boys go without him. But when he sat down with Acevedo, he told the first sergeant that he didn't think he was going to make it back from this war. The soldier, nicknamed "Drum," had survived the First Gulf War with the 82nd Airborne Division and hundreds of infernos, including 9/11, with the New York City Fire Department. But his premonition about this one was so strong that he even took out another life insurance policy in Kuwait. Acevedo told him it was money wasted, but Drum was certain. As late as the night before he was killed, Drum shared the same presentiment with his roommate. "Listen, I'm not gonna make it out of here. When I'm gone you need to step up and take care of the men like I have tried to do."

When Crosby finally sent the battle roster number over the radio—ENG3762—it only confirmed what everyone already knew.

But the second number to come over the radio hit Acevedo hard. Specialist Wilfredo Urbina—URB5348—was, in the civilian world, another firefighter. Like Drum, he had been depressed for the past few weeks and was having trouble focusing on the work ahead. In a private conversation with the first sergeant the day before the mission, Urbina said he liked when Acevedo rode with them. "When you're with us, it feels like everything's gonna be okay." But Ace hadn't been with them, and the first sergeant felt ashamed. Maybe if he had been there he could have done something.

More likely Ace would have been a casualty, as well. The insurgents had all the advantages in the engagement. The Americans had so few routes to choose from that the enemy knew he was likely to catch a patrol on one of the big roads that bordered the area of operations. In the past twenty-four hours, dozens of patrols were surging through the area, more U.S. forces than any of the Iraqis had seen in months. The American presence was so great that it had stymied the enemy's usual efforts to launch mortars and rockets. But the insurgents were not without options. Several patrols had already driven down the road that bordered the north side of the Grand Canal, and the enemy's analysis showed the Americans would use it again. As most Iraqis

were driving to work or to the market that morning, an insurgent con-
nected a remote-control detonator to a bomb that was already buried
under the road. The device was simple—just a few wires rigged to a
black Motorola radio, the kind parents might use to keep track of their
kids at Disney World. He set the frequency, then headed to the south
side of the canal, hiding behind one of the massive berms that paralleled the waterway, until the Americans came through. The canal was
about one hundred yards wide, nearly as long as an American football
field, and any unit that might think about searching for him would
have to drive miles in either direction to find a bridge to cross. The
Iraqi was effectively in no more danger than the Air Force pilots who
dropped laser-guided bombs from thirty thousand feet—and he was
every bit as accurate as the smartest weapon in the U.S. arsenal. He
had only to wait a couple of hours for a patrol of Humvees to drive
into his engagement area. He calmly watched the trucks pass before
setting his sights on the last vehicle in the pack. A break in the north
berm served as his trigger point, and when the last vehicle reached
the gap, the insurgent keyed his radio. It was a perfect hit, the explosion sending the bulk of the vehicle airborne. It soared twenty meters
before the hulk landed upside down further along the road. The Iraqi
quickly left his hide site and disappeared into the normal life of the
city.

But if the enemy was hoping the attack would break the 69th's will
to fight in Taji, they were mistaken. The Wolfhounds responded by
flooding the area for the next three days—walking the streets, frisk-
ing civilian bystanders, and searching homes. Slack's ire was so great
that he even conducted a one-man assault, grenade in one hand and
rifle in the other, on a house he suspected as the home of insurgents
who triggered an IED and RPG ambush on the commander's convoy.
As usual there was no sign of insurgents in the home, and nobody
knew anything. But the pressure was on, and the Iraqis noticed. The
new American unit in their backyard was acting differently from
many of the other units they had seen. In a discussion Slack had with
a senior tribal sheik in the area, the Iraqi looked at his Rainbow patch

and said, "Yes, I know this patch. This is Special Forces, yes?" Slack, who had grown an Arabic culture–appropriate black mustache by then, laughed off the remark, then turned serious. No, he explained, the patch meant they were from New York and eager to avenge the 9/11 attacks.

The tempo didn't slow down until December 3, when the Wolf-hounds conducted a memorial service for their fallen comrades. While the Blacksheep held the ground in Taji, the rest of the battalion gathered at Camp Cooke. In addition to the 69th men, a platoon-sized element of Drum's old friends from the 27th Brigade, who had been serving with the 108th Infantry, drove down from their area of operations north of Taji. When their fellow New Yorkers entered the chapel, the entire battalion broke out in tearful embraces. Most of them were already friends; some were family. All the men mourned for Drum and Urbina from deep in their guts.

When the Fighting 69th suffered its first losses in World War I, a prominent poet and *New York Times* writer who was a sergeant in the unit, Joyce Kilmer, wrote a poem titled "The Rouge Bouquet" to be read at the memorial ceremony. Since the first recitation of the requiem by Father Francis Duffy on Saint Patrick's Day in 1918, the regimental commanders have recited the poem at the memorial services of every 69th soldier who died in combat, usually adding the fallen soldier's first name to a passage in the second stanza. Slack first read the poem at the November 2001 memorial service for Lieutenant Gerard Baptiste, the 69th soldier who was killed while serving as a firefighter at Ground Zero, and now penciled two new names onto his printed copy of the requiem. After Captain Drew and his men eulogized the soldiers, Slack stood to read "The Rouge Bouquet":

> *"In a wood they call the Rouge Bouquet*
> *There is a new-made grave to-day,*
> *Built by never a spade nor pick*
> *Yet covered with earth ten meters thick.*
> *There lie many fighting men,*

Dead in their youthful prime,
Never to laugh nor love again
Nor taste the Summertime.
For Death came flying through the air
And stopped his flight at the dugout stair,
Touched his prey and left them there,
Clay to clay.
He hid their bodies stealthily
In the soil of the land they fought to free
And fled away.
Now over the grave abrupt and clear
Three volleys ring;
And perhaps their brave young spirits hear
The bugles sing:
'Go to sleep!
Go to sleep!
Slumber well where the shell screamed and fell.
Let your rifles rest on the muddy floor,
You will not need them any more.
Danger's past;
Now at last,
Go to Sleep!' "

"*There is on earth no worthier grave*
To hold the bodies of the brave
Than this place of pain and pride
Where they nobly fought and nobly died.
Never fear but in the skies
Saints and angels stand
Smiling with their holy eyes
On this new-come band.
St. Michael's sword darts through the air
And touches the aureole on his hair
As he sees them stand saluting there,

His stalwart sons: Gerard, Christian, and Wilfredo
And Patrick, Brigid, Columkill
Rejoice that in veins of warriors still
The Gael's blood runs.
And up to Heaven's doorway floats,
From the wood called Rouge Bouquet,
A delicate cloud of buglenotes
That softly say:
'Farewell!
Farewell!
Comrades true, born anew, peace to you!
Your souls shall be where the heroes are
And your memory shine like the morning-star.
Brave and dear,
Shield us here.
Farewell!'"

The dogtags that Crosby had carried after the attack now hung from a pair of helmet-capped rifles pointed bayonet down into a pair of combat boots, the universal representation of fallen soldiers. After reading the poem, Slack and Command Sergeant Major Brett came out from behind the podium and stood in front of the rifles. They each rendered a slow hand-salute and then stepped forward, clutched the dogtags, and prayed for the soldiers' souls, for the surviving members of the battalion, and for the strength and ability to kill the insurgents who flouted any sense of military propriety, who didn't wear uniforms, who didn't have the courage to stand and fight, and who had so cowardly taken Slack's soldiers' lives.

THE ECONOMY OF FORCE

Jay Olmo cringed as the sour notes of "Amazing Grace" rose from Lieutenant Rathburn's bagpipes. The sounds reminded him of his friend Christian Reardon and his memorial service back in Kuwait.

It didn't seem the right tune to hear as he and the rest of Reardon's old squad walked from the chapel to their Humvees for another day of driving around in the parched farmlands west of Taji.

The Scouts were supposed to be Slack's eyes and ears, out conducting reconnaissance operations. But the battlefield environment in Taji hardly permitted that kind of work. Where in Taji could an American sneak around and pretend not to be seen? Even if a Scout could get into an area undetected, the dogs would give his position away within minutes. So, short of a good reconnaissance mission, Slack and Crosby used the Scouts as light cavalry to cover down on the 69th's western flank, an area that ranged anywhere from six to ten miles as the crow flies, but up to a two-hour drive from Camp Cooke. The mission made doctrinal sense to the officers, but Olmo and the rest of the Scouts felt slighted once again, for they bore responsibility for an area that was roughly equal in size to the Assassin and Blacksheep areas combined. On top of that, the Scouts were just a single platoon with only twenty-eight men, compared to more than one hundred for the line companies. Talk about the guys on the short end of the stick—the Scouts were the economy of force platoon, inside an economy of force battalion, inside an economy of force brigade, inside an economy of force war. The unit's martyr complex inflected its every word and mannerism. They were convinced that Slack was treating them poorly, as the sordid underside of the battalion that got all the shit equipment and all the shit details. Yet despite their bitching, the Scouts secretly relished the role in which they'd been cast. They thought they were every bit as tough as Hollywood's *Dirty Dozen* and played the part of cavalier soldiers well.

Olmo had shaken off the eerie drone of the bagpipes by the time he and his squad rolled off Camp Cooke. They were headed out west on a standard framework patrol designed to deter insurgents from launching rockets. Olmo sat in the front passenger's side of his Humvee, traditionally the vehicle commander's seat. Lwin was driving and Ali was on the gun. The rest of the squad was behind them in Staff Sergeant Irizarry's vehicle, where Izzy was in the commander's seat,

Specialist Reed drove, and Sergeant Melendez was on the gun. Specialist John Cushman, the Scouts' medic, also rode with Izzy. The squad's two trucks were part of a four-vehicle patrol led by the Scout platoon leader, Lieutenant Ramnarine, who commanded his vehicle. Specialist Makish, another of Olmo's cronies from the old Alpha Company, commanded the fourth vehicle in the patrol. Every member of the section was confident as he headed out into sector. They had come to know the ground well and had brought in their first weapons cache and detainee the day before. Having just left a memorial service, the men were eager to settle scores.

But if the enemy was on the job that day, he was lying low. The Scouts roamed the rocket box for more than an hour before pulling up to a rubbled house that they occasionally used as a target to test fire their weapons. The men took some practice shots. Shooting is a perishable skill, and the insurgents had yet to give them any good targets.

Ziyad Hassan Ali Hamadi, a tall and lean oil worker in his late twenties, didn't plan on making himself a bull's-eye, either. He and the other local members of the al-Khalifawi clan had noticed an uptick in the number of U.S. patrols in their sparsely populated area, but nothing had really come of the American incursions. The family was an integral part of the insurgent funding network in Taji. They extorted money from contractors who worked on U.S.-backed projects as well as from the commercial oil traffic that traversed the area en route to the Mushada oil refinery, which sat astride the primary pipeline that ran into Baghdad from the north. They also made money from selling and distributing weapons to the insurgency, whose hardcore Iraqi and foreign leaders transited the area regularly. Ziyad and his brothers, who were low-level operators in the network, had even heard reports that the top mujahadin "prince" had recently been in their area—none other than al-Zarqawi. But if the Americans knew about the activity, they hadn't yet done anything about it. The occupiers never stayed in the region long enough and hadn't placed enough troops there to get in the way of the clan's normal criminal and insurgent activities. But that all changed when one of the patrols stopped at a family member's house the previous day. The Americans entered the home without reason, treated the residents disrespectfully, and then rummaged through the place in search of weapons. What did they find? A couple of grenades. So what, every house has a couple of grenades. It was no reason to put a blindfold on the owner and cart him off in a Humvee. Now they would take him to Abu Ghraib prison—and Ziyad and all his friends knew what went on there. Their brother would be leashed like a dog and stripped of his clothes and his manhood. They may as well have killed him in his own home; it would have been a better death.

Ziyad and the rest of his family were fed a regular diet of anti-American news. They got it from the television, from the newspapers, and from the flyers the mujahadin—the so-called Sunni freedom fighters—were passing out among the people. The Americans were raping Iraqis in prison. They were strapping innocent Iraqis to the steering wheels of bomb-laden cars and making them destroy mosques and markets. They were killing women, children, and elders. They were not trying to help Iraq; they were trying to establish a foothold in the country in order to rob the nation of its resources.

Oh, Muslims! Iraq and all Muslim countries that have been occupied are ranting for you to rescue them . . . find the holy warrior and fight behind him, devote yourself to him, he who raises the Islamic flag and starts the jihad again . . . then the root of American, British, Jewish invaders will be pulled from all Islamic countries . . . become stronger in this life until doomsday and the enemy won't be able to use his army to invade your countries!

Neither Ziyad nor his brothers had become deeply involved with jihad. In fact, they despised many of the Salafist zealots who were swarming into their country from Syria and Saudi Arabia. God forbid people like them ever got into power, for they'd have everybody in the mosques and bowing to Mecca five times a day. That said, the jihadists and the Khalifawis and Salems and other members of the Al Dulaimi tribe in central Iraq shared some of the same goals. First, they needed to make certain that the new government failed, thus keeping the nation's wealth in the hands of the Sunni tribes. Second, they all wanted to keep the Iranians and their Shia dogs out of power.

As for the Americans . . . call them infidels, call them occupiers, call them whatever you wished. But they had to go. It was they who had turned over the country to the Shias and Iran. And now they had detained a family member. It was time to kick them out of Taji—just as the proud Iraqis had done in June and July when they crushed their Humvees and tanks with bombs. Although the soldiers abandoned the area then, it now looked as if they were back. Ziyad got word from a senior clansman: the same four Humvees that ransacked the house yesterday had returned to the area. Ziyad was determined to hit them with one of the bombs they had planted for just such a defense. The Iraqi quickly made his way to the main road where they had had success back in July. The weapon, which was comprised of several large artillery shells, was buried just off to the side of the asphalt-covered road. Because he didn't have a remote detonator, Ziyad ran the wires through a culvert under the road that drained into a canal that paralleled the artery. He followed the drainage path through a break in the canal berm, which he would use as a sight to trigger the bomb. Ziyad then hooked up a detonator and lay behind cover less than forty yards from where the bomb was planted. He would engage the last vehicle in the patrol and slip across the canal before the Americans knew what hit them. Then he would walk home from the area as if nothing had ever happened.

As the patrol of Humvees approached, the insurgent lay low and still, exposing only enough of himself to see the vehicles as they passed his trigger point. As he heard the distinctive sound of the Humvees approaching, Ziyad's heart raced. If ever there was a time to pray, it was now. He clutched the detonator, chanting *Allah Akbar, Allah Akbar, Allah Akbar* as the first truck passed his position. He waited, blood surging through his veins, until the last vehicle entered his sight.

Olmo was wearing his vehicle commander's headset when the

blast went off. The muffled explosion sounded as if his trunk had bumped open and then slammed shut, as it often did when they bounced through a pothole. The noise was far louder for Ali, who was on the gun. He turned and looked back, only to see black smoke and a tire flying through the air, and shouted down into the turret, "Jay!" At the same time Ramnarine's voice came over the net. "Fuck! One of my trucks just got hit! Turn around."

The guys had talked over and over again about what they would do if they ever got hit. The plan was for every vehicle that wasn't damaged to continue on for a bit, get out of the engagement area, then try to move back to the blast scene from the flank—ideally flushing out the forces that had triggered the ambush. That plan went out the window as soon as the IED went off. Ramnarine's truck was second to last in the movement and closest to the blast site. He slammed on the brakes, ordering his men, "Watch out for secondaries." Insurgents had often used one IED to fix the patrol, then fired off several more to kill the responders as they exited their vehicles. In Olmo's truck, Ali turned his .50-caliber machine gun toward the side of the road and fired several bursts down the shoulder to see if anything else would blow. When nothing did Olmo told Lwin to swing the truck around and head back to the blast site.

Izzy's truck had been hit, and as Olmo pulled up to the mangled Humvee, his eyes fixed on Melendez, one of his best friends since the two soldiers had been at West Point. The entire front end of Izzy's truck was gone, and Melendez's body slumped out of the turret, arms outstretched and knuckles hanging just above the blackened asphalt.

Olmo began opening his door even before the truck stopped, pushing it so hard that the armored steel slab bounced back and slammed him against the vehicle as he exited. He recovered and ran directly to Melendez. "Come on, buddy," he said, as he began to feel for his wounds. Ali looked down on the scene from his gun. Normally quiet and reserved, he shrieked as he never had before. "Get a fuckin' medevac!"

Specialist Cushman had been sitting in the back of Izzy's vehicle and had crawled out by the time Olmo reached the wreck. The medic's face was split open like a coconut and was spilling out blood. He looked at Olmo and then Melendez, and said, "He's dead. Don't worry about him." Olmo didn't believe him and began slapping Melendez's burned and charred face. "Come on, buddy. Don't fuckin' die on me." Melendez grunted. *I knew he was fuckin' alive!* Olmo climbed atop the vehicle and started to cut off his friend's body armor so he could get him out of the crushed Humvee.

Specialist Makish had been in the lead vehicle of the movement and reached the blast site just after Olmo. He went straight for Izzy. The bomb had blown off Izzy's door and most of his crew compartment. Both of the soldier's legs above the knees were gone, and his right arm was missing. Makish lifted him out of his seat and gently laid him on the ground. The sergeant's torso and vitals were intact, and he was conscious. Izzy looked up at Makish. "I'm pretty fucked up here, right?"

"No, you'll be fine," Makish assured him. The wounded medic came over, and the two soldiers started working on their squad leader, applying tourniquets to all his extremities. When one tourniquet snapped, Makish pulled off his belt to fashion another one.

"I don't know if I'm gonna make it, guys," Izzy said.

"Shut up, you'll be fine, you'll be fine."

Lwin rushed over to help but froze when he saw the extent of Izzy's wounds. Makish slapped him to try and bring him around, but Lwin was shaken. Makish ordered him to pick up security at the perimeter with Ali and the other soldiers.

Specialist Reed had been driving the Humvee, one of the less armored M1025s with an add-on kit. The firewall had been blasted back into his lap, and although the soldier was pinned inside the vehicle, he hadn't suffered the same level of trauma as Izzy. As Olmo struggled to get Melendez out of the vehicle, he told Reed to hang tight and try to work his way out of the rig if he could. When soldiers finally managed to help him out of the vehicle, both his legs looked like the letter W.

Ramnarine was back at his truck working the radio and shouting instructions to his soldiers on the security perimeter. He requested a medevac and asked the 69th to launch its quick reaction force (QRF). Both assets were moving in minutes. When the pilots of the 4th Aviation Brigade got the call, they also sent two of their scout helicopters, Kiowa Warriors, to help the lieutenant.

As the helicopters and QRF made their way to the engagement area, Specialist Jared Frenke, Makish's gunner, scanned the fields looking for any sign of the triggerman. Several minutes after the blast, he spotted an Iraqi male wearing a black shirt and khakis emerging from behind the berm on the far side of the canal, immediately adjacent to the blast site. He thought about shooting, but the man could have been just some Iraqi walking in the field, nothing about his mannerisms indicating that he was involved in the attack. But still, it didn't add up. The field wasn't being cultivated and was far from anything else in the area. Frenke kept his eyes on the Iraqi as he walked toward a distant house. *Fuck . . . that could be him.* The soldier yelled to the man in Arabic. *"Ogaf!"* But the Iraqi didn't stop. Frenke fired a warning shot to get his attention, but the man kept walking. Finally the gunner aimed a couple of rounds into the dirt near his feet. The Iraqi barely flinched, though he did change direction and headed for the closest house.

Ziyad was trying his best to play it cool and hoped the Americans would lose interest. But as he entered his cousin Achmed's house, several helicopters converged on the area. One of them landed near the attack site, but two of them started to circle over the house in which he was holed up. Ziyad knew he had been spotted and asked Achmed for clothes. He gave Ziyad a blue dishdasha, which the triggerman slipped over the khaki pants he had been wearing. Ziyad tried to leave the house, but each time he walked out the door one of the choppers buzzed over him, and the soldiers fired rounds toward the building. The better part of an hour passed, and the damn helicopters remained flying overhead.

When the 69th QRF finally arrived at Ramnarine's location, the officer and Frenke, who had been keeping an eye on the suspect, hopped in with the relief force and headed for the house. The soldiers went to the front of the building and ordered everyone outside. As women and children exited from the front door, one of the Kiowa pilots saw two men attempt to flee from the back of the house. They sent the word down, and the 69th soldiers ran to the back and ultimately apprehended the two men—Ziyad Hamadi and his cousin Achmed Souan. Both men and several others the Wolfhounds detained came up hot when the GIs tested their hands for explosive residue with a product called EX-Spray. When the soldiers later found the wires that led to Ziyad's hide site, they knew they had their man.

But the capture was little consolation for Olmo. Half his squad was wounded. What was he going to tell Melendez's mom? And Izzy . . . the sergeant had become something of a father figure for all the guys. Whenever anyone needed an encouraging word it came from Izzy. Christ, the guy had four of his own children. How would they react? As much as Olmo loved to play the streetwise tough guy, an emotional fog swept over him as the Scouts drove back to Camp Cooke. The soldier cried as he never had before and cringed with every bump in the road and headlight on the street. He wanted to curl up in a ball and shut out the world. He was covered in his friends' blood and could still smell the cordite and could still hear—over and over and over— the frightful sound of Ali yelling for a medevac. When they got back to Camp Cooke, the other Scout section ran to the soldiers. The men hugged and cried together. They told Olmo and Ramnarine that they had tried to drive out to be with their comrades, but had been blocked from leaving the base. Slack had ordered the gate guards not to let the rest of the Scouts out for fear they would wreak havoc on the countryside. It was a wise command decision, for in their frenzied state of rage, had the Scouts made it to the suspects first, none would have been taken alive.

Captain Daniels eventually called the men up to the battalion TOC. He wanted to give them an update on the wounded. In addition to the shrapnel wounds everyone had sustained, Melendez had broken his

back; Reed, his legs; and Cushman, his jaw. All three would be evacuated to Germany and would survive. But Izzy didn't make it, passing
away on the flight to the hospital.

"Go to sleep!
Go to sleep!
Slumber well where the shell screamed and fell.
Let your rifles rest on the muddy floor,
You will not need them any more.
Danger's past;
Now at last,
Go to Sleep!"

10: THE INFANTRY

COUNTERINSURGENCY

Seconds after Olmo learned Izzy had died, Major Cerniauskas pulled the team leader aside. "I know what you're going through, man," he said. "But we got to talk about it now. We gotta talk about this while it's still fresh in everyone's mind." The officer intended to conduct an after action review (AAR), a standard military procedure designed to help the unit learn, but Olmo wanted nothing to do with it. "Go fuck your mother," he shouted. "This is not the time."

But it was the time. Both Ramnarine and Daniels told Olmo they had to discuss it. The soldier hated them for it but took his seat. He told Lwin and Ali to grab food from the chow hall and come back to relive the nightmare.

That's how it felt for everyone in the Fighting 69th. Like a fucking nightmare that wouldn't end until they were all dead. Most of the soldiers had rebounded after Drum and Urbina were killed. They recognized that casualties were a part of war, and the men were more angry than afraid. But with Izzy's death—so close to the others—a wave of mortality rolled over them. The soldiers lost their sense of invincibility. Death could come to any of them at any time.

Several days later the Assassins were hit again, this time with one of the largest IEDs yet, its blast leaving a crater four feet deep and six feet wide in the middle of the road. The driver of the vehicle had noticed something strange and slowed the moment before the earth exploded, and though the force of the bomb lifted the Humvee and tossed it twenty-five yards from the point of impact, nobody was hurt. The 1114 worked as advertised, so long as the insurgent had poor aim. The Assassins smiled at their good fortune and mugged for photos in the crater.

But not all the men were so relieved. First Sergeant Acevedo had been worrying about many of his leaders, who had not developed as he had hoped. Guys he had been carrying for fear they wouldn't be replaced reached their limits and broke. One of Acevedo's platoon sergeants, an NCO who had been with the Assassins at Ground Zero and West Point, folded under the stress. After the deaths, he refused to leave Camp Cooke with his own men. At the same time Acevedo and Drew realized that two of their lieutenants weren't making the grade. All three men were cut from the team to be reassigned by the battalion.

When Slack had first gotten word that the 69th would go to Iraq nearly a year before, he knew that the time had come for the chickens to come home to roost. The policies of the Army and State of New York had resulted in an underfunded, underequipped, undertrained, and undermanned unit. Most of the problems had been fixed by an influx of cash and hardware in the months after mobilization. But the lack of training—especially leader training—and the legacy of nurturing inept soldiers were still all too obvious in Task Force Wolfhound. In addition to Major Major and the senior NCO and two officers pulled from the Assassins, the Scout platoon sergeant, a captain, and three more lieutenants from the headquarters company would ultimately be reassigned in the early period of the Iraq tour.

The effects of the weekend warrior legacy and the violence of Iraq seemed to hit the Assassins hardest. Drew and Acevedo lost their executive officer, a platoon leader, and a platoon sergeant to competency issues. They lost one of their top squad leaders to an IED. Most of the positions would never be replaced, and consequently the junior and senior leaders who did remain had to pick up extra duties.

But just as the stress of combat and the failure of certain soldiers threatened to shake the task force apart, Slack and the other key officers and NCOs pulled the unit back together and helped the Wolfhounds stay frosty.

The commanders had all learned one basic truth about the enemy: He wasn't stupid. Whenever he thought he had an advantage against the 69th, he would attack. When it looked as if the Americans had the advantage, he would stay in his house and drink chai. Commanders Slack, Daniels, Drew, and Kazmierzak accordingly responded to the early attacks by ensuring they had whatever advantages they could. There was really only one, however—firepower—and the 69th pushed as many forces into the sector as they could. First they focused on the population centers. As they developed their own intelligence, they concentrated on certain families and certain houses. The Wolfhounds acted on the slightest hint of intelligence—targets that were so poorly developed they often didn't even have the name of a suspect, or, if they did have the name, they often didn't have his location. Most times the searches resulted in nothing. At other times the task force found weapons or garnered some shred of information that led to a better understanding of the area. The battalion also welcomed informants, and if the turncoats wanted money, the Wolfhounds would gladly draw from their own personal bank accounts. The shotgun approach seemed to be working in December: in the weeks following Izzy's death, the 69th detained more bona fide insurgents than all the other units in the Tiger Brigade combined.

By Christmas the battalion had gone without casualties for three weeks, and the soldiers were feeling good. Even after rolling one vehicle into a canal and trading fire with insurgents, Assassin Lieutenant Stan Westmoreland was able to joke with a reporter from the *Stars and Stripes* newspaper, "I've been shot at more this Christmas than all the other ones combined."

The task force's best holiday present came in the form of intelligence. An Iraqi they had detained during a random search was singing like a canary. The informant gave up several members of the Salem family, key players in the same clan that had attacked the

Scouts and killed Izzy. Cerniauskas gave the mission to Kaz and the Blacksheep, who moved against the target on December 27, a house just a mile and a half from where Izzy was killed. When they reached there, the residents pleaded ignorance. But instead of offering tea and claiming their innocence like most suspect Iraqis, the three Salem brothers at the house seemed cocky. The twenty- and thirty-something Iraqis laughed at the Americans as the soldiers scoured their property with metal detectors, hoping to find evidence of a weapons cache buried below the surface. The GIs wanted to pummel the suspected insurgents but swallowed their pride and held back. The Salem property turned up nothing—a "dry hole," in soldier parlance—but when the Blacksheep confronted the informant, whom they had brought along blindfolded, the man reasserted his claims. The Salems had a ton of weapons there, he insisted, and asked the soldiers to lift his blindfold so he could see where he was. After a quick survey of the area, the informant told the soldiers they had the right men but were looking at the wrong house; the Salems lived next door. With that the Americans brought their metal detectors to the adjoining dwelling, and the Salems stopped laughing immediately. When the first metal detector went off, the brothers hung their heads. The soldiers found their weapons—a massive cache of rockets, bomb-making equipment, ammunition, and rifles. The soldiers took a picture of the insurgents with their arsenal and sent it to General Chiarelli with the note: "Merry Christmas from the Salem family."

The end of the year was also supposed to bring about the reunification of the Fighting 69th. The Banshees' force-protection mission in Baghdad was scheduled to be completed on December 31. The Tiger Brigade couldn't cut the entire company loose from its assignment, however, and instead General Basilica sent Slack one of his engineer platoons, "The Red Dogs," and pulled one of the Banshees' light-wheeled recon platoons for duty up in Taji. The eighteen-man unit was ultimately chopped to the Blacksheep, giving the mechanized unit a section of Humvee-mounted soldiers that could go places the massive Bradley Fighting Vehicles couldn't.

CHARLIE 24

Choosing the best routes had proven to be a daily struggle for the Blacksheep. There were only three places at which the unit could cross into the Taji AO. Once inside, the options were just as limited. The Louisianans weren't able to zip up and down narrow canals like the Scouts and the Assassins, as they needed more solid roads to traverse, but there simply weren't that many to choose from. Some of the routes that would have been ideal for armor had been labeled "no go"—Route Red Legs being the perfect example. The paved thorough-fare was among the sturdiest in the region, but recent history had demonstrated that its roadbed seemed to hold as much TNT as it did gravel. Yet because it passed directly through the Blacksheep's portion of the battalion AO, at a minimum the Cajuns had to cross the bomb-sown road to get to the other side. The Blacksheep just had to hope that the enemy wasn't expecting them to cross when they actually had to. However, as night fell on January 6, 2005, insurgents were watching.

Kazmierzak usually patrolled his area twice a day—once during daylight hours and once at night. He had come off his first patrol at 3:00 p.m., went to the mess hall for an early dinner, and returned to his command post at around half-past seven. Minutes later *that* voice came over the radio, that high-octave, fast-paced, chopped voice.

"Contact, IED!"

Kaz recognized the speaker as Sergeant James Scaruffi. He picked up the handset and asked for more information. "Comeux . . . his track was hit . . . it's on fire . . . I don't see anybody moving . . . I'm looking for the triggerman."

Kaz knew from Scaruffi's tone that the hit had been a bad one. He told his guys to get ready to roll and then rushed out of his command post to the battalion TOC. "I got a Bradley hit. Get on my company net." Slack's office was on the other side of the TOC. Kaz ran over, cracked the door, and told the commander he had a track down. "It sounds catastrophic." Kaz left Slack's office for his motor pool and climbed aboard his Bradley. It took him fifteen long minutes to get his section spun up and rolling toward the gate. Major Cerniauskas had called the base fire department and asked them to send a pumper truck along out to the site to fight the blaze. The firefighters were American contractors who knew well who the 69th was—the guys who had stopped the mortars and rockets. They rushed to their truck—a regular old, unarmored, red fire engine straight off Main Street, USA—so quickly that they beat Kaz to the gate. A section of Humvees from the Assassins linked up with the responders as well. The convoy rolled outside Camp Cooke and blasted straight up Route Red Legs. As they neared the attack, Kaz saw an orange glow on the horizon—the burning hulk of the armored personnel carrier. He got more details from Scaruffi as he neared the engagement area: the Bradley had been thrown into the air and now lay upside down in the canal that lined the road.

Kaz made it to the scene about forty-five minutes after the initial engagement. The sun had gone down hours before, but the fire from the vehicle lit the entire area. He jumped from his vehicle and headed to where some of his soldiers were gathered nearby. They had been standing on the road watching the vehicle burn—watching their friends burn. A few of the guys were in hysterics; a few more were catatonic. Kaz told them to get back to their track. The Assassins picked up security of the area.

The commander stared at the burning wreck. Rounds from the vehicle's main gun were cooking off, posing a hazard to anyone close at hand. But Kaz didn't budge, and neither did the firefighters, who pulled their truck down the road and started to spray foam on the flames. As they subsided, Kaz's worst fear materialized: there were no survivors. A gaping wound showed where the vehicle's soldiers would have been sitting. He pushed himself back to his vehicle and picked up the radio.

"Wolfhound Mike, this is Black Six."

"Black Six, Wolfhound Mike—go ahead, over."

"It's a catastrophic kill. The vehicle is melted down in a ditch. The fire is out and is still smoking, over."

"Roger."

Kaz returned to the smoking Bradley and thought about the crew entombed inside vehicle number Charlie 24: Sergeant First Class Kurt Comeux, Sergeant Christopher Babin, Corporal Bradley Bergeron, Corporal Warren Murphy, Corporal Huey Fassbender, Specialist Armand Frickey, and Specialist Kenneth VonRonn. *Oh my God—seven men.* They were all gone.

Kaz didn't have time to lament. Anger took over, and he looked up from the vehicle and through the smoke toward the village, just five hundred yards away. It was Awad al Hussein, home of Sheik Abed, the senior member of the Al Dulaimi tribe in the area and a two-faced contractor who took American money for infrastructure projects, only to flip it back to the insurgency. He told the Americans that he knew about everything that happened in his town, so if an attack took place, Kaz knew it was because Abed had sanctioned or even directed it. Perhaps it was a response to the Blacksheep's capture of the Salem brothers just a week earlier.

The captain clenched his fist, and shifting his eyes from the center of the town, he studied the terrain around the vehicle. The triggerman would have to have had good visibility to score a direct hit on the Bradley. There were only two structures with a good line of sight of the blast. The captain was ready to roll.

As Kaz was contemplating his next move, Slack pulled up to the scene in his Humvee. He exited the vehicle and walked toward Kaz without looking at the blast. Kaz gave him a quick and complete brief of everything he knew, but Slack could see the man was hurting. He put his hand on Kaz's shoulder and looked into his eyes. The captain was enraged and determined. Slack, well aware of what was on his mind, ordered Kaz to keep clear of the village. "The triggerman is long gone. We need to recover your men."

A soldier called to the officers as they talked. "There's a body in the canal." Slack and Kaz hurried to the waterway, slid down the slope, and waded into the putrid pool where most of Specialist Fassbender's remains had come to rest. Slack hugged the soldier's torso close to lift him out of the pond. As he and Kaz carried Fassbender up the slope, the other soldiers nearby heard Slack speaking to the fallen soldier. "It's okay, son. You did a great job. We're gonna take care of you. We're gonna bring you home."

It was September 11 all over again.

The high explosives and steel shrapnel contained in IEDs were devastating to their victims. As at Ground Zero, many U.S. soldiers killed in Iraq could be identified only through DNA. Since the deaths of Drum and Urbina, Slack had sought to do the same thing for his men that he had done for the victims of 9/11—give them back their dignity. He pledged to his soldiers never to leave one drop of American blood on the soil of Iraq. When Drum and Urbina were hit, Slack crawled on his hands and knees looking for remains. He then took a shovel and scraped up the blood-soaked sand, transferring it into a body bag. After he and Kaz pulled Fassbender from the water, Slack and every soldier available waded back into the canal and scoured the surrounding fields in search of remains. The men set up twenty-four-hour security at the site and brought in mobile light sets to aid the cleanup crews. When dogs tried to scavenge the area, the soldiers shot them. Once the vehicle had been retrieved and Slack was as certain as he could be that the 69th had recovered every personal effect and ounce of flesh they could, the commander directed Daniels to bring out a fuel truck, saturate the area with diesel, and put the land to the torch. General Basilica rushed north to the 69th headquarters after the attack. When he learned the Wolfhounds were burning down the countryside, he asked Slack if he could send more fuel.

After the Bradley was brought back to Camp Cooke, Command Sergeant Major Brett continued the mission, crawling through the hulk until he was certain he had recovered any trace of the soldiers. Then for two days he mopped and scrubbed the charred metal clean with bleach.

The catastrophic kill on Charlie 24 became a *Black Hawk Down* moment for the Fighting 69th. The Bradley was the biggest, strongest piece of war-fighting gear in the battalion. With armor nearly as thick as a tank's, it was a symbol of the Wolfhounds' strength. If the enemy could destroy a Bradley so easily, it became perfectly clear to Slack that no vehicle could survive on any road in Taji. The enemy's timing was perfect; his power to destroy the vehicle was awesome. If a soldier was unlucky enough to be hit, he was going to die. Slack could read that knowledge in the men's faces the following day. His entire battalion was worried because everybody who would have to cross one of those five stinking bridges into Taji was well aware that death, in the form of getting atomized by a massive IED, was their fate. If the 69th stayed there long enough, the odds that every one of them would be killed or wounded were really damn good. It was happening all over the place. It was happening on every major trail in the area. The men wouldn't dare go down the road along the Grand Canal any longer because that's where Engeldrum and Urbina had been killed. They couldn't travel up and down the main north-south road, because that's where Izzy had been attacked. Americans were getting hit all around the town of Hora al Bosh and on the little goat trails barely wide enough for a Humvee. Even the road where the Bradley was hit was a tertiary trail off Route Red Legs. As for Red Legs itself, it was a death trap. By now it was pocked with so many bomb craters that it looked like the surface of the moon. There was simply no place left to go.

The carnage from the Bradley was the worst thing Slack had seen in Iraq. And for the first time in the war, perhaps the first time in his life, the commander wasn't sure what to do. He believed the enemy had gotten so good that the 69th was close to being defeated in the area. The battalion no longer had the freedom of the roads, and the enemy was clearly watching them, doing his own pattern analysis. If he sent his men outside the wire again, Slack feared, he would be sending them to their deaths.

The commander had come to the same conclusion as the units that had patrolled Taji before the 69th. They had been willing to press on after losing Humvees, but when they lost an Abrams main battle tank, the toughest piece of kit in the U.S. inventory, they knew the gig was up. Taji was just too dangerous. It wasn't worth the risk. Slack was ready to fold.

When the Blacksheep's first sergeant, Cliff Ockman, and several of his NCOs walked into the commander's office back at Camp Cooke, the men looked grim. Slack had never seen Ockman so depressed. The entire company was screwed up, an emotionally beaten-down group of soldiers. Slack was ready to tell them to take the day off or to take a short, slow, and safe patrol in the local area.

"We're going back out, sir," the first sergeant announced. "We're going back out hard." Slack took a deep swallow. After the first deaths, he had pushed his battalion back into the breach. But now he didn't have the strength to order the Blacksheep or any of his soldiers to return to the fight. But he didn't have to; the men now understood their duty better than before. They refused to give up. They refused to let the insurgents have the last word. What would the Blacksheep tell the widows and orphans back in the small town of Houma? "We gave up. It was too hard. We didn't want to risk any more casualties to avenge your husband, your dad, our high school classmate." What would Olmo, Lwin, and Ali tell Sergeant Melendez when they saw him back on the block? "After you got hit we avoided the area. We captured a couple of guys, but didn't bother with any other insurgents. Fuck the people in the Green Zone, let them get hit with rockets. That's their problem."

No fuckin' way.

When Slack left his office, he saw that the entire battalion was loading up their vehicles, inspecting their equipment, wiping down their guns, and rolling back out into the killing fields. The commander was heartsick. *Look at all these brave, young, wonderful guys—company commanders and platoon sergeants and first sergeants and squad leaders. They know what they're up against. They know what can happen to them. And they're all saying, Let's go.*

The 69th wasn't fighting an insurgency; they were fighting a gang war. That fact was now obvious to all the battalion's cops and all its kids from the projects. It was obvious to the tight-knit Blacksheep clan out of Houma. When the 69th hit them, the Iraqis hit back. You take one of ours; we'll take seven of yours. The soldiers didn't have to do a lot of soul-searching on their next course of action. They would escalate. The Iraqis of Taji had given the Wolfhounds a reason to fight, and the 69th was going to give them a bellyful.

THE HEART OF DARKNESS

The coppery taste of death was on the back of every soldier's tongue as the 69th went to work. Another Bradley got hit, wounding one. The Scouts got rammed with a car bomb, wounding three more. But the soldiers said fuck it, resigning themselves to their fate, and in doing so the 69th regained its functionality. The men still flinched at every bump. They still ground their teeth and shut their eyes when they passed a lone parked car. But they drove on. The Fighting 69th stayed frosty. In the days after Charlie 24 was hit, the battalion went into overdrive. They pressed informants for more information. They threatened sheiks and the heads of families with horrible violence— acts that the Iraqis knew the 69th was fully capable of committing. Something in the soldiers' eyes told the locals that the Americans were serious, that they were highly dangerous. When Slack was pressing one Iraqi for intelligence, the commander's Shia interpreter, who hated the Sunnis of Taji, told Slack he was wasting his time. "These people are willing to die for nothing," his interpreter said. Slack looked deep into the Iraqi's eyes and retorted, "Well God damnit, tell him *I'm* willing to die for nothing!"

The aggressive posturing of the Americans was only part bluff. The men had truly come to hate the Iraqis of Taji. Even the "innocent" civilians were not to be trusted because they turned their eyes away from the murderous activity around them. "We didn't see not'in'." People who lived next to massive weapons caches claimed they couldn't possibly imagine how the weapons had gotten there; they never saw anybody nearby. Kazmierzak thought they were cowards, an attitude that was shaped during a patrol when he witnessed an

Iraqi man pummeling his two-year-old son in front of their home—kicking him and punching him. When the man threw a bicycle at the baby, Kaz halted his track, jumped off, and marched up to him, giving him a shove. The father was unrepentant. Kaz grabbed him by the shirt and pulled him spittle-close. "If you touch the kid again, I'm going to kill you. If you don't believe me, just go ahead and take a swing at him." All of it was translated by Kaz's interpreter. The child lay bleeding and crying while its mother watched stoically from a distance. Kaz didn't care about cultural differences. Any people who would beat their two-year-olds were savages. As time passed the officer and soldiers across the battalion practically begged Iraqis to give them a chance to kill them. They wanted to avenge their friends.

But the Iraqis never fought back, never stood up to the Americans openly. Instead, they avoided a decisive fight with the soldiers. Even if the Americans knew a man was an insurgent—if, for example, an informant had given him up—there was nothing the 69th could do unless they found evidence. Without evidence, the Army lawyers would tell the 69th they needed to release their detainees the next day and compensate them twenty dollars each for their trouble.

The situation was beyond frustrating for the soldiers. Many of the men had seen movies of Americans executing German prisoners in a rage after Normandy or read reports of summary executions of Nazi prison guards at concentration camps. Nobody but a soldier who has been bathed in his best friend's blood could understand such behavior. The men of the Fighting 69th did understand it, and many had reached the same mental state. Slack believed there had been some close calls. If he had not stopped the Scouts from leaving the base after Izzy was killed, if he had not ordered Kazmierzak to stand down after Charlie 24 was hit, it could have gotten ugly for any Iraqi within small-arms range. As much as he hated the bastard insurgents, the commander didn't want to see any of his own men swing for the death of any Iraqi. As much as he could, he urged his men to show restraint. In a rare address to the entire battalion in January, he stood atop a flatbed truck and commiserated with his soldiers. He felt the same way they did; he wanted to cut down as many insurgents as possible. But they were American soldiers and needed to abide by the laws of land warfare.

"As much as you may think that you and your buddies on the scene at that moment may say, 'This fucker needs to die. At the very least he needs to ingest his own teeth . . . ' Don't do it. Maintain the moral high ground. Cuff him. Lock him up . . . When that urge strikes you to take your muzzle and jam it down his throat—don't do it. Step back." Slack urged his men to let the judicial system work. "We're putting the dirtbags away. They're going away for a long, long time, and we don't need to fuck 'em up to do it."

Intelligence became everything in the struggle. And as the Wolfhounds pressed the population and as a handful of locals agreed to give up their neighbors for cash, the battalion was able to develop a good understanding of the network in Taji. When they gathered enough information to act, the task force rolled into Awad al Hussein, the village adjacent to where the Bradley was destroyed. The troops searched the entire village, seizing weapons and apprehending the individuals who had enough reporting against them to make a detention stick. By mid-January the battalion had sent more than two hundred insurgents to Abu Ghraib prison—a conviction rate of more than 60 percent of every civilian detained. Enemy activity in the Taji sector dropped drastically. Indirect-fire attacks remained suppressed. The enemy's IED campaign waned.

Now, when the Blacksheep ever did get to go home, they could tell the families of their fallen brothers that they got the bastard who killed their fathers, husbands, sons, brothers. The Wolfhounds generated enough intelligence on the triggerman and his associates that higher levels of command took interest in the gang. Two weeks after Charlie 24 was struck, the insurgent who detonated the bomb was killed in an engagement with a U.S. and Iraqi Special Forces team. The man had been a lieutenant colonel and engineer officer in Saddam's Republican Guard. The operators tore a medal off his well-kept uniform and passed it on to Slack, who wore it close to his heart from that day forward.

The efforts of the battalion drew lauds back at Camp Cooke, whose soldiers benefited directly from the 69th's efforts. They hadn't had to wear body armor on the base since the Wolfhounds arrived, and only a scattering of mortars still fell onto the camp. Not one soldier was wounded by indirect fire since the 69th came to town, and the soldiers who were stuck on the base were truly grateful. When 69th men walked into the mess hall, other troops let them go to the front of the line. When 69th men came off patrol, other troops thanked them for their work. The commander of the 4th Aviation Brigade expressed his appreciation to General Basilica weekly for sending the Fighting 69th to Taji. No other unit had taken it to the enemy in the AO as successfully as the Wolfhounds. One civilian worker and former Army Ranger approached Major Crosby to tell him that Iraq was his fifth contingency operation, and that the 69th was as good as any unit he had ever served with, in some cases more so. General Chastain from the 39th Brigade all but sang the battalion's praises from the rooftops. Major General Chiarelli, commander of the 1st Cavalry Division, told Slack that the Fighting 69th was the most effective unit under his command, though he'd never say it in public for fear of alienating his own Big Army commanders.

But no sooner did the battalion start making a difference than were the effects of inadequate troop strength felt. The Iraqis were set to hold their first democratic elections since the invasion on January 30, and Chiarelli needed more troops inside Baghdad to secure the city and its polling stations. As an economy of force battalion, the 69th was pulled from Taji for election-security duty in central Baghdad. The countryside where ten Wolfhounds died and more than a dozen soldiers were wounded was effectively handed back to Sheik Abed, his clan of black market insurgents, and the jihadists who fled Baghdad to reorganize during the election surge.

The soldiers had mixed emotions about leaving. On one hand, they were relieved, as if they had been given a pardon off of death row. But on the other hand, they feared that all their work and all their suffering had been in vain. Counterinsurgency doctrine called for units to clear, hold, and build. The 69th had unquestionably cleared the area, but they never had a chance to hold the place, let alone rebuild its infrastructure and support for the new government.

That said, how many incidents did the 69th prevent while they were on duty? How many soldiers' lives did they save from mortar fire at Camp Cooke? Did they disrupt a rocket attack aimed for President Bush when he visited troops in Baghdad on Thanksgiving Day? Did Mike Kazmierzak save the life of a toddler from his savage father? As with their seemingly pointless security duty in New York City and at West Point in 2001 and 2002, the task force's success could not be wholly measured in how many insurgents it captured. Rather, it's what didn't happen that was more significant. When the 69th Infantry was on the job, American soldiers in Baghdad were safer.

11: INFORMATION OPERATIONS

HAGAR THE HORRIBLE

Both the Sunni and jihadist insurgents made their opinions on the elections clear. In conversations with 69th soldiers about the vote, Baghdad-area Sunnis claimed the entire event was just a ploy to bring the Iranians and Kurds to power. They believed that the U.S. needed to appoint a strong dictator who could bring peace to Iraq and maintain its territorial sovereignty. They feared the election was just the first step in the ultimate partitioning of the country. Al-Zarqawi was more dramatic. In Internet statements he said that Al Qaida had declared war on the "evil principle" of democracy in Iraq, and declared that anyone who voted was the enemy. Death threats were posted around Shia neighborhoods, and intelligence reporting indicated that every insurgent element in Iraq was planning major attacks against polling stations and the American and Iraqi forces that protected them. When Task Force Wolfhound loaded their vehicles in Taji for the fifteen-mile convoy to the center of west Baghdad, they were ready for a fight. Weapons were greased, soldiers put fresh batteries in their radios and optics, and Captain Daniels inspected the construction of the portable outhouse his men had built for him. It was perfect.

The HHC commander had been given the job of setting up the 69th's forward operating base for the election mission. The headquarters would be in the Al Adl mall, an abandoned six-story structure that sat astride a sectarian divide. The building provided a good view of the battalion's main area of responsibility, an IED-pocked cloverleaf intersection. But the place had nothing in the way of plumbing, with not a commode in sight. At Camp Cooke the men used Porta-Johns that were cleaned and emptied daily by civilian contractors. But KBR didn't have a contract for the mall, which meant not only no mess facilities or running water, but no latrines as well.

Slack wasn't overly concerned about the issue, given his focus on more pressing matters, such as the element of surprise, force protection, and fields of fire. They were important concerns, to be sure, but what was going to happen when five hundred soldiers needed to relieve themselves? If the guys were in the woods, they could dig a trench or a hole. But in the middle of the city? Daniels ordered his maintenance platoon to build wooden toilets for the men—and a private one for himself, if the soldiers didn't mind.

The soldiers didn't mind in the least. If Daniels had wanted a shower stall they would have built that for him, too. The captain had earned his men's respect in spades over the past five years, and they were willing to do whatever he asked—so long as the officer didn't try to con them. If the men had to pull a shit detail they would do it promptly, but they wanted to know it was a shit detail up front. Since every detail was shitty, the men were used to it, anyway.

The HHC was the least sexy unit in the battalion. The line companies and the Scouts got the big missions and the cool trucks and radios, the headquarters company got everything else. The HHC provided the guys who stood guard at the gymnasium, who counted heads at the mess hall, who built the shitters. Yet as mundane as their work was, the task force could not have run without them. With every new mission came a new set of tasks, which Colonel Slack quickly levied against his HHC. And why not? "Hagar the Horrible" and his men had never failed the battalion yet.

When Slack arrived in Taji, he realized he needed a security detail of his own with which to maneuver. He gave the requirement to Daniels, who built a team of mortarmen and cooks to follow the fearless 69th commander into combat. When Slack realized he needed someone to drive the twenty miles back and forth to Camp Liberty to pick up the mail and get supplies every day, he gave the requirement to Daniels. The captain dug up three beaten Humvees with first-generation armor and blown-out shocks, and tagged his support platoon—from then forward, Team Hagar—to make the daily "thunder runs." When Slack got pissed off and wanted to raid an insurgent-held village RIGHT NOW, he told Daniels to get soldiers moving. The captain, who didn't command combat-maneuver elements, as did the leaders of the Blacksheep and Assassins, rounded up whatever cook, recovery-vehicle operator, and mechanic he could find.

The men weren't always at their most confident on these jobs. During one impromptu mission, one of Chris's medics was shanghaied for use as a driver. He complained to Daniels about Slack: "Captain Dan . . . that guy's gonna get us all killed! What the hell am I doing here, anyway? I'm a medic and I don't even have a Band-Aid." But what the Horribles lacked in confidence or training, they more than made up for in moxie. The HHC was full of New York originals who never shrank from a challenge. They were eager to participate and volunteered for missions before Daniels had to task them.

Even the mechanics signed up for extra duty. Chief Bill Solmo's maintenance platoon were among the hardest-working soldiers in the battalion and "worked some fuckin' wonders," in the words of Jay Olmo. As resource-starved Guardsmen, the mechanics had long become experts at scrounging equipment for repairs. In Iraq, the experience served them well. When men like Olmo dragged in blown-up and damaged trucks, the mechanics went to work on the vehicles like doctors and nurses in a trauma center. With the 69th's self-imposed operations tempo, the mechanics couldn't afford to wait for replacement parts to arrive at base but had to get the trucks up immediately. One of Solmo's soldiers trolled Camp Cooke looking for parts, even stripping equipment from a Wal-Mart-sized parking lot of abandoned Iraqi military hardware. Every other mechanic was roused from sleep or from the mess hall and thrown into the ward, often going for days without any significant amount of sleep. Their efforts were critical.

Nine times out of ten, the maintainers got the trucks back up and ready for combat patrols within twelve hours—often much less. More combat power in sector meant fewer indirect fire attacks on Camp Cooke and a smaller window for insurgents to stage IED attacks. The mechanics didn't stop there. Whenever Daniels needed to round up forces RIGHT NOW, the soldiers waved off sleep and climbed into anything with wheels or tracks and rolled into the fight. There were few infantrymen among the mechanics and the rest of the HHC, most of whom were trained to support combat from behind the lines. Yet Daniels's soldiers were the first to be hit with an IED. They were on Slack's machine guns whenever the commander rolled. And they expended more ammunition than all the line companies combined. About the only thing they didn't do was rate the Combat Infantryman Badge.

The CIB was the ultimate mark of honor for an infantryman. Yet if a soldier hadn't been to infantry school, he wasn't authorized the award. The rule was a slap in the face to the guys in the HHC. Slack, for example, was the only infantry-schooled soldier in his Humvee crew, which consisted of his gunner, a fifty-five-year-old cook; his driver, an engineer; and his backseater, an anti-tank man. Yet Slack was the only one eligible for the CIB. The injustice was so great that the commander contracted with a local vendor to make framed and rather ornate stained-glass plaques with a picture of the CIB and each non-infantry-schooled soldier's name. When the men were in an engagement that would have rated a CIB had they been classified as infantry, Slack and Daniels presented them with the unofficial but highly meaningful Fighting 69th CIB Plaque.

The award had even been made up for Lieutenant Brian Liona. While the junior intelligence officer and Manhattan architect did not conduct regular combat patrols, there was every indication he would accidently wind up in the middle of an engagement. The diminutive officer once handed a videotape to one of the personnel specialists and asked him to put the content on a CD so he could mail it home to his mother. When the specialist played the tape he was dumbfounded and called Daniels in to have a look. Liona had been in Baghdad on intelligence-related business and had some spare time. Armed with his rifle, the soldier decided to hail a civilian taxicab in the Green Zone, and then asked for a sightseeing tour around Baghdad. The lieutenant taped the entire ride and provided commentary for his mom at every corner. "Here is a regular city block in the middle of Baghdad. I don't know what all the fuss is about. It's not that bad." When the taxi reached an American checkpoint, startled soldiers from the 101st Airborne Division pulled the lieutenant from the vehicle and escorted him back to where he had started.

Liona was in his glory in Baghdad, a city that was absolutely spellbinding for an architect. Its more affluent neighborhoods were filled with beautiful homes that were a cross between Miami Art Deco and Graceland kitsch. When Task Force Wolfhound stormed into its mall posting in the black of night on January 28 with hundreds of soldiers and scores of armored vehicles, Liona was eager to get a look at the rest of the area. Not really thinking about the element of surprise, force protection, or fields of fire, the lieutenant sought out the electrical panel and started flipping all its switches. Baghdad may have suffered from an inadequate power supply, but there was plenty of juice that night to light up the old shopping mall like a Christmas tree—and blow the battalion's cover. If insurgents planned to attack, they'd know right where to aim, perhaps giving Liona a chance to get his CIB Plaque.

Of course, the enemy wouldn't attack that night or any other. The insurgents in Baghdad were not inclined to attack hundreds of nervous Americans with automatic weapons and air support. When an armored column of the new Iraqi army rolled into the area the next day to bolster security, the target became even less appealing. The Iraqi unit—which was all Shia, and knew very well that it was in the middle of a hostile Sunni stronghold—would be quick to the trigger at the first sign of impropriety (from the Sunni side of the street, anyway).

The daunting collection of firepower allowed Daniels to relax. After the line companies headed out into the surrounding neighborhoods, the captain adjusted his ad hoc security force of recovery vehicles and cargo trucks, then headed for his private commode, labeled CAPTAIN DANIELS ONLY, without a care in the world.

Slack, more tense, listened to the radio chattering nonstop about planned Sunni attacks and suicide bombers and unprotected polling stations. The commander flexed his line companies and the Scouts from one area to the next to make sure the insurgent genie remained in the bottle. The Assassins conducted a raid; other soldiers blasted a vehicle that rushed the men's position. But despite these efforts, Slack's concerns seemed about to materialize. As he looked west toward the horizon, the commander saw thousands of people marching slowly toward his position. They carried flags and marched in a disciplined formation. Worried that they would overrun his task force, Slack gave his troops a warning order: "Prepare for contact." As he considered calling for backup the mass of Iraqis moved closer, until Slack finally realized they were not militants. These people were smiling and singing, pumping their arms and cheering. Slack's Shia interpreter, who was a Canadian resident and had by then become the commander's trusted cultural adviser, told the colonel that they were Shias on their way to the polling stations to vote.

Because vehicle traffic had been banned for fear of car bombers, anyone who wanted to vote had to march, and the route to the polling stations led from distant Shia neighborhoods directly through the 69th's position. About a mile out, the marchers had to pass through several Sunni areas, whose streets were lined with local toughs looking for trouble. They had pushed debris into the street to block the way, then set it ablaze. Kaz sent his Bradleys to intervene, and the giant armored vehicles easily crushed the hasty barriers and extinguished the flames. The Blacksheep then stood guard along the route, muzzles aimed straight into the rabble, daring the hooligans to try any other interference. The Sunnis yielded.

When Daniels was done with his other business, he joined Slack to watch the marchers pass. Neither of the men had ever seen anything like it. There were thousands of Iraqis of all ages marching, with fathers carrying children and mothers supporting elders. When the group reached the new Iraqi army positions, the soldiers began to fire their rifles to the sky in jubilation. Daniels likened the scene to New Year's Eve in Times Square. After two and a half months of savage combat and bloodletting in Taji, the joy of the election sparked a flame in the captain, which began to melt the ice that had shrouded his heart. A wave of warm joy spread over the entire task force. The men who had been all but frothing at their mouths in mortal combat just days earlier found themselves smiling and cheering along with the Iraqis heading to vote. The soldiers slung back their rifles and started passing the marchers their water bottles. When the GIs ran out of bottles, they sent for trucks to deliver more. The Americans had their pictures taken with civilians and shook their hands as they passed by. When one of the men asked a voter why he was risking his life to dip his finger in the ink, the Iraqi replied that he was voting for the future. "*Inshallah* [God willing], we will make a better place for our children."

Due to the massive surge of American troops and the nascent Iraqi security forces into the heart of Baghdad, the elections went off far better than anyone had dared hope. There were attacks and casualties, but nothing that took away from the joy of the civilians who did vote. Plenty of journalists had gathered in the area, and all the American soldiers had standing orders to direct them to the voting Shias and Kurds, and away from the soldiers. Thus, as people around the world turned to their televisions to view the expected carnage, they saw instead the ecstatic voters, who held their purple-stained index fingers high into the air. It was a rare public relations victory for American forces and the new government.

THE MOST DANGEROUS ROAD IN THE WORLD

Information operations (IO) are one of the more important aspects of modern warfare. The discipline generally refers to the effective management and use of information to achieve a commander's objective. When officers in Iraq referred to IO, they were typically referring to combat marketing and public relations. Their goal was to publicize milestones such as infrastructure improvements and humanitarian operations in order to reinforce the legitimacy of the new government. But the Americans had been chronically unable to register any public relations wins. Conversely, they had been stacking up PR losses since the day after they helped Iraqis tear down the statue of Saddam. The failure of American forces to prevent the looting of the country's treasures in the period following the fall of Baghdad was the first significant blow in coalition efforts to win the hearts and minds of the Iraqis. By early 2005, publicity about every school U.S. forces built was trumped by news of the death of civilians in a U.S. raid or in a vehicle accident with a military convoy. Publicity about the new Iraqi army and police force was trumped by news of rampant neighborhood crime. Publicity about the humane face of Western-style leadership was absolutely destroyed when the Abu Ghraib prison scandal broke. The 69th had been given frozen chickens to distribute to the needy families of Taji in hopes of demonstrating goodwill. Slack just shook his head at the notion; the Fighting 69th was just pissing in the wind when it came to PR.

The insurgents, in contrast, were public relations masters. Along with creating fictional propaganda, they seized on every failure of the Americans and the interim Iraqi government and exploited the missteps at every opportunity. Orators railed against U.S. forces at the mosques. They printed up anti-occupation flyers and posters. They filled the newspapers and radio stations with eyewitness accounts from people who had lost their children during an American raid. The insurgent marketing machine rivaled any used in modern warfare.

The most effective weapon the insurgents employed against the U.S. occupation was video. If news networks around the world had the option of running footage of a happy villager clutching a frozen chicken or a wailing mother lamenting the loss of a loved one amid the carnage of a suicide bomb, more often than not the journalists chose the latter. The drumbeat of horrific stories coming out of Iraq damaged coalition efforts to rein in the country. Reports of dead soldiers weakened the resolve of many smaller nations that had committed troops to Iraq. In late 2004 and 2005, countries that had committed support to the coalition began to pull their men and their dollars. The enemy's IO campaign was so effective that the insurgents made information operations their primary strategy for long-term success. And the main effort of their campaign was a short span of highway that the Americans had christened "Route Irish," after the Notre Dame football team. But by February 2005, however, most people around the globe knew the freeway by its more mediagenic moniker: "The Most Dangerous Road in the World."

A four-lane highway with a fifty-meter-wide median and hundred-meter-wide, garbage-strewn grass shoulders, Route Irish was the main thoroughfare from the Baghdad International Airport to the center of the city and the Green Zone. Everybody who was anybody drove it. Western diplomats, Iraqi officials, generals, journalists, contractors, and soldiers traversed the road day and night, offering insurgents a convenient shooting gallery of lucrative targets. Contractors customarily took it at high speeds, swerving in and out of traffic, often peppering civilian vehicles with bullets. American convoys cleared traffic with bursts from their machine guns and bumps from their grilles. Iraqi civilians drove through the garbage on the shoulders and median to bypass congestion. It was every man for himself on Route Irish, a Wild West melee in the middle of the capital and an embarrassment to top U.S. brass, who struggled to answer the question: How do you expect to secure Iraq if you can't even secure a few miles of highway? Middle Eastern observers had long argued, "As goes Baghdad, so goes Iraq." In 2004 and 2005, Route Irish was added to the equation. "As goes the Airport Road, so goes Baghdad." The highway became a bellwether for U.S. effectiveness. Major General William Webster, whose 3rd Infantry Division replaced the 1st Cavalry in Baghdad after the elections, told his subordinate commanders that Route Irish was the only road in Iraq that President Bush knew by name.

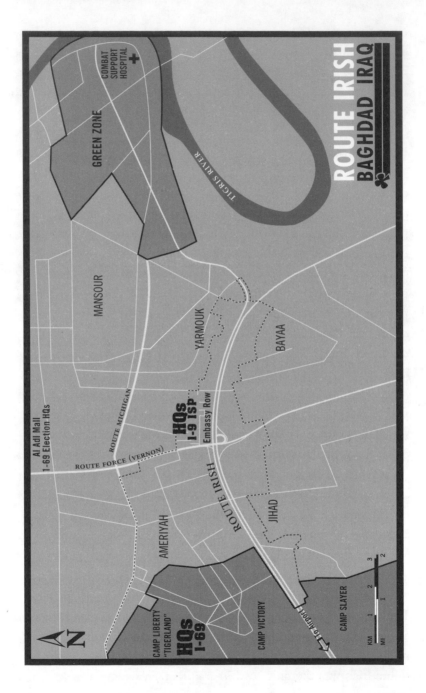

In the five months leading up to the January elections, insurgents sprayed bullets at highway drivers sixty-three times, fired RPGs seventy times, and planted IEDs forty-two times. And, perhaps most disconcerting, they attacked military and civilian convoys with car bombs twenty-five times. Seventeen coalition soldiers and civilian contractors who were patrolling or traversing the road were killed, while seventy-five more were wounded. A large number of the attacks were caught on video and sent around the world to reinforce the apparent failure of the coalition. Insurgents called sympathetic media outlets before attacks and suggested cameramen might happen by the road at a particular time. And when they didn't record the videos, U.S. soldiers or contractors themselves might post them as trophy footage on the Internet.

Yet people still drove on the highway, especially Westerners. They had to; it was the only way to get into the Green Zone. Try as the soldiers of the 1st Cavalry Division might, they just didn't have the resources to get the upper hand on Route Irish, and the attacks by insurgents continued unabated.

As if to prove one of Slack's favorite maxims—that no good deed goes unpunished—commanders assigned to the 3rd Infantry Division selected the Fighting 69th to take over Route Irish when the highway's current security forces rotated back to the States in February. Some have speculated that the 69th got the job because of its impressive record in Taji. Others have suggested the Wolfhounds got the mission because it would be appropriate to have an Irish American unit in charge of defending Route Irish. A third reason could be found in a history of the 69th in the Civil War. In the introduction to the 1994 edition of *The Irish Brigade and Its Campaigns,* historian Lawrence Kohl quotes a telling passage from an English war correspondent: "When anything absurd, forlorn, or desperate was to be attempted, the Irish Brigade was called upon." Route Irish certainly qualified.

The most likely reason the 69th got the job, however, is that they were available. The task force was pulled from the Tiger Brigade and reassigned under the 2nd "Commando" Brigade of the 10th Mountain Division. Instead of sending the Wolfhounds back to the economy of force in Taji, the brigade and division commander opted to shift them to Irish, which had been designated one of four strategic areas in the Baghdad area of operations, due to its PR significance. They were a canny choice by the Big Army commanders, for if the National Guard battalion performed well, it would be a great victory for the total force concept and for the regular Army officers whose careers were on the line. If the 69th failed, however, well, they were just National Guardsmen, after all. What more could anyone really expect?

Although the soldiers were well aware of the Route Irish myth, they reasoned that there was no way it could be as bad as Taji—a belief backed up by the numbers. The unit that Task Force Wolfhound would replace, the 1st Cavalry Division's 4th Battalion of the 5th Air Defense Artillery, had suffered four killed on the highway over a period of seven months; the 69th had lost ten men in only two and a half months in Taji. Perhaps the most reassuring factor for the men, however, was all the concrete in downtown Baghdad. Most of the massive IEDs that insurgents had triggered on the 69th had been easily buried under dirt roads. It would be far more difficult to bury the same bombs under concrete. In addition, the area was far smaller than what the 69th had been responsible for up north. The battalion would patrol about six miles of the primary highway, most of a two-mile spur that led to the Green Zone, and the neighborhoods, or *muhallahs*, that bordered the highway and provided cover and concealment for insurgents shooting at the road. The relatively focused mission would allow the 69th to mass its forces in ways it couldn't do in Taji.

Task Force Wolfhound moved from Camp Cooke to Camp Liberty near the Baghdad Airport and, after a brief battle handover with the air defenders, who patrolled mostly in Bradley Fighting Vehicles, the 69th assumed responsibility for Route Irish on February 15. Instead of dividing the area among his companies, Slack opted to patrol the highways in three eight-hour shifts. The Blacksheep would be on call from 7:00 a.m. to 3:00 p.m., the Assassins from 3:00 p.m. to 11:00 p.m., and an ad hoc company team comprising the battalion's engineers and light-wheeled recon platoons, called "Team Comanche," had the overnight shift. While such a division ensured there was unity of command in the small AO at any given time, it also resulted in a major reshuffling, or "task organizing," of the force. In addition to creating Team Comanche, Slack needed to balance his group to meet the enemy threat. Insurgents typically attacked during a three-hour window in the morning and another in the afternoon. To ensure that the Assassins had enough power and the Blacksheep enough mobility, Slack swapped one of Kaz's Bradley platoons for one of Drew's Humvee platoons. The Scouts first worked for the line companies on Irish, then took over duties as a full-time quick-reaction force.

Many of the ADA soldiers told the Wolfhounds that Route Irish wasn't all it was built up to be and was not exceptionally dangerous for the American forces that patrolled the road. Most attacks, they explained, targeted the supply convoys and modestly armored security contractors rather than the heavily gunned security forces. As long as the 69th maintained a good presence on the highway and kept would-be car bombers away, the men would be fine.

The advice proved accurate. As the 69th got into their battle rhythm throughout February, the enemy essentially laid off. Insurgents sprayed rifle fire at the road a few times and lobbed ineffective RPGs only twice. They planted nine IEDs on the highway and in the *muhallahs,* but the 69th found eight of them, and the one that did explode was too small to do any significant damage. A VBIED was also launched against a defense contractor but failed to cause any casualties. "The most dangerous road in the world" didn't seem all *that* bad.

For the men of the 69th the change in pace was welcome. Captain Drew was exhausted from the combat in Taji and the workload he had to pick up when his key leaders were killed, wounded, or reassigned. As he talked about the new mission with another captain at the Camp

Liberty mess hall, he exhaled deeply, saying, "Thank God." He reinforced the message when a *New York Times* reporter interviewed him.
"Quiet is good," he told Kirk Semple.

Slack gave Semple a somehwat different take on the matter, complaining that the task force had gone from being a lethal combat force
in Taji to something akin to highway patrolmen. "I'm agitating to get
off the mission . . . It's been deathly quiet, deathly quiet." As with all
his deep beliefs, Slack's opinions on the mission of the infantry and
the role that the Fighting 69th should play in times of war had remained consistent throughout his stint with the unit. Route security
was the doctrinal mission of military police, not the infantry. The job
had even been relegated to an air defense battalion before the 69th
arrived. Route Irish was simply not the best use of an infantry battalion that Slack believed had finally achieved the beginning levels of
wartime proficiency. The 69th should have been out in Anbar Prov-
ince, where the Marines were trading barbs with hardcore insurgents
around the clock, not conducting shift work on a highway. If there
was a fight, the Wolfhounds should be in it. Otherwise, what was the
point?

Many of the 69th's soldiers understandably didn't see it that way.
Slack's comment to the *Times* struck many soldiers as over the top,
especially considering the extent of the battalion's losses in Taji. Both
Acevedo and Drew slowly shook their heads when they talked about
Slack's preferences, patently disagreeing with their commander and
wondering if Slack was assigning his own willingness to accept risk
to the battalion as a whole. When Acevedo had warned him once
about handling sweating explosive material in a cache the Assassins
had found in Taji, Slack all but juggled the material and told Acevedo
not to worry. "I've made my peace with God," he said. "But you should
step back, because I'd hate to see anything happen to you." Since the
moment he stood stoically among falling mortars at the Citadel, Slack
had regularly accepted high levels of risk. On several occasions he approached suspect IEDs and car bombs on foot rather than waste valu-

able time for a call to the overtaxed explosive ordnance disposal (EOD) teams. His relentless searching for the enemy led his soldiers to nickname him the "hardest working squad leader in Iraq." Back at the Tiger Brigade headquarters, the staff officers would take note of the names next to the blue icons on their BFTs. It appeared to them that Slack was out on the streets patrolling around the clock. "Is your commander ever *not* on patrol?" one officer asked Crosby. Slack's operations tempo and his cavalier approach to danger finally led his first gunner to ask for reassignment, while it caused others across the task force and brigade simply to wonder if the commander was insane.

But the same actions that some regarded as mad had also earned Slack the respect of many of his soldiers. Mike Kazmierzak had served under West Point graduates and highly successful commanders in the Big Army's 2nd Infantry Division and 101st Airborne. Yet Slack was the most impressive commander for whom Kaz had ever worked. The colonel led from the front, accepted every risk his own men did, and treated his soldiers with respect and dignity during life and death. For Kaz, that was a combat commander's duty, and he looked to Slack as a role model. Most grunts had come to a similar conclusion. Even the Scouts, who once despised the commander, warmed to Colonel Slack as the war dragged on. *How can you not respect a man who has enough balls to tug on the wires of an IED?* Olmo thought. In both New York and south Louisiana culture, machismo trumped just about every other trait a man could have, and Slack all but sweated testosterone.

If other officers thought leading from the front, accepting the same risks as their men, and seeking to kill the kind of people who attacked the World Trade Center was insane, then Slack indeed was out of his mind. The Tiger Brigade was welcome to relieve him at any moment; the State of New York had made that abundantly clear. If General Basilica was concerned about Slack's actions, he could have pulled him from the battalion and appointed a more cautious commander. But he chose not to do so, and, in fact, senior Tiger Brigade officers began to privately ask some of their more passive commanders why they weren't as aggressive as Geoff Slack and the guys from New York and Houma.

Though Slack believed fervently in everything he told the *Times*, he was also cognizant of the IO value of his comments. He believed Americans wanted to view their commanders and soldiers as aggressive, no-nonsense warriors. If activity had continued to remain quiet on Route Irish, the article entitled "New York Nerve, Tested on Meanest Streets" would have almost certainly given readers confidence in their forces. But as with many PR efforts undertaken by U.S. forces, the story in the *New York Times* proved another failure. On March 4, 2005, the same day the newspaper hit the streets back in the States, both the suffering families of the 69th and eventually the entire global community learned that Route Irish was no longer "deathly quiet." Instead of inspiring confidence in the Fighting 69th, Slack's comments only worried task force family members and provided fuel for one of the biggest public relations failures for U.S. forces in Iraq.

12: ROUTE IRISH

LAST MAN STANDING

Olmo, Lwin, and Ali had their own name for Route Irish: the Highway to Hell. The crew had rigged speakers to their Humvee and blasted the AC/DC song of the same name every time they rolled out the gates of Camp Liberty on patrol. But despite the heavy-metal theme song, the Scouts found duty on Irish rather agreeable. There was hardly any enemy contact on the road, and the fear that served as background to everything they did in Taji was gone. If anything, the soldiers got bored on Irish as they drove up one side of the road and came back down the other in a continuous racetrack loop that was essentially only broken when they stopped in the Green Zone or just inside Camp Victory to use the latrine. The men tried to disrupt the monotony with their music—everything from salsa to hip hop to classic rock—and with talk of home, women, and food. Though the GIs in Iraq almost certainly ate better than any other army in history (many joes were gaining weight), they got tired of the repetitive KBR menu and longed for a good steak or barbecue over the coals back in Flushing. Short of that, the soldiers settled for the other fast-food options that had been set up around the Victory Base Cluster. There was a Burger King at Camp Liberty, local Iraqi food at Camp Stryker, and a Pizza Hut at Camp Victory proper, where the Army's corps headquarters was based. Lwin and Ali made the run to the Hut on a regular basis, pleasantly surprising their team leader, newly promoted

Sergeant Olmo—whom they simply called "Jay" per the Scouts' no-rank tradition.

As the only three members of their original squad who hadn't been killed or evacuated due to wounds, Olmo, Lwin, and Ali grew especially close. They knew how one another would act in a fight; they could complete one another's sentences. On top of the rapport that any vehicle crew or fire team acquires through combat operations, Lwin and Ali even shared a room. When Olmo asked if they were sick of each other yet, the men shrugged and said, "Not at all." About the only time the three men were ever apart was when one was sick or had an appointment and needed to stand down for a patrol. That was the case with Olmo on March 2, when the team leader, who had hurt his elbow in a vehicle accident, needed to stay back to heal. Another sergeant jumped into the vehicle as commander in his place, and the Scouts rolled out the gate for a patrol of Irish with the Assassins.

Olmo spent the day recovering in a tent the battalion had set up for whoever was on the quick-reaction force. About six hours after the patrol left for Irish, a soldier from the battalion TOC ran to the tent to tell the QRF that one of the trucks on patrol had been hit. Olmo didn't know who it was but he ran to his room to get the rest of his gear. His team had been in a fight, and the sergeant needed to get there. More news about the contact had reached the QRF by the time Olmo returned. As the sergeant looked to hop aboard an empty seat in one of the QRF vehicles, he noticed that none of the soldiers could look him in the eye. In fact, they all seemed to be going out of their way to avoid him. *What the fuck's going on?* Then it struck him: it must have been his truck that had been hit.

Lwin and Ali, patrolling with Sergeant Daniel Maiella, were headed east on Route Irish near the turnoff for the extension that ran to the Green Zone when insurgents hit them with an IED that was unusually effective for its small size. Explosively formed penetrators (EFPs), which were in regular use in Israel, had recently begun showing up in attacks in eastern Baghdad. The weapons, which intelligence officers believed were coming from Iran, were typically about the size of a coffee can and featured a thick metal "lid" that coned into a dimple an inch deep in the center. When the EFPs were detonated, explosives reshaped the metal into a compact projectile of molten steel that could penetrate the thickest armor the U.S. had. A Humvee was simply no match.

The Comanches, the ad hoc team that Slack built to patrol Route Irish in the overnight hours to prevent the placement of IEDs, had bumbled across an EFP just a few days before. The weapon was hidden inside an opaque plastic bag and was so small that the soldiers didn't think anything of kicking the unknown object down the road. When the package came to a stop, a battery pack and Motorola radio flopped out of it, causing the soldiers to scatter for cover. The weapon did not detonate, but the men of the Fighting 69th quickly wised up to this new threat. Still, all it really did was make the men nervous, for how could one spot a coffee-can-sized weapon on roads lined with garbage that included scores of metal cans?

The EFP that insurgents detonated against Lwin and Ali's truck sat just a few feet away from the vehicle in a pile of brush along a narrow center median. The penetrator shot from the can and entered the Humvee behind Lwin, who was driving. The molten steel killed the Burmese American instantly. Ali was sitting in the gun turret facing rearward. When the round exited Lwin it blew off Ali's hindquarters, before sending shards of steel into Sergeant Maiella's chest cavity and head.

Captain Drew, who heard the explosion from the other side of Irish, knew immediately that one of his trucks had been hit. The officer's heart stopped. *Not again!* The commander raced his own vehicle to the site of the blast. Unlike the massive IEDs that had claimed the lives of the soldiers in Taji, the EFP left most of the Scouts' vehicle intact. Soldiers were climbing to the top of the vehicle to get Ali, who was slumped over the red-stained turret. As Drew ran for the truck, he saw that the gunner was still alive and bounded atop the vehicle to help lift him out. Other soldiers freed Maiella. Both wounded men were carried from the smoking vehicle and loaded into one of the Bradleys, which rushed them to the Combat Support Hospital (CSH or CaSH), in the Green Zone. The hospital was only about three miles away, but the turns and the American checkpoint slowed the vehicle's progress.

By the time Olmo arrived at the attack site aboard a recovery truck, the wounded soldiers had been removed. The sergeant didn't yet know who was hurt or how bad. He sought one of the medics. The doc spoke before Olmo could.

"Jay, I'm sorry."

"What the fuck's going on, Vasquez? Tell me!"

"Lwin is gone. I mean . . . he's gone. There was nothing I could do."

"Ali?"

"I think he might have a chance. They put him and Maiella in a Bradley and rushed them to the CaSH."

Jay joined the rest of the Scouts and drove to the hospital. When they reached the emergency room, he learned Maiella would likely survive. Shrapnel had entered his chest cavity under the left arm but had miraculously not damaged any vital organs. Ali was not as lucky. Olmo saw his friend splayed out on a gurney, his wounds beyond the help of tourniquets. The Muslim soldier had bled to death in the back of the Bradley.

Word of the killings had spread through the family members of the battalion by March 4, the same day the article about the 69th appeared in the *Times*. *Is it still too quiet for you, Slack?* dozens of family members thought. "My son is being led by a gun-slinging maniac," one father concluded.

CHECKPOINT 541

The deaths of Lwin and Ali were especially hard on Mike Drew, who had never fully recovered emotionally from the loss of his first two soldiers. Who could? Then, in January, the commander learned that two of his twenty-one-year-old men who had been cross-assigned to a Louisiana battalion had been killed. Private Francis Obaji, the Nigerian immigrant who had joined the 69th after watching the Trade Center fall, and Specialist Alain Kamolvathin, another immigrant soldier, from Thailand, died after their Humvee rolled into a deep canal. Now two more soldiers were dead on Drew's watch. Any relief the commander felt after first arriving on Irish vanished. Drew and the rest of the Wolfhounds were back on death row. The men credited their peaceful first month to luck. As their early success in Taji was short-lived, the 69th assumed the attack on Lwin and Ali was just the first in another campaign to bloody the unit.

The Army did its best to protect its soldiers with technology. In addition to their thick armor, the 69th was fielded electronic jamming equipment designed to foil remote-detonated bombs. However, the Wolfhounds figured the enemy would simply change tactics. He was getting smarter every day. What million-dollar smart bomb in the American arsenal could be as intelligent as a dedicated suicide bomber at the helm of a VBIED? Some EFPs didn't even require a triggerman but used a laser beam similar in style to ones that prevent an electric garage door from closing on an obstruction. The moment anything crossed the beam, a signal triggered the device, removing any human error in the process. As Drew rolled out on patrol March 4, he had come to the realization that there were simply too many ways for insurgents to kill his men. In the 69th's crowded quarter of Baghdad, death could come at any time, in any form, from any dimension. Trying to defend against all the possible attacks around the clock was exhausting.

The commander needed to get inside the enemy's head and war-game every course of action an insurgent might be considering at any given moment. Would he choose an RPG or a VBIED? Would he drop a grenade from an overpass into the Humvee turret? Would he try to place an IED behind that tree over there? What about the other one? Yet the moment Drew figured out what the enemy might conceivably do, the battlefield situation changed. Perhaps an imam would call for attacks against Americans during Friday prayers, or a car accident would provide cover for an insurgent to plant a bomb. As Drew further analyzed his new AO, he concluded that the battlefield that was Route Irish was perhaps the most fluid in Iraq. Every traffic jam, every new car, every shift of the wind, changed Drew's decision-making factors. About the only constant on the highway was Task Force Wolfhound.

The insurgents could easily tell which vehicles belonged to the Wolfhounds by recognizing and tracking the numbers the battalion painted on their vehicles. If the insurgents struggled with Arabic numerals, they were familiar enough with the four-inch-tall black shamrock painted on the doors. But all of that simply served to confirm the obvious: The U.S. soldiers that patrolled Route Irish were the only people in the coalition that crawled along the airport road at speeds from ten to twenty-five miles per hour. They were the ones whose gunners scanned down each avenue that ran into the highway's access roads. They were the only ones who actually left the highway to prowl the *muhallahs* on either side of the strand. Most American units blasted down Route Irish using their speed for safety. The 69th and the security forces that owned the road before them, however, calmly moved about the place looking for a fight.

Drew knew the 69th's offensive posture made the unit one of the less attractive targets for enemy forces to attack on Route Irish. The trucks with the shamrocks knew the road and the neighborhoods intimately from hours and hours of patrolling. Sometimes they knew the area better than the insurgents themselves, who often came from outside the region, attracted to the highway by its fat collection of targets. The insurgents preferred to target the caravans of Western SUVs, lightly armored logistics convoys, and U.S. and coalition units, whose actions betrayed their inexperience on the route. That said, if a U.S. patrol did move into the crosshairs of an enemy triggerman and there seemed little danger of an effective American counterattack, that trigger would certainly be pulled, as it had been against Lwin and Ali and dozens of 1st Cavalry assets before the 69th.

Those rare attacks were more targets of opportunity, however, than deliberately planned efforts. But just as a good quarterback can spot and take advantage of a weakness in an opposing defense, Captain Drew knew that a good insurgent would seek openings to exploit the 69th's weaknesses on Irish. The captain knew the enemy was studying his every move. And he knew the enemy was agile enough to hit his Assassins if the Americans gave him the chance.

By 8:30 p.m. on March 4, about forty-eight hours after the deaths of Lwin and Ali, Drew was expecting the enemy to attack at any moment. His entire company had been stationary for an hour, and the commander feared its immobility would result in his loading up yet another body bag. It was the most vulnerable he and his Assassins had yet been on Irish. He called the Wolfhound TOC and asked—for what felt like the eighth time in the past forty minutes—for permission to move his forces. "Negative, Assassin Six," the radio operator responded. "You've got to stay in place for at least another twenty minutes."

Drew had gotten word earlier in the night that he needed to have Route Irish closed to civilian traffic by 7:30 in order to protect a high-ranking dignitary who would be transiting the road from the Green Zone to the airport. It was a simple enough mission for the officer; halting civilian traffic in Iraq was as easy as raising your hand. The Baghdad population had been well trained by two years of occupation to stay clear of U.S. Humvees. A sign on the back of each U.S. vehicle warned locals to stay back one hundred meters, or they would be shot—a warning that had been reinforced by several lethal incidents over the years. When civilian vehicles did get too close, the soldiers used escalating levels of force to drive the message home. Hand signals came first. If those failed, the soldiers pointed their weapons toward the vehicles. If the cars still advanced, the soldiers fired warning shots into the ground near the violator. If the car continued to approach, the soldiers then attempted to disable the vehicle with rounds to the engine block or tires. If that failed to halt the car, the Americans often concluded the driver was a car bomber intent on ramming their Humvee, and the gunner then engaged the driver of the vehicle.

While the tactic had regrettably resulted in civilian casualties, it also decreased the effectiveness of suicide car bomb attacks on Americans. Yet the massive smart bombs were still a threat, and several Americans had died from suicide car bombs in Baghdad. Insurgents had hit the unit the 69th replaced on Irish twice, killing and wounding troops in both engagements.

Drew had posted his vehicles in hasty blocking positions at every entrance point to Route Irish to close the road, and so far all civilian traffic had avoided the soldiers' positions. The sight of the military vehicles alone typically caused the drivers to stop and turn around; if not, hand signals and then flashes from high-powered lights as it got dark did the job. Dozens of civilian vehicles had already been turned at every blocking point, and Drew was confident that the unnamed dignitary could pass through Irish safely.

Yet as every minute passed, Drew grew more certain that insurgents were observing his actions from any one of the multistory buildings that surrounded the highway. Lessons learned from Taji and passed on from prior Route Irish forces led the 69th men to believe they could only remain static for about fifteen minutes before the enemy took advantage and engaged. Drew had now been in place far longer than that, and to make matters worse, a U.S. Special Forces unit had flipped a vehicle on an exit ramp off the highway near one of Drew's positions, presenting yet another static target. When the captain got reports that the Special Forces were engaging an unknown target north of Irish, the commander was certain his forces were now sitting ducks. He called his units and reminded them to stay alert and behind cover. He reminded his men of the descriptions of two possible car bombs they were supposed to keep an eye out for—sedans, one black and one white.

As Drew and his men grew more tense, John Negroponte, the U.S. ambassador to Iraq, exited his vehicle at Camp Victory. He had left the Green Zone shortly after Drew reported the highway secure and safely arrived at the main U.S. base just after 8:00 p.m. However, the artillery battalion that would generally have reported such a move failed to notify the 69th or the Commando Brigade. The Wolfhounds were also unaware that Giuliana Sgrena, an Italian journalist who had been held hostage by insurgents since early February, had just been turned over to an Italian intelligence agent in a Sunni *muhallah* north of Route Irish.

Nicola Calipari, a senior officer in the Italian military intelligence and security service known as SISMI, had just secured Sgrena's release with a large ransom, which one U.S. officer later estimated to be in the neighborhood of $5 million. He loaded the journalist into a silver four-door sedan and had his driver, another intelligence officer named Andrea Carpani, drive the party back to Camp Victory, where an Italian delegation—and, by one report, Ambassador Negroponte—waited to welcome Sgrena back to freedom before shuttling her back to Italy.

Calipari and Carpani risked the move through Baghdad without a security team and were nervous as they headed for Route Irish, the fastest way back to the airport. As they approached the highway from the north, Carpani drove and talked to Italian officials on his cell phone. Near Irish the officer heard gunfire and saw tracer rounds flying in the air. The fire came, in fact, from where the Special Forces team had rolled their truck, as the U.S. soldiers had been in sporadic small-arms contact with insurgents since they first crashed. Carpani, however, believed the rounds were being fired at him and yelled into his phone, "They're attacking us." He stepped on the gas pedal and accelerated toward Irish. As he steered onto the exit ramp at some fifty miles per hour, the Italian officer saw the U.S. Humvees and waved to them, hoping they would recognize him and let him pass.

Specialist Mario Lozano was manning a machine gun at the blocking position when the Italians approached at just before 9:00 p.m., ninety minutes after the Americans first moved into position. He flashed his high-powered light on the vehicle to get it to stop, but the car didn't yield, as dozens of others had that night. Fearing a car bomb attack, the soldier quickly switched to his M240B machine gun and fired, first to the ground and then at the engine as the vehicle continued on. Several of the soldier's rounds slammed into the car, most of them overshooting the engine block and crashing into the passenger compartment as the vehicle sped on. One bullet struck Calipari in the head, killing him almost instantly, while another struck Sgrena in her shoulder. Glass shards grazed Carpani. The driver finally slammed on the brakes, bringing the vehicle to a halt about thirty yards from the American position.

Drew, who was at another blocking position when the incident occurred, rushed to the scene when his soldiers called in the contact. Calipari's body was pulled from the car by the time the captain arrived, and his medics were treating Sgrena. Both Drew's operations sergeant and Carpani spoke Spanish. The driver told the NCO who the Italians were and explained why he was speeding down the ramp. Drew passed the report to the Wolfhound TOC, then instructed his men to get Sgrena to the CaSH for further treatment.

The commander then walked over to where Calipari lay. One of his soldiers handed the captain the Italian's identification card, which listed him as a major general in the Italian army. Drew exhaled and hung his head. Another soldier was dead. There seemed no end to the bloodletting in Iraq. He said a silent prayer for the fallen officer and returned to his operation.

Drew knew full well that the engagement was a tragedy, but he didn't begin to comprehend the scale of the crisis until shortly later. As he was getting Sgrena loaded into a Humvee for the drive to the CaSH, the TOC called to let the captain know that news of the incident had already hit CNN. The wounded journalist was still sitting on the Baghdad asphalt, yet the story was on television. *What the hell is going on here?*

The engagement on Route Irish would quickly become an international incident. Colonel Mark Millie, the commander of the Commando Brigade, headed out to meet Drew and Slack at the site. He asked Drew to walk him through the engagement and told the captain that it sounded as if he had done everything according to procedure. Nonetheless, he instructed the Wolfhounds—who had already cleaned the area up, as they did with every incident on Irish—to re-create the scenario. The area would be treated like a crime scene, and the brigade commander named Major Crosby as the preliminary investigator. Crosby began his inquiry immediately but was later replaced by a general officer as the magnitude of the incident rose.

In the weeks that followed the engagement, the Big Army dug into the Wolfhounds in a manner that most 69th soldiers strongly resented. Many of the men believed that the investigators at every level approached the battalion as merely a group of weekend warriors and judged them guilty before they could even be proven innocent. The battalion's level of training was reviewed in microscopic detail. When was the last time the men had qualified on their weapons? When was the last time the men had received instruction on the rules of engagement? How qualified for command were Geoff Slack and Mike Drew? Had the Guardsmen ever served in the *real* Army? Had they ever been to Ranger School? Everything the battalion had achieved in Taji was forgotten. Now the men who had fought so hard against the insurgents were being treated and questioned by their own Army in a manner that was in many respects more harsh than that afforded to the insurgents the battalion had captured.

The investigation was a distraction for Mike Drew. He had lost soldiers to horrible deaths. He had been saddled with junior leaders who had to be replaced for incompetence. And now he had officers questioning every action he had undertaken in his military career. By now Drew couldn't move without a Big Army officer raising his eyebrows. Though his actions were beyond reproach, Drew told Slack he thought the Army was looking to make him a scapegoat. Slack urged him to stay frosty.

Slack understood Drew's concerns. He had been scrutinized as closely as the captain and fought around the clock to defend his battalion and his soldiers. For almost fifteen years Slack had struggled to rebuild the Fighting 69th, and now his entire body of work seemed in jeopardy. As Drew sought solace from the colonel, Slack sought comfort in the Tiger Brigade. Though the 69th was working for the 10th Mountain Division, General Basilica and the Tigers maintained their paternal support for the battalion. Basilica could see the stress and the hurt on Slack's face. He knew the Big Army was running the 69th through the wringer, and it pained him that the Wolfhounds were not under his command. He tried to help Slack on both personal and professional levels, but at times he felt powerless. If the 69th had been under Basilica's command when the shooting occurred, the battalion would not have been treated with the same disrespect. But short of that he pledged his complete support and told his commander to hang tough.

VEHICLE-BORNE DEATH

Captain Kazmierzak and the Blacksheep were not unduly impacted by the investigation of the Italian incident, what the men now universally referred to as "the Italian job" after the film of the same name. Baghdad was a dangerous place. People got shot or blown up every day—soldiers, civilians, journalists, diplomats. About the only person whom Kazmierzak was certain would not be killed or wounded was himself.

The captain had seen seven of his men perish and knew the enemy was capable of destroying his massive Bradleys; he just didn't think the enemy would get *him*. It's not that Kaz believed he was smarter than the enemy, but he simply felt that the bad guys didn't have his number. He was invincible, and that belief enabled him to operate without fear—and to become the American scourge of west Baghdad in the eyes of some of the region's suspected insurgents and criminals.

The captain opted against his Bradleys and patrolled the highway at the head of a more maneuverable three-Humvee section, driving up and down the road and in and out of the neighborhoods. If he sensed insurgent activity, he jumped on the radio and vectored his forces to a possible target, usually a building. His dismounted soldiers would storm the place as if putting on a class for the infantry school at Fort Benning. As they cleared the buildings, Kaz would walk forward, his rifle hanging down in his right hand, and dig into every corner of the place. When he found anyone who signaled "insurgent," he grabbed hold of the suspect as if the man had just blown up a Bradley. The Iraqis could feel Kaz's hot breath in their faces as the captain warned them against attacking Americans and would try to turn away, but Kaz would force them to look him in the eye. "If I have to come back here, you're going to Abu Ghraib," he told them. The commander would have preferred to just kill them, but knew he and his men needed to follow the rules of engagement.

The captain's favorite targets along Route Irish were the criminals who lined the curbs of the highway and its access roads, selling black market gasoline. Instead of spending a day in a line at an authorized government gas station, many Iraqis would pay more to get a quick bit of fuel from roadside vendors. Kaz didn't care about enforcing fuel-distribution laws but was concerned about the traffic jams when someone stopped to refuel. Congestion on Route Irish provided insurgents the perfect cover to place IEDs or to launch RPG attacks, and the commander made it his mission to rid the highway of the black marketers. On his first encounter he gave a warning. On the second encounter he confiscated the fuel. If it happened a third time, the commander went berserk. In one instance he and his men chased down the black marketers, dumped their gas, and then searched every house in the area, dragging out steel drums and pouring out their contents until the streets flowed with petroleum. Black market fuel sales soon ceased in the entire area.

However, if the criminals in the capital operated in the same fashion as those in Taji, the time would soon come for them to strike back against the Blacksheep. On the heavily patrolled concrete streets of west Baghdad, massive bombs were packed into cars, not buried under the roads. Soldiers were urged to look for cars that seemed overly weighed down, that failed to yield to American vehicles, or whose drivers seemed hypnotized or were perhaps muttering prayers. As Kaz patrolled a neighborhood south of Route Irish on March 15, he saw a suspicious-looking car near a gas station south of Route Irish. The unmanned black four-door sedan was riding so low to the ground that it could only mean one thing: VBIED. The commander noticed the vehicle shortly after conducting a regular assessment of the gas station, something the Americans did to keep tabs on the state of essential services in the city. The station itself looked fine, but one of the men there seemed out of place. When Kaz questioned him, the Iraqi was evasive, and something about him was all wrong. Kaz took his picture but as he didn't have enough information to detain the guy, he left the area and decided to drive by every now and then to see if the civilian was still hanging around. He saw the car on his first trip back and didn't think much of it. On the second trip, he and his men believed they had found a bomb.

Kaz's first move was to seal off the area. The textbook called for a standoff distance of three hundred meters, which was usually impossible in the close quarters of the city. The Blacksheep parked their vehicles about two hundred meters out and began to set up a blocking position with orange cones and signs that were so conspicuous that anyone who approached, even someone new to driving in Baghdad, would know to stop. If they didn't, the men would engage, much as Specialist Lozano had two weeks earlier. After Kaz called in the possible VBIED, he remained near the armor protection of his vehicle and scanned the surrounding area. Civilian traffic had largely stopped at a safe distance, but one car started to pull into the danger area from a side road. Kaz didn't want to see an innocent civilian get hurt and hurried into the path of the vehicle. He signaled the driver to back up, but the man just stopped short and avoided looking at Kaz. *What the fuck is wrong with this guy?* Kaz thought. *Does he not see me? Does he not understand my signals?* The driver clenched his steering wheel, and then came the explosion.

Kaz saw the flash and felt the crush and sting of the bomb as he sailed backward through the air about ten feet. The commander could make out people running through black smoke in the distance. Although he was dazed and his ears were ringing, blocking out all other sound, the commander tried to gather himself. He did not feel any pain but saw that his thumb was missing and that there was blood on his legs. He tried to shout but could only mumble, "I need a medic . . . Hey . . . I need a fuckin' medic." The commander moved to sit upright, but as he lifted himself, blood began to squirt vertically in a thick stream out of his leg. "Hey . . . I need a fuckin' tourniquet." Kaz pressed down on his leg where the blood was shooting from his femoral artery. A soldier dragged him to a sidewalk, where Kaz looked up to see a medic and his executive officer, Lieutenant Daniel Fritts, who had been patrolling with him that day. He knew the men were amped up and told his soldiers to stay calm. "Go to work. Put a tourniquet on me and we'll be fine."

As the Blacksheep worked on Kaz, a medevac helicopter pilot who happened to be flying over the area started moving toward the blast site. The pilot had seen the explosion and assumed correctly that there were casualties on the ground. He looked for a clear area of the street to set his chopper down. The only place that looked available was the portion of the street the Blacksheep had cordoned off. The helicopter came in for a landing just behind the black sedan that had caused all the concern in the first place. As the medics hopped off the chopper, insurgents blew the vehicle. The pilot quickly pushed the chopper back into the sky while his medics, who were not wounded in the blast, ran for one of the 69th's Bradleys that had responded to the initial blast. The chopper suffered only minor damage, and when the pilot got word his men had been safely recovered, he nosed the bird back to the Green Zone. Insurgents followed the second blast with small-arms fire, and though the Blacksheep gunners looked for targets, they couldn't find a thing in the crowded area. Civilians were everywhere.

The soldiers were also working on Kaz's dismounted security team leader, Sergeant Jacque Ballay. The soldier's job was to go wherever Kaz did, but now he lay on the deck with shrapnel to the head. The men loaded him into one vehicle and Kaz into another. Lieutenant Fritts was now in command of the company and led the team on a ground evacuation to the hospital. Ali had died from massive blood loss on a similar drive just two weeks earlier; this trip was nearly two miles longer.

Kaz seemed uncannily desensitized to any significant level of pain, but as the team headed for the CaSH, he could feel himself bleeding out and getting weaker. "C'mon guys . . . you gotta go faster," he urged them from the backseat. Though the medic had placed a tourniquet on his leg, the captain could still feel warm blood pooling around him. As his men checked him over they found another large hole in his stomach, which they had missed earlier. The men added another dressing, but the blood continued to flow, and the captain started to lose consciousness.

Fritts urged the drivers forward, but as they approached the site where Lwin and Ali were killed, the Humvee carrying Sergeant Ballay, which had been damaged in the blast, began to falter. The lieutenant told the three-vehicle section to pull over in front of a colorfully painted monument in the middle of the street that the men simply called "the mural," a standard rallying point for the Wolfhounds. After the convoy stopped the men cross-leveled Ballay into Fritts's truck. The lieutenant called another unit to meet the crew at the crippled Humvee, then set off again for the hospital. He hated to leave a small team of men alone on the most dangerous road in the world, but he needed to balance that risk against saving the two wounded soldiers in his Humvee. If he didn't get them to the hospital quickly, at least one of the men would certainly die.

Ballay had serious wounds but was not bleeding as heavily as Kaz. The captain had already filled the back of the Humvee with warm, sticky blood and was fading in and out of consciousness. Kazmierzak, who was a bachelor, came to as the men entered the Green Zone. He looked at the soldier who sat in the back of the vehicle with him. "Make sure you find my parents," he said. "Tell them I love them."

At the same time that Fritts rolled into the hospital parking lot, one of the soldiers he left at the mural doubled over inside his vehicle. Sergeant Paul Heltzel, a veteran of the First Gulf War, clutched his chest, the concussion from the blast having caused him to go into cardiac arrest. Adrenaline hid his symptoms until he reached the mural, but they manifested severely as the soldiers waited for a relief force. Help arrived within five minutes, but the soldier was in rough shape. Heltzel died less than an hour later.

Slack had already been on his way out to Route Irish when the blast occurred and now headed straight for the engagement area to try and make sense of the event. As he looked the site over, he concluded the enemy had either deliberately ambushed Kaz, or the Blacksheep had disrupted a car bomb attack intended for another target or even for another location. Whatever the case, Slack was livid and immediately ordered searches and tactical questioning of anyone suspicious in the area. He called for an intelligence team that specialized in dealing with civilians and for more medics to assist the civilians that had been hurt in the blast. In addition to the Americans, one civilian had been killed and another dozen wounded. As Slack prepared to leave the site, Colonel Millie from the Commando Brigade pulled up to the area. The brigade commander had just gotten a casualty update from the CaSH. He told Slack that Heltzel was dead and that his company commander wasn't going to make it.

The news was devastating. In the past thirteen days the battalion had lost three men, had several more wounded, and was suffering through an investigation that would have shaken the confidence of George S. Patton. Slack swallowed hard.

Lieutenant Fritts and the rest of the Blacksheep were feeling the pain as well. The acting company commander returned to Route Irish shortly after learning that Heltzel had passed.

Though the 69th had pushed everything they had into the sector, the Blacksheep were still in charge of the highway. But Fritts didn't think his men were mission capable. He called Slack on the radio and told him he had a lot of soldiers who were emotionally banged up and wanted to get them off mission and back to Camp Liberty. Had the

engagement taken place in Taji, Slack would have certainly backed
the idea. But Route Irish was a different beast; the mission never
ended on the highway. On his way to the blast site, Slack found an
IED. Another section reported a potential VBIED farther down the
road. The Fighting 69th clearly could not afford to let up on Irish.
Every company and platoon was committed to the route daily. If the
Blacksheep came in, who would relieve them? Slack told Fritts he
couldn't spare the lieutenant's company. "If you have a casualty, bring
him in," he said. "But I need you to hang on for a few more hours.
Hang on until you can turn it over to Captain Drew." Fritts paused
before responding. The lieutenant and many of his other soldiers were
covered in blood. They had lost yet another comrade, and their commander was on his deathbed at the CaSH. The Blacksheep's minds
were not in the game, but they would have to get over it.

"Roger, sir," Fritts responded. "We have the sector."

Kaz was still alive when Slack reached the CaSH, but the captain's
prognosis was not good. Doctors reported that Kazmierzak had a
5 percent chance of survival. The soldier needed so many trans-
fusions that the hospital was rapidly running out of its entire stock of
A-positive blood. Doctors at the CaSH told Slack they had to have
more immediately, and the commander ordered every soldier on Route
Irish with A-positive blood to get himself to the hospital. Another
dozen Wolfhounds with the same blood type mobilized at Camp Liberty and headed for the CaSH as well. Doctors didn't show any signs
of optimism until nightfall. After he survived for ten hours, they raised
Kaz's chance of making it to 10 percent. It would be another week before they predicted he would indeed survive.

SAINT PATRICK'S DAY 2005

Slack lay in his bed ill. He was emotionally and physically drained
from nearly 150 days of combat operations and the sight of more blood
than he ever could have imagined. Thirteen men under his command
and two more 69th troopers under Cajun commands had died in

combat. More than a dozen others were wounded. Then there was the ongoing Italian investigation. How could anyone stay frosty? But the commander had to. It was, after all, Saint Patrick's Day, and General Basilica had planned a unit celebration for the 69th on par with a jubilant Mardi Gras celebration the Tiger Brigade had held in February. Slack slowly lifted himself from his bunk, pulled on his boots, and headed into the sun, making his way for the battalion formation that would march to a Mass at the Camp Liberty chapel that would honor the Wolfhounds. When he reached the men, he counted only some fifty soldiers. Everybody else was either patrolling Route Irish, working on their vehicles, or getting ready for the next mission. He gazed blank-faced over the group for a moment, then decided to go on patrol. "Go on to Mass without me, if you'd like," he told them, and then walked away. He knew General Basilica wanted to show respect to the unit and its traditions, but there was simply no time for it. The 69th would mark Saint Patrick's Day with RPGs, IEDs, snipers, and mortars on Route Irish instead.

The celebration back in New York was likewise muted. A small rear detachment of new recruits, wounded soldiers, and others marched while others drove to Dover Air Force Base in Delaware to meet the bodies of Lwin and Ali as they rolled off a cargo plane inside flag-draped coffins.

13: TASK FORCE WOLFHOUND

FRESH LEGS

Lieutenant Joe Minning left the Banshee Company command post at 9.00 p.m. on March 19 and walked around the building to a courtyard full of M1114 up-armored Humvees. His sergeants were already there, anxiously waiting for him. After four months of separation from the task force, the Banshees were back in the Fighting 69th and gearing up for their first regular patrol on Route Irish.

Minning briefed the platoon's mission in the darkness by the light of a headlamp strapped over the faded black New York Yankees baseball cap that seemed stitched to the officer's head whenever he wasn't wearing a helmet. The soldiers would patrol the western half of the 69th's area of operations on Route Irish and inside its adjoining *mu-hallahs* from 11:00 that night until 7:00 the next morning. Twice during the shift the men would also set up blocking positions at all the entry points to the highway to permit the safe transit of an armored shuttle bus called the "Rhino" from the Green Zone to Camp Victory and back. Minning told the men to expect Colonel Slack at their blocking positions. It was the Banshees' first full night on the job, and the battalion commander would check up to make sure his long-lost company was alert and had established its positions in accordance with the 3rd Infantry Division standard operating procedure, which called for all sorts of lights and mobile barricades designed to prevent another Italian job. Once the Rhino bus and its security entourage passed, the platoon would break down the blocks and patrol the road for the rest of the overnight hours. With a citywide curfew in effect, the night should be quiet. Minning handed out copies of the patrol order and asked the men if they had any questions or comments.

"The coffee sucks," one of his sergeants joked. Minning agreed, and the soldiers groused about some of the other things they missed from their last assignment.

While the Banshees were happy to be back with the task force, they longed for the niceties of their first four months in Baghdad. While the main body of the 69th was wearing itself thin in Taji, Minning and his troops had been posted to a former Saddam Hussein palace that now served as home to select U.S. and Iraqi Special Forces units in Baghdad. Minning's men lived in outbuildings around the compound, and the company headquarters was located in the penthouse of the main palace with distant views of the well-irrigated green fields that surrounded the city. Members of the unit lifted weights in a waterside villa and relieved themselves in Saddam's golden commodes. The Special Forces enforced a strict "casual Sunday" policy, which allowed the Banshees to wear civilian clothes once a week and provided the New Yorkers with Land Rovers and Polaris four-wheelers to zip around the compound. They served dinner and fantastic coffee in a former five-star hotel for the Ba'ath Party elite, which made the soldiers wonder why Saddam would ever challenge the U.S. and risk losing all the opulence.

Minning had been disappointed when he learned back in November that his company would get a lame base-security mission. But as the weeks wore on, he began to adapt to life at the SF camp. When word came that the Banshees would finally be reunited with the Wolfhounds, he dejectedly realized that he loved not only the trappings of the compound, but the mission itself.

The lieutenant's company had been tasked to secure the compound, and the elite soldiers they protected provided them virtually all the tools they needed to get the job done. The Special Forces gave the Banshees a two-hundred-man-strong security company of Iraqis to serve as gate guards, tactical vehicles to patrol the land surrounding the base, unmanned aerial drones to observe the villages nearby, access to funds to reward locals who provided information, multiple weapons ranges to remain proficient in marksmanship, and intelligence support from the U.S. Special Forces Command headquarters. In some regards, the company had more support than the rest of the 69th had had in Taji, which was almost a crime, given that the Banshees didn't have to deal with a very active enemy. While Minning and his soldiers diligently patrolled their small area, met with village leaders, and captured suspected insurgents, except for a VBIED attack against one of their positions and occasional mortar and rifle fire, they encountered few insurgent attacks. The enemy that lived outside the Special Forces compound was primarily engaged in surveillance and reporting. The insurgents hid in plain sight and left the U.S. forces alone so that both the good guys and the bad guys could continue their missions.

The Banshees successfully secured the base, but their experience in Baghdad looked on the whole a lot more like a well-resourced training exercise than wartime duty. The unit did most of the same things it did during its three-week rotation at the National Training Center in California, but this time they did it with real Iraqi civilians, real Iraqi villages, and real bullets. Yet the mission proved no more lethal than the rehearsal. In addition, when Minning's men weren't on patrol, the lieutenant was able to negotiate with Special Forces teams to get his soldiers advanced weapons and explosives training. Expecting at any moment to rejoin the rest of the 69th in Taji, the Banshees also attached some of their soldiers out to Special Forces teams across central Iraq to gain valuable experience in areas where the enemy was more active. Before Colonel Slack had departed for Kuwait, he had hoped to get another few months of training for the battalion prior to entering the fight. It wasn't in the cards for the task force as a whole, but extra training is exactly what the Banshees got. By March 2005, 82nd Airborne veteran Joe Minning believed his platoon and company were as well trained as any conventional unit in the Big Army.

They were also well rested—a fact not lost on Slack.

While his task force was running on fumes in Taji, Slack all but begged General Basilica to arrange the return of his company. He needed the manpower and a group of fresh soldiers who were not fatigued from the stress of daily combat and casualties. But the math didn't work until the Wolfhounds hit Route Irish. Because it was a strategic mission, the airport road rated more troops than the economy of force mission in Taji. The 3rd Infantry Division ultimately facilitated the move. In early March a company from the Hawaii National Guard relieved the Banshees, who left the comfortable SF compound for Camp Liberty. The unit immediately began a relief in place with Team Comanche, the ad hoc company Slack created to secure Route Irish during the night hours. When the Banshees took over, the key elements that made up the Comanches were plugged into the Assassins and the Blacksheep to beef up their strength.

It was a major shot in the arm for the war-weary task force. The influx of the Banshees increased the battalion's maneuver strength by 30 percent. At full capacity the company could push twelve Humvees operating in three four-vehicle sections onto Irish. In addition the 69th outfitted the unit with eight M113 armored personnel carriers (APCs). The M113 was a Vietnam-era infantry vehicle that had long been the butt of jokes in the 69th. The track was covered with thin aluminum armor and boasted just a single machine gun. The Big Army had largely phased the vehicle out of its inventory for its infantrymen, replacing it with Bradleys in the 1980s. But the fourth-string National Guard units still trained on the old tracks—though no one thought they would ever actually use them in war. The men figured they would get Bradleys if the balloon ever went up. But you go to war with the Army you have, and since the 69th had dozens of M113s, they loaded the pariahs onto the trains and shipped them to Iraq. The task force used them in a support role in Taji, but none of the line units had employed them as a primary combat platform until the Banshees returned to the battalion. Refitted with additional armor and cages that could mitigate the blast damage of an RPG, the new M113s actually became a favorite among the Banshees. The tracks were capable of carrying a nine-man infantry squad at speeds of up to fifty miles per hour, though in most cases the unit would use them as mobile observation posts with just four soldiers on board, including the driver and vehicle commander. Either way, the tracks gave Minning an armored component that he could use if the shit hit the fan. Like the Bradley, the M113 also served as a strong psychological weapon: there was nothing like driving fifteen tons of steel into someone's backyard to make a point.

As good as the updated APC was, however, Slack would have preferred more Bradleys. He wanted to use the Banshees during the day to give the other two companies a break from the higher levels of activity and the extreme heat, which was already starting to top 100 degrees. But in his mind the M113 was still too vulnerable for daytime operations, where the armored vehicles would serve as deterrents in static observation posts for long periods of time. With the exception of major battalion surge operations, Slack was compelled to leave the Banshees as the nighttime patrol force. He weighted the unit with the best night-vision and thermal-imaging equipment in the task force, and challenged the company to clear Route Irish during its overnight patrols of IEDs that insurgents might have slipped onto the road during the chaotic daytime traffic.

The mission lifted the spirits of Minning's platoon. The Banshees had felt helpless when the battalion was suffering and bleeding without them, and were glad to be part of the team again. Task Force Wolfhound had lost twelve soldiers to IEDs in five months. If the Banshees did their job properly, the company would reduce the IED threat against the rest of the Fighting 69th as well as the hundreds of soldiers, contractors, and civilians who transited the route daily. Like any infantrymen, Minning's troops were also full of moxie and eager to get into the fight. They were confident in their unit and themselves, and wanted to take it to the enemy who lingered on the fringes of Route Irish.

By 10:15 on the night of their first patrol, Minning had replaced his baseball cap and headlamp with a helmet and body armor. His men were likewise in kit and sat in their idling vehicles waiting for the order to roll. Minning walked past his line of trucks, received a thumbs-up from each vehicle commander, and then jumped in his own Humvee, which the lieutenant had nicknamed "the Jedi Knight." The name was stenciled on the vehicle above its windshield, and a small Yoda doll had been strapped to the front grille. Such decorations were frowned upon by the U.S. command in Iraq, but since they worked almost exclusively at night, the Banshees freely customized their trucks. Some had names like "the Short Bus," while others boasted colorful green shamrock stickers that some of the unit's supporters in the States had sent over. Once Minning was settled in the Jedi Knight, he picked up his radio and ordered his platoon forward with a "Let's roll."

Lieutenant Rathburn, whose primary mission in Framework Operations was to work with the HHC to keep the company's rolling stock up to snuff, was standing nearby as Minning and the rest of the company got their vehicles ready to roll. As the men fired their engines, the company executive officer tuned up his bagpipes once again. Although his renditions of "Amazing Grace" had been forever emblazoned on the souls of the 69th men, for this occasion—the return of the Banshees—the officer produced an inspired rendition of the 69th Infantry Regiment's traditional marching tune, "Garryowen." The battalion had largely skipped its Saint Patrick's Day celebration that year, but the belated march into combat of the Banshees' shamrock-marked armored vehicles to the old Irish tune trumped any Fifth Avenue parade the regiment had seen in recent years and seemed to signal a turning point for Task Force Wolfhound in Iraq. At full combat strength for the first time in theater, the Fighting 69th could go back on the offense.

THE TRIAL

Sergeant Jay Olmo alternated glances between his digital map of Baghdad and the unfamiliar intersections his Humvee approached as he and the other Scouts rolled north of Route Irish into the upscale Mansour district of west Baghdad. The unit was operating outside its normal area, and Olmo, slightly disoriented, was a touch nervous. The Scouts were driving at top speed through the city with an informant who claimed to know where a group of insurgents had gathered to plan attacks against U.S. forces. The prospect of catching the bastards in the act thrilled the soldier, but the risk of following a walk-in informant was high. For all Olmo knew, the Iraqi could be leading the 69th men into an ambush.

Major Chris Cerniauskas, the battalion's Cajun operations officer, was more trusting. The informant had first approached the officer during a random house search near Route Irish. The Iraqi told Cerniauskas that he had been an insurgent fighting the Americans but had had a change of heart when his friend Faiz was killed in a VBIED attack on Route Irish. Faiz was an interpreter for the American social worker Marla Ruzicka. He had been driving her to visit Iraqi families when insurgents detonated a car bomb against a convoy of defense contractors that was rushing to the Green Zone. Ruzicka, whose mission in Iraq was to aid the innocent civilian victims of the conflict, was not the target of the attack, but both she and Faiz were caught up in the blast and killed.

The informant was devastated by the loss and knew the insurgent cell responsible. He told Cerniauskas that he could lead the Americans to the target. But they had to do it immediately. Because Colonel Slack was back in New York on the standard two-week leave all soldiers received in Iraq, Cerniauskas, an aggressive fireplug of an officer who earned the nickname "Major Chernobyl" for his frequent bombastic outbursts, took the proposal to Major Crosby, who was acting as task force commander. Real-time intelligence was nearly impossible for line units to come by in Iraq, so when the 69th got such a hot lead as the result of a random search, Crosby judged that a hasty mission was worth the risk and gave the order to raid the insurgent cell immediately.

The mission was precisely the kind for which Olmo had joined the Army. The soldier had fire in his gut and a full load of ammo. His heartbeat quickened as he approached the target house, thrilled by the high-speed, heavy-metal movement to combat. Every ounce of Jay Olmo's mind and body was tingling, leaving the soldier more alive than the uninitiated would ever be. He didn't want to be killed in the assault, but everyone had to go at some point. If it was his turn to die, this was the way to do it—on the attack and poking the enemy full of holes. Izzy, Lwin, and Ali had never had that chance. They never saw their killer, never knew it was coming. And that was how most soldiers in Iraq died—joking with their pals about the last movie they saw or the last steak they ate when, in a blink, their guts were torn open or their lights simply turned off. They died with their boots on, but almost never had a chance to shove those same boots up the ass of the cowardly enemy.

This is just like we always talked about, guys. I wish you were here with me.

The informant pointed out the building where the meeting was being held, and the U.S. fleet quickly "surrounded" the three-story complex. Olmo was the first outside his vehicle as it skidded to a halt on the sidewalk. Since the rest of his squad was either dead or convalescing back in the States, the sergeant had fallen in with other Scouts and quickly led the team into the front door and straight up to the third floor, as the informant had directed. Olmo turned left at the top of the stairs and immediately saw a lookout standing in front of the target doorway, some fifteen feet away. The man dodged into the room, followed closely by the Scouts, their M4s leading the way. Olmo was first in and immediately saw an Iraqi male reach for a gun. Olmo fired two rounds from his rifle, striking the man in the stomach and in the hip, but the insurgent made for an open window. Major Crosby, who was standing outside the building at street level with the rest of the assault force, saw the bleeding insurgent step out of the window and onto a ledge. He struck the man with two more rounds, and the insurgent fell from the ledge, through an awning and onto the street. Back inside another insurgent rushed Olmo, punching the GI in the head. Before the soldier could fight back, Batiste struck the insurgent in the face with the butt of his rifle, spilling the man's teeth out onto the floor as if someone had scattered a handful of Chiclets. None of the other three insurgents in the room made a move. The raid was over, and the GIs lowered the electric current running through their systems.

The Wolfhounds detained the Iraqis and headed back to Camp Liberty. Remarkably, the man Olmo and Crosby shot was still alive, and after dropping him off at the hospital, the soldiers returned to headquarters, where a group of American intelligence officers quickly took custody of the detainees. The 69th men were jubilant. The enemy in Iraq had proven remarkably elusive and had resolutely avoided any decisive engagements with the Americans. When the Wolfhounds did get a good score, it made some of the sacrifices they had borne a little easier to digest.

Olmo was pissed, however, unable to believe the guy he shot was still alive. It was the first time he had come face-to-face with an active and armed enemy—the first good chance he had had to avenge Irizarry, Lwin, and Ali—and the soldier botched it. He had aimed too low.

The sergeant felt the same way about Izzy's triggerman. The 69th had captured the insurgent responsible, but Olmo wished he had been given the opportunity to kill him. Now, six months after Ziyad had murdered his squad leader, the Tiger Brigade lawyers were telling Olmo the insurgent might go free.

Olmo was confused. *What did lawyers have to do with the insurgent?* The 69th had captured the guy at the scene and sent him off to a military jail. How was it possible the perp could go free? Major Rico Alvendia, a lawyer in Tiger Brigade, explained to Olmo and the other

Scouts that Ziyad—and every other insurgent the battalion had detained—had to go to trial before an Iraqi tribunal, Central Criminal Court of Iraq. This was not like the early days of the Afghanistan war, when insurgents were often whisked out of the country to the prison at Guantánamo Bay in Cuba. In its efforts to restore legitimate government to Iraq, the U.S. reestablished the Iraqi judicial system and gave it jurisdiction over attacks against coalition forces. Instead of trying the "suspected" enemy combatant in a military trial, Ziyad was assigned an Iraqi defense lawyer and given a court date. The Iraqi defender had dug up a series of eyewitnesses who said Ziyad could not have been involved in the attack against Izzy, as the suspect was at work when the incident occurred. At a sort of grand jury trial without the jury to determine whether there was enough evidence to prosecute Ziyad for the attack, the defense made a strong case for outright dismissal. Though Alvendia and the other U.S. lawyers had prepared the Iraqi prosecutor with mounds of evidence, the Iraqi magistrate who convened the hearing found the American case entirely circumstantial. Nobody had actually seen Ziyad detonate the bomb, and several Iraqis had provided the defendant with an alibi. Alvendia, who sat in the grand jury trial while his Iraqi counterpart argued the case, was certain the case would be thrown out. But in the end the judge decided there was just enough information to move forward. Still, he warned the prosecution to bolster its argument.

To Olmo, the whole situation was absurd. This wasn't *Law & Order;* it was a fucking war. Ziyad was the goddamn triggerman. Execute the motherfucker.

Olmo found the very idea of an Iraqi court for attacks against Americans to be strange. When Alvendia told the sergeant that he had to testify at Ziyad's trial, Olmo was convinced the Army had lost its way. In what war had U.S. soldiers ever been pulled from combat to testify at a civilian trial? In what war did U.S. soldiers ever have to convince a jury that the people they had captured were, in fact, enemy combatants?

While the GIs were like cops called to testify against the perp they had captured, and the Iraqi defense lawyers were like public defenders looking for weaknesses in the Americans' case, that's where similarities with the American legal system ended. The insurgents were not tried by juries. Rather, a three-judge tribunal heard the cases and decided the defendants' fate. In the United States, judges are meant to be neutral authorities who can dispassionately arrive at a fair verdict. But Alvendia, a slight officer with dark hair and a neutral accent that belied his background as a civil litigator in New Orleans, worried that the same dynamic was not at play in Ziyad's trial. The Iraqi legal system has a long history, which can be traced to the Code of Hammurabi, a lengthy set of laws that dates back to Babylon around 1700 BC. Even under Saddam's rule, judges were generally respected for their objective application of law. But because several judges and prosecutors in the U.S.-backed Iraqi court had been executed by insurgents in 2004 and 2005, Alvendia worried the judges would be afraid to convict an Iraqi civilian for the death of an American soldier. Such a ruling could as easily be a death sentence for the judge himself.

As bizarre as the legal process might have seemed to an infantryman engaged in daily combat in Baghdad, Olmo was eager to cooperate. If the insurgent escaped penalty, the soldier would never be able to look Izzy's wife or children in the eye. On the day of the trial, the Scouts loaded up in their Humvees and drove from Camp Liberty to the zone with Tiger Brigade legal representatives. Once inside the zone, the vehicles parked off a nondescript street and stepped through a hole in a wall onto a soccer pitch–sized open field. Now seasoned combat veterans, the soldiers fanned out in the event of an indirect fire or small-arms attack. The legal team advanced in a huddle, oblivious to any danger. The court sat at the far end of the field in a former museum where Saddam housed gifts from other heads of state. The men were impressed when they entered the back door of the building. Like most of Saddam's structures, its interior featured tall ceilings with elaborate moldings. The floors were of marble and the walls were trimmed in dark-stained wood. Both Iraqi and American security guards moved about the place.

The soldiers were led to an anteroom where the men shed their body armor and stowed their weapons. Ushers then led them inside the courtroom, which could have been any courtroom in the United States. Judicial clerks sat in the front near a court reporter and several security guards. Olmo and the other soldiers were still dirty from their drive and hike to the court, and sat sweating as they waited for the trial to begin. When Iraqi police led Ziyad and his brother, who was charged with aiding and abetting, into the room, bile rose at the back of Olmo's throat. He leaned forward in his seat, and another Scout put his hand on Olmo's back to calm him.

The people rose when the three judges, heavy-set middle-aged men, entered the room. Each wore a black robe with a white sash; the attorneys wore the same robe with green sashes. It was all very formal, with nothing suggestive of war except the presence of soldiers, who shifted uncomfortably in their seats as the prosecution team rolled a TV into the center of the room. Alvendia had asked the 69th to put together a video about Izzy, so-called impact evidence. When the images and music played, Olmo and the other Scouts wanted to cry as they had at the soldier's memorial service, but resisted the urge, refusing to show their mortal enemies any sign of weakness. The video ended, and without warning the judges called Olmo to the stand. Speaking through translators, the soldier answered the prosecutor's questions and recounted the events of December 3, 2004. He did his best to keep his fury in check, but it finally rose to the surface when the prosecutor asked Olmo if he could identify the triggerman in the courtroom. Olmo leaned forward and thrust an accusatory finger toward Ziyad. "Yeah, it's that motherfucker right there."

The court adjourned for deliberations after the testimony. Olmo and the Scouts needed to get back to Route Irish and left the hearing without any resolution. Alvendia told the men everything looked good; Ziyad and his brother would get what was coming to them. But, in

truth, the attorney didn't believe his own prediction. In his summa-
tion, the prosecutor, who was supposed to be fighting on Izzy's be-
half, had all but recommended Ziyad be released. He cited the lack
of hard evidence and suggested that the perpetrator could indeed have
been someone else. Alvendia was bursting, wanting to jump up and
take over the case, but he couldn't. Though the Americans could prep
the lawyers, they had to step out of the picture once the big show
started. When he returned to the courtroom, Alvendia was all but certain the insurgents would walk.

He was wrong. The judges did drop the charges against his brother,
but they found Ziyad guilty as charged and sentenced him to fifteen
years in an Iraqi prison, which Alvendia viewed as a virtual death sentence, given the rough conditions in Iraqi jails. It was the first conviction in the Iraqi court for an IED attack against Americans, and the
New Orleans lawyer was thrilled. He rushed back to the Fighting 69th
command post at Camp Liberty to pass on the great news, only to find
Olmo and the Scouts were not overly impressed. "Just fifteen years?"
Olmo asked. "We should have killed him when we had the chance."

Nonetheless, it was a victory—like the hasty raid in Mansour and
the shooting of the insurgent in the gut. A few weeks after that impromptu assault, the Wolfhounds learned from various intelligence
sources that the men they captured were indeed high-level planners
and their apprehension no doubt weakened the enemy's network in
western Baghdad. Olmo was pleased with the outcome, and when he
learned that the Iraqi he had shot had later died in the hospital, he
was downright ecstatic. No matter how many insurgents he put in
jail, nothing short of death would count as true justice for what the
enemy had done to his friends. The generals might tell the GIs that
killing the enemy was not usually the most effective way to win a
counterinsurgency fight, but it felt pretty damned good for the guys
with their boots on the ground.

REVENGE OF THE ASSASSINS

The images of the attack against Lwin and Ali returned to Mike Drew's mind virtually every time he drove past the blast site. But by June 2005, Drew rarely worried another bomb would be waiting for him there. In the days following the March attack, the task force had set out to radically redesign Route Irish. To prevent insurgents from hiding roadside bombs in the bulrushes along the road, the battalion began lining the highway with an unbroken string of Jersey barriers like those used on highway-construction areas in the States. If the insurgents placed anything on the side of the road, it would stand out easily against the smooth concrete barriers. If they opted to place something on the backside of the barrier, a bomb would be less effective and difficult to set off remotely due to the poor line of sight.

As with most nonstandard missions in the 69th, the job of placing the barriers fell to Chris Daniels and Horrible Company. They hauled the Jerseys out to Route Irish every night and positioned them along the road. Their only limiting factor was a shortage of material. The Horribles ultimately started plucking the three-foot-tall walls from outside every building in Camp Liberty and Camp Victory, including the headquarters of the 3rd Infantry Division. When word reached the division commander that the long-suffering Fighting 69th was swiping Jerseys from his headquarters, the general thought it was a good idea. He sent word to Slack that the 69th could have whatever barriers of his they could find.

Every night the HHC slung more walls, and every day on Route Irish, Captain Drew felt more secure. He and his soldiers still found a handful of improvised bombs, but they were usually small, and none caused casualties. Between the route clearance, the constant patrolling that the Banshees (and the Comanches before them) conducted every night, and the barriers the Horribles had placed to block enemy bomb attacks, the IED threat on Route Irish was effectively neutralized. After Lwin and Ali were killed in early March, not a single soldier in the task force—for that matter, not a single coalition soldier or defense contractor—was wounded by an IED in the 69th Infantry's area of responsibility on Route Irish.

The enemy still posed a threat on and around Irish, of course. Insurgents switched tactics in April and May, favoring RPG and small-arms attacks against the 69th. One RPG ricocheted off an Assassin Humvee and smacked into the head of one of Drew's machine gunners before exploding on the shoulder of the road. The gunner's helmet took most of the blast, and the soldier suffered only the loss of a chunk of ear. Another machine gun attack caught a stationary defense contractor, killing two men, an event that was recorded by a dashboard camera and posted to the Internet, further adding to the legend of Route Irish. In late May and early June, the enemy tested the Banshees in the early morning hours, luring the unit into three coordinated ambushes, one of which caused the company's first casualty. An IED blew ten feet away from Lieutenant Rathburn, the battalion bagpiper, as he investigated suspicious activity on foot. Miraculously, the soldier was only lightly wounded and was again playing "Garryowen" that night.

Staff Sergeant Peter Hahn of the Blacksheep was not as fortunate. Insurgents conducted a drive-by shooting against his Bradley Fighting Vehicle, which was stationary along the broad shoulder of Irish. There was too much civilian traffic to use his main gun against the enemy, so Hahn rose up out of the track's turret to return fire with his rifle. As soon as he hit daylight, a single bullet slammed into his right shoulder above his armor, deflected off bone, and sliced through his chest cavity, killing him almost instantly.

But despite the casualties and regular low-grade attacks, the men of the Fighting 69th believed they had gotten the upper hand on Irish. Still, the battalion struggled to defend against car bombs. Denied use of their most effective weapons, the IEDs, the enemy increased his VBIED attacks against the highway, causing civilian and defense contractor casualties to rise. The strike against the Blacksheep just before Saint Patrick's Day was the first in a major surge by the enemy on the highway. Between April and June, not a week passed without a car bomb attack against nonmilitary targets on Route Irish. About half blew during Drew's shift with the Assassins, adding more vivid images of carnage to his psyche. He was the first American soldier to identify Marla Ruzicka after she was hit with a suicide bomb on Irish, and the sound of her voice whispering for help would never leave the officer.

As horrible as the images of both the military and civilian casualties were, Drew had rebounded from the Italian Job. When Kazmierzak was blown up, Drew's attitude changed. The Blacksheep commander had been the senior line company commander in the task force, and Drew knew he had to step up to take his place. The Louisianans would have a new commander, and the Banshees were returning to the battalion. Drew, as the 69th's most experienced line captain, had to carry the torch for the new officers. The NYPD sergeant turned Army officer struck back out onto Route Irish with a vengeance. He and the Assassins picked up their presence in the *muhallahs* surrounding the highway, raiding suspected insurgent homes, questioning locals, and ultimately pushing the enemy and his RPG and small-arms attacks farther away from the highway. Soon after, the enemy was forced to attack the 69th from long range with mortar fire. But even that was a risky venture.

As Drew trawled Irish one scorching summer day, he saw mortars striking near the highway. The explosions were kicking up a large amount of debris and dust, creating a thick smokescreen for Drew to maneuver undetected. He told his driver to gun the Humvee and sped off the road to where he thought the enemy might be firing from. As he moved at high speed, mortar rounds continued to thump in near Irish. The enemy was either stupid or hadn't seen him. The commander rounded a corner and began scanning down Baghdad's long city streets until he spotted the mortar team less than a half mile from the highway. The insurgents were dressed in civilian clothes and still firing when Drew made the turn onto the road they were using. The enemy had rigged a mortar in the open hatchback of a small white car. When they saw the Humvees, the men dropped their weapon back into the car and rushed into the vehicle. Having left the engine running, the insurgents were able to get in gear quickly and start rolling, but it was too late for them. Within moments, bullets from Drew's machine gunners started to rip through the vehicle, the Assassins pouring it on as never before. The insurgent car careened into a telephone pole as the Americans continued to fire. Though the target was immobilized, Drew let the men shoot. There would be no trial in the Green Zone for this group.

When the Americans finally ceased fire and approached the vehicle, Drew looked at the remains of the two insurgents as his soldiers pulled an arsenal of weapons, including a sniper rifle and the mortar tube, out of the car. So this was the enemy—the guys who planted the IEDs, who shot the RPGs, who lobbed mortars. In eight months of combat, it was the first time Drew had caught the bastards in the act. For all the commander knew, however, he could have seen the men a thousand times before. He could have talked with them, eaten in their homes, treated them in an accident. The insurgents in the car could have been anybody in Baghdad or Taji—and to Drew they were everybody in Baghdad and Taji. But this time they were dead. As flames sparked up and engulfed the vehicle, the captain smiled. Except for his wedding day, it was the happiest moment of his life.

IRAQIZATION

Drew's aggressive maneuver against the mortar team impressed Slack, but it wasn't the only sign his battalion had become a veteran combat unit. By June the commander realized he was giving less and less guidance or instruction. The Fighting 69th that he had derided as a young officer, the battalion that once struggled to get soldiers to a drill weekend sober, the task force that he thought performed poorly at the National Training Center in California the previous September, was now functioning like a well-oiled machine. They acted as effectively on detailed plans as on gut instinct. The bark had been peeled back on the men, revealing raw nerve. The violent and aggressive band of soldiers knew their jobs cold.

In late June, when a massive car bomb detonated on Route Irish killing a dozen Iraqi soldiers, Slack hurried to his operations center to direct the battalion's response. But the reaction was already under way by the time he showed up. The commander eased back, crossed his arms, and watched in amazement as his operations officers and sergeants took reports from the field and issued others to the higher headquarters. The Assassins were on the scene treating and evacuating casualties. Sergeant Olmo and the Scouts were already rolling out to Irish as a quick-reaction force. Captain Daniels and his Horribles were moving out to clean up the highway. Captain Mike Melancon, the new Blacksheep commander, had just come in from Route Irish with his company but immediately he turned the unit around and headed back out to sector. Lieutenant Minning woke his Banshees early and ordered them to their vehicles to prepare to assist in the battalion response. Slack had never seen anything like it. Without a word, he left the operations center. Where he would have once rushed to his own Humvee, the commander walked out of the headquarters, stood at the base of a flagpole that flew the 69th Infantry Regiment's green regimental colors, and smoked a Camel. Slack had all but worked himself out of a job. The only thing left for him to do was solve the VBIED problem.

The battalion could protect itself from car bombs, but the defense contractors and other Westerners on the road were still getting hit. Videos of the attacks continued to pop up on Arabic news stations, making for an untenable situation for the American command in Baghdad. The 69th, which had returned to duty with the Louisiana Tiger Brigade in April after the 10th Mountain Division left Iraq, worked with the Tigers to come up with a solution. Some officers proposed walling the highway off with sixteen-foot barriers. But the plan was logistically difficult and not politically attractive. Others opted for random vehicle stops, called "snap checkpoints," to catch a car bomber in the act, but that usually placed soldiers too close to a car bomb. The solution they finally agreed upon was the same solution the U.S. military had been proposing to eventually end the war: hand it over to the Iraqis.

The 3rd Infantry Division gave the Fighting 69th a brigade of Iraqi Special Police (ISP) to train up for security on the route. The ISPs, the Iraqi version of military police, had recently been formed at Camp Cooke and were led by General Mohammed Bassim. But just as the 69th had been rushed to the war in 2004, the ISPs were prematurely posted to Route Irish to help stem the car bombs. When they arrived on Irish in June, Slack was shocked at their state of readiness. Most of the Iraqi soldiers, or *jundis,* were illiterate farmers from the backwaters of the country, and many were sick due to a lifetime of neglected health. They had little training and even less equipment. Their AK-47 rifles were rusted relics. Their wheeled armored vehicles didn't run. The soldiers had no body armor and refused to wear their helmets. But as motley as the group looked, Slack found the soldiers to be highly motivated and eager to make a difference.

The commander also had something of a personal connection with the ISPs. Each Iraqi unit was trained and advised by a U.S. Military Training Team, a "MiTT" for short. The team assigned to the ISPs on Irish happened to be comprised of the same soldiers who had managed the training for the 69th back at Fort Hood the year before. When the team arrived in Baghdad to link up with the 69th, however, the teachers became the students. The Wolfhounds were salty veterans, and the advisers sought them out for advice and support.

American units had been working with the new Iraqi security forces since the nascent units were established in 2003. But in many cases the Americans did not have the manpower or equipment to set the new army up for success. Even the Wolfhounds had given short shrift to the Iraqi army units with which they had previously worked. Supporting the host-nation forces was often an additional duty for the Americans. When the 69th was in Taji, for example, the Tiger Brigade ordered the New Yorkers to supply a dozen soldiers of various ranks to support the training of the new Iraqi army back in Baghdad.

Already short of troops to accomplish their primary mission, Slack had to chop more men away for a job that didn't help his main effort. Consequently, the commander sent the soldiers he could most do without. Training host-nation security forces is a doctrinal mission for the U.S. Special Forces, the best-trained soldiers in the Army. Yet because of the small number of troops in Iraq, the job was often left to marginal soldiers, relegating the training of the Iraqis to just another economy of force mission.

But when the ISPs hit Irish, economy of force was the furthest thing from Slack's mind. Instead of a "secondary" duty, training and equipping the Iraqi unit became the 69th's new main effort. Slack pulled up Jersey barriers he had established to help protect his own forces and had Daniels place them in defense of Iraqi positions. The line companies reduced their focus on Irish to conduct joint training patrols with the Iraqis. The battalion doctor gave the Iraqi soldiers medical treatment. The maintenance platoon pulled broken Iraqi armor into the 69th motor pool and went to work. The medical platoon trained the Iraqis in combat first aid. Captain Joe Whaley, the battalion logistics officer who had moved mountains to outfit the 69th in Texas, now applied his efforts to equipping the Iraqi unit. The Wolfhounds worked with the ISP advisers to get the soldiers more body armor, more uniforms, hardened bunkers, and camouflage netting. Battalion soldiers even made the dangerous run back up to Taji to scrounge equipment for the ISPs, losing one truck to an IED in the process.

Slack still cruised Route Irish but spent more time at the ISP headquarters, located inside the former Kuwaiti Embassy just north of the airport road. The commander sat with General Bassim, sharing cigarettes, drinking Sprite, and discussing the VBIED problem. Like most successful military plans, its solution was simple: The Americans would build fences and string wire along the shoulders of Route Irish to force all civilian traffic to use the on- and off-ramps to the road. The Iraqi *jundis* would then position themselves at the ramps and screen every car that entered the highway.

For an American soldier, inspecting a car driving onto Irish would be tantamount to suicide. A car bomber would gladly martyr himself to kill one or two GIs, and some reports even suggested insurgents (or their survivors) could be paid a thousand-dollar bounty for the job. But why waste a good VBIED on an illiterate *jundi*? It wasn't worth it, in the eyes of the enemy. Car bombs were essentially strategic weapons for the insurgents; if they could kill twenty Iraqi soldiers with a single car bomb, a suicide attack might be in the cards. But using them to kill one or two *jundis* was a waste of an asset. Given that most Iraqis wanted nothing to do with a suicide attack, when insurgents did find someone willing to blow himself up, they needed to get a big payoff.

Once the ISPs hit the road, the key task for the 69th was to protect the ISPs from sniper fire, drive-by shootings, mortars, and indirect fire—enemy tactics the 69th had largely already neutralized. In addition, Slack had the Horribles build hardened battle positions at each ramp and challenged the line commanders to befriend the Iraqis and get them anything they asked for. The only problem the Americans encountered was an initial reluctance among the *jundis* to wear body armor and helmets in the blasting summer heat. The Iraqis would often put the gear on only when the Americans were around. But on one such occasion, a vest stopped a sniper round, saving the life of an Iraqi officer. From that point on the other ISPs quickly adopted the armor without further convincing.

The simple strategy, which Slack called the "Bassim Plan," in honor of the ISP commander, worked. Some Iraqi soldiers were killed in the early days of their mission, but as they learned to use their equipment and the defensive positions the Americans built for them, attacks against them all but ceased. As hoped, the threat of discovery by a *jundi* deterred further VBIEDs. Not a single car bomb detonated in the 69th and ISP area of Irish after the Iraqis began checking cars.

The 69th was having similar success in the fervently Sunni stronghold of Ameriya, north of Irish. The Iraqis of the middle-class neighborhood had grown up hating the Americans due to an airstrike against a dual-purpose military and civilian bunker during the first Gulf War. The site was marked with a stirring monument of a burning Iraqi woman—"The Screaming Lady," as the Americans called her. Trying to conduct effective counterinsurgency in the town was understandably difficult. But again, the 69th turned to the Iraqi army. After Slack dissolved Team Comanche, he sent the unit's commander to be the senior adviser to the Iraqi army operating in Ameriya. Captain Timothy Joseph "T. J." Hoy, another 69th mustang who had already pulled a tour of duty with the 10th Mountain Division in Afghanistan, integrated the Iraqi and American operations in the *muhallah*. By the summer of 2007, Slack instructed Hoy and the other commanders to make the Iraqis the lead element for any operation in the area. While the indigenous forces weren't always the picture of professionalism, they could spot telltale signs of insurgent activity that the Americans could never detect. On one patrol, an Iraqi captain ordered a raid of a house in Ameriya simply because the water hose outside had been left running. That sign didn't mean a thing to Hoy's advisers, but the Iraqis were certain something was amiss: nobody left water running in Baghdad. Someone must have run when he saw the army turn down his street. When the soldiers searched the house, they found one of the largest weapons caches the 69th had seen in the war.

With the Iraqis squeezing the insurgents on the 69th's flanks and screening vehicles on Route Irish, the so-called most dangerous road in the world was fully in check by the end of July for the first time since the insurgency began in earnest in April 2004.

14: BOOTS OFF THE GROUND

69 MINUTES

When General Basilica called Slack into his office in early August and led off with a compliment, the Wolfhound commander knew something was up. The general first reported that the 3rd Infantry Division hadn't asked about Route Irish in weeks—the ultimate sign of success as far as Basilica was concerned. The road had settled, so much so that the division commander was able to switch his attention elsewhere. Convoy commanders who had once deliberately avoided Irish began driving the highway again. They, too, had watched the drop in enemy-activity reports about the road and concluded that Irish was now the safest way to Camp Victory.

"Congratulations," Basilica told Slack. Then the other shoe dropped. Since no good deed goes unpunished, Basilica announced that Slack would be responsible for hosting a team of journalists from *60 Minutes,* a news program not especially known for glowing reports about the military. Slack shuddered at the thought. He figured the journalists were doing an investigative piece on the Italian shooting and intended to ambush 69th soldiers until they got the story and the quotes they wanted. Further, Slack was still smarting from his comments to the *New York Times* back in March. The interview about the "deathly quiet" highway had been one of the low points for the commander, and he wasn't keen to put himself under the spotlight again. Slack told Basilica he couldn't do it, but the general was adamant: the Fighting 69th would welcome *60 Minutes* and would give them whatever they needed.

When the reporters arrived at the Wolfhound headquarters, CBS News reporter Lara Logan explained that they had no interest in the Italian shooting; the magazine had already covered the event. The focus of this visit, rather, was the highway itself, "the most dangerous road in the world." What was it like to work on Route Irish? How were the Americans trying to secure the road? The journalists wanted to patrol with the 69th day and night. They wanted to interview the soldiers and the commanders. They wanted to join the battalion on any raids it was conducting.

At first blush Logan didn't look like the type of salty war correspondent one might expect to find embedded in Iraq. She was a slight and rather comely South African woman whom the men might have expected to see at the annual Victoria's Secret fashion show back at the 69th Regiment Armory in the States—not in the middle of a war zone. But Logan was, in fact, a veteran war correspondent and, with only a handful of visits home, had been in Baghdad since before the start of the war. She had connections with scores of Iraqi civilians and had already conducted hundreds of patrols with U.S. forces. According to one account, she was even in a U.S. vehicle that was struck by an IED. The Wolfhounds, save a handful of media skeptics, were impressed.

Jay Olmo was one of those skeptics. A few negative experiences with the media had soured the soldier's opinion of the press in Iraq. In one instance, Al Jazeera had reported on a raid the Scouts had conducted without bothering to get the American side of the story. Instead, the Arab outlet interviewed only the Iraqi residents of the home that had been entered, who made false allegations against the American soldiers—accusing the GIs of destroying their property and disrespecting their Koran. In another incident, an American journalist embedded with the Fighting 69th reported on the death of the seven Blacksheep in Taji before the Army had a chance to notify the next of kin of the victims, causing several days of confusion and an incredible amount of stress among the families back in the States. When Logan and her cameraman were looking for seats in a Humvee for a patrol on Irish, Olmo claimed his truck was full and begged off.

Mike Drew was likewise uneasy about the media. The official U.S. military report about the Italian shooting had been leaked to the public that summer. Though the report cleared the GIs of any involvement, the document listed the names of every soldier involved. Reporters in the States had been calling Drew's home at all hours, seeking comment from his wife. Upset about the intrusion and the lingering story of the Italian agent, the captain asked Slack to be excused from any involvement with 60 Minutes.

The rest of the battalion, however, was eager to have the journalists accompany them. The men were proud of the work they had done on Irish and wanted to show the fruits of their labor. The only problem was, the success of the 69th didn't exactly make for exciting reporting. Logan interviewed the soldiers during planning sessions and rode with them on patrols that lasted from eight to fifteen hours. But after a week of taping the Fighting 69th on Route Irish, the reporters had failed to capture any significant combat. The most dangerous road in the world was, it seemed, fairly quiet, prompting the journalists to extend their visit a second week. By now the soldiers had begun to suspect that the journalists were waiting to capture a car bomb attack on the route. But again, no insurgents accommodated them.

The battle for the airport road was finally over, and the U.S. and Iraqi Special Police had won. The American command in Baghdad had essentially taken a page from retired General Colin Powell's rules: use overwhelming force to defeat the enemy. Between Task Force Wolfhound and the Iraqi Special Police brigade, there were now more than one thousand combat soldiers committed to security of the five-mile stretch of the airport road and its neighboring *muhallahs*. An insurgent couldn't take a leak near Route Irish without being seen by a U.S. or Iraqi soldier. To the extreme gratification of the 69th and the pleasure of the thousands of people who traveled Irish daily, the enemy decided to go elsewhere.

Unfortunately, there were not enough forces in the rest of Baghdad to evict the insurgents from the city full-stop. The enemy simply shifted its attacks from Route Irish to the other main roads in western Baghdad. Wolfhound soldiers could now stand in the middle of Route Irish without fear, while watching thick black smoke from car bombs and IEDs rising from points north and south. When Slack, riding with Logan, heard one major blast north of the airport road, he rushed to the scene to determine whether the unit in contact needed any help. A remotely detonated car bomb had blasted an American patrol driving along Route Michigan, just two miles north of Irish. As fate would have it, the blast caught a section of Mike Drew's Assassins that had been operating under a Louisiana command. Fortunately, the soldiers suffered only minor wounds in the blast.

The platoon from the Banshees that had been detached to a Louisiana battalion the summer before was not as fortunate. On August 7, insurgents launched a coordinated ambush against a section from the platoon in northern Baghdad. Specialist Anthony Kalladeen, a former Marine who had volunteered to deploy with the Fighting 69th, and Specialist Hernando Rios, a soldier who had arrived in May as a replacement, were killed when an armor-piercing EFP ripped through their Humvee. Other soldiers were wounded. In the firefight that ensued, the rest of the section expended all their ammunition before they were reinforced by another platoon of New Yorkers from Demon Company, the unit of the 101st Cavalry that had been swapped for the Blacksheep. The Demons, who had lost one of their own in a vehicle accident in December—Specialist David Fisher—successfully broke the enemy ambush by sheer presence. They helped the bruised Banshee squad reconsolidate and move back to Camp Liberty for medical help. Kalladeen and Rios were the eighteenth and nineteenth soldiers who had served under the 69th Infantry flag at some point since May 2004 who were killed in Iraq with the Tiger Brigade. Slack read "The Rouge Bouquet" one last time. Lara Logan, who sat at the back of the chapel as Slack recited the requiem, cried with the rest of the task force, endearing herself to many of the soldiers in the nearby pews.

The experience led her to ask Slack during a lengthy sitdown interview in the battalion operations center about the unit's deaths.

"The hardest question you have to answer to a family or to a young soldier who has lost a friend is, 'What is that all about? What are we doing here, sir?'" the commander said. "I can only tell them what I believe, that we are buying time . . . for [Iraq's] military, for this government to stand up and put itself together."

Logan assumed Slack was just spinning the party line and asked him what his own opinions were. If she had known the commander better, she would have realized his opinions on most matters were often lockstep with the Army's own. Moreover, the commander wasn't about to pick up the political football Logan tossed in his lap.

Slack had long avoided the politics associated with the Iraq war. He didn't think it was the soldier's place to comment on policy and lambasted any of his soldiers for discussing the subject. The first time that Chris Daniels met Slack back in 1997, the future battalion commander shouted down a fellow officer for making a joke about then-president Bill Clinton. Slack believed that badmouthing the civilian leadership of the U.S. military was a dangerous path for any soldier to take. "Oh, God, it would be terrible if our Army ever voiced its opinion about politics," he told one of his captains back in New York. "And if you ever talk politics you better be out of uniform and out of this armory. You can't be in a New York State military facility in uniform and sit around and trash the elected leadership, because senior people, when they say that, junior people listen." Though many Americans opposed the war in Iraq, Slack believed Americans continued to love their soldiers precisely because they didn't take a political stand. The moment the Army began to do so, the same people who cheered American soldiers would most likely turn against them in a heartbeat.

Logan did not make politics a focus of her interviews; had she done so, however, she would probably not have found many soldiers willing to trash the war or the politicians who had sent them there. Rather, she would have found a group of men who genuinely believed in their hearts that they were helping both their fellow soldiers and the people of Iraq. Three months before he died, Specialist Kalladeen captured the sentiments of most of the soldiers in a letter he wrote to his college newspaper in Purchase, New York:

> Being out here, I feel like I am actually doing something to help change Iraq for the better. Since I have been here in Iraq I have seen a lot of things happen. When I first got here, the base would receive mortar attacks just about every day. At times, we would have to wear our vests and helmets every time we left our rooms. We could hear fire fights off in the distance. Many civilians were taken hostage and some were beheaded on TV.
>
> Things started to change after the Marines stormed Fallujah a few months ago, killing about 2,000 Insurgents and taking away their stronghold. The next major event was the elections on January 30. The Iraqi National Guard and police are starting to conduct operations on their own. Improvised Explosive Devices are getting less and less effective. I forgot one thing; the Sunnis who were making up most of the Insurgency are being encouraged by their own clerics to join the National Guard, Police and Army to help stabilize the country.
>
> There are a lot of good things that have been going on in the region. I am not going to get into them; all you have to do is turn on CNN to find out what it is. Every time we stop for a break, we always have kids and sometimes adults coming up to us asking for chocolate, a soccer ball, toothpaste and brushes. They come to us without fear. I give them what I can, when I have it. Seeing those kids smile and wave at us tells me what I am doing is meaningful.

Though Kalladeen referenced CNN as a source to see the good things the soldiers were accomplishing in Iraq, most GIs believed the news media hadn't been able to capture effectively the sentiments of the rank-and-file troops. Why was *60 Minutes* featuring the airport road and not the children with whom Kalladeen was kicking soccer balls? One soldier with a journalism degree tried to explain the issue to his mates: "It's pretty simple," he said. "If it bleeds, it leads."

It was that basic tenet of journalism that had prompted the *60 Minutes* team to divide its efforts on Route Irish in hopes of catching dramatic action. But they were largely stifled. The most dramatic footage they captured was a clip of Colonel Slack walking up to a suspicious object in Ameriya near the highway to confirm whether the item was or was not an IED. The item did turn out to be a bomb, and the incident surprised Logan. Why would the commander approach a possible explosive? "It's either I do it or they do it," Slack said. When the *60 Minutes* piece aired some months later, a number of people asked soldiers in the 69th if Slack had been hamming it up for the cameras. The answer was a resounding no.

In broadcasting the risk Colonel Slack took with the IED, *60 Minutes* captured the essence of the Fighting 69th, from Ground Zero to Baghdad. Whether rushing to the World Trade Center on 9/11 or braving a mortar barrage in Taji, the commander had sought to provide an example for his officers and NCOs. His men should be bold, courageous, lead from the front, and respond to any enemy attacks with an overwhelming show of force. It was the same leadership style the Fighting 69th officers had espoused since the Civil War, and the unit's leaders in the new millennium had followed suit. From Colonel Slack and Captain Drew down to First Sergeant Acevedo and Sergeant Olmo, the men of the Fighting 69th always leaned forward—and made up for their own lack of experience with an abundance of moxie and frostiness. To compensate for their lack of forces in Taji, the leaders of the 69th pushed their men beyond their limits, often working them around the clock. The intense tempo of operations left the unit no choice but to get better. The casualties it suffered forced it to learn effective counterinsurgency tactics. From a shotgun approach at the outset, which some soldiers likened to "driving around just waiting to get blown up," they progressed to a targeted approach based on the intelligence the unit gained in the field. The same principles it had learned in Taji guided the unit to even greater success on Route Irish. Enemy activity was so light by August that the Big Army battalion from the 3rd ID that was sent to relieve the 69th on Route Irish conducted its reconnaissance of the airport road on foot without the protection of its armored vehicles. If they had pulled that stunt in April, there might well have been many more widows and orphans back in the States.

Though Slack knew Route Irish was far more secure than it had been seven months earlier, he was hesitant to risk any more of his own men in such a dangerous gambit. As the unit approached its last day of work, the commander urged his captains to choose their battles carefully: "Do your job well, but don't go off half-cocked looking for a fight in someone else's sector." The 69th was too close to the finish line to take another hit.

The Wolfhounds began their relief in place with the 6th Squadron, 8th Cavalry Regiment on August 21. For the next ten days the battalion's footprint on Route Irish diminished a little more every morning, until August 29, when only one 69th soldier remained on patrol in western Baghdad. As fate would have it, the honors went to Lieutenant Al Trentalange, a short and scrappy New York City firefighter who had been one of the first 69th men at Ground Zero. As it had been on 9/11, Trentalange's last duty in Iraq was fraught with danger. He was the lone American officer advising a platoon of Iraqi army soldiers on a mounted patrol in Ameriya, the Sunni enclave where Slack had walked up to an IED as the *60 Minutes* cameras rolled. As Trentalange and his team rounded a corner, the section drove into an RPG and machine gun ambush that wounded several Iraqis. The officer fought back with the green soldiers, beating back the enemy. He helped the *jundis* get their mates to the hospital and then hung with them for another hour before making his way back to Camp Liberty. When he returned to the 69th command post to report the incident, the TOC was empty save for a few soldiers who had been huddling around a lone radio, listening to the contact.

"Pretty sporty, huh?" one officer asked.

"Yup," he replied curtly. "Now let's go home."

The balance of Task Force Wolfhound reconvened the following morning at a transient base camp on the southwest side of the Victory Base Cluster. Though it was August 30, General Basilica and Colonel Slack had arranged a 9/11 memorial Mass. Father Alejandro Sanchez, the 69th's Puerto Rican chaplain, led the service. He prayed for the lost members of the regiment and the Tiger Brigade, and for a safe return to New York. Though he had served the battalion well, the Roman Catholic priest had never become the gifted speaker and ubiquitous spiritual guide that Father Francis Duffy had been in World War I. For their regular dose of inspiration and eloquent homilies, the men of the Fighting 69th in 2005 turned instead to their commander, who addressed the assembled task force following the Mass.

Slack, who had shaved his Iraqi-style mustache, stared out at his battalion before reading from a letter a 69th soldier had written back in 1862. The letter was to the father of an Irish soldier killed in Virginia and included a response to the grieving parents' request to have the remains of his son disinterred and returned to New York City. The soldier wrote that such a move would be difficult, as the men were in a mass grave, and their remains would be fully intermingled with those of their comrades within a piece of land that had "been consecrated by our blood."

The letter reminded Slack of the intermingled remains he had seen at Ground Zero and along Route Red Legs in Taji where the soldiers inside Charlie 24 had died. Though most of the carnage was recovered, a little bit of those people would always remain in the grounds there. As with the Virginia battlefields, the places had been consecrated by American blood, and Slack hoped that he and the families of the soldiers left behind would be able to some day return to pay their respects. For Taji, he had a vision of a shade tree and a nice stone marker along the canal where the Bradley came to rest. But he doubted such a memorial would ever exist, at least not in his lifetime. Until then, the men and all the people lost on 9/11 would have to live on in the soldiers' minds.

At 7:00 a.m. on August 30, 2005, Task Force Wolfhound formally turned over Route Irish. With the Iraqi Special Police fully trained, the 6/8 Cav was able to cover the highway effectively with fewer forces than the 69th. Within months, the Iraqis took control of the highway outright. Attacks rose slightly from time to time, but the airport road never reverted to the state of a shooting gallery that had made it famous. While *60 Minutes* did not comment on the Army's success, other news outlets did. In September, *USA Today* ran a story about the 69th efforts under the headline "Number of attacks decreases on Baghdad highway to airport." A similar *Washington Post* headline a few weeks later read: "Easy Sailing Along Once-Perilous Road to Baghdad Airport; Army Steps Up Presence to Quell Attacks."

Route Irish was a striking success for the Army's plan to turn security over to Iraqi forces, but the experience also demonstrated the effort needed to make that venture a success. The U.S. military would need far more forces to replicate the victory the Fighting 69th and the Tiger Brigade ultimately achieved on Route Irish. But it would be two more years before the Big Army surged thousands more troops into Baghdad. In the meantime, the safest place in the entire city may well have been the center median of Baghdad's airport road.

THE ENEMY AT HOME

The same day that the Fighting 69th turned Route Irish back to the Big Army, Hurricane Katrina made landfall on Louisiana, home state to nearly a third of Task Force Wolfhound. The men watched the news coverage in disbelief. Some of Slack's key operations sergeants had come to him from the New Orleans–based Washington Artillery. The unit and its soldiers lived and worked in the Lower Ninth Ward of the city. Many lost everything.

General Basilica was concerned about the state of his brigade. One of the unit's strengths was its strong network of support for families back in the States, which gave most of the soldiers the ability to fight without the distraction of problems back home. But now Basilica believed the enemy had gotten behind them. He began regular telephone and video conference updates with officials back in Louisiana and held town meetings at the camp chapel to disseminate whatever information he had to his soldiers. Still, nothing short of getting the brigade home could calm the unit. But the general was up against the commercial airline industry and the thick bureaucracy of defense logistics. Though the Tigers were now out of the war, Basilica could not convince the airlines to move the 256th out of Iraq any faster. Although the 69th was the first unit scheduled to leave the country, the New Yorkers volunteered to give up their seats if it would get the Louisianans home early. But the Army would not allow the change. Despite the severity of the storm, the Tiger Brigade did not leave Iraq one day sooner than the redeployment schedule originally called for.

The Brigade finally began arriving in Louisiana in mid-September. The leadership that had served in Iraq was the same leadership that would typically have responded to a hurricane. Though the State of Louisiana had mobilized about four thousand Guardsmen in advance of the storm, they were eager to get the Tigers back. After eighteen months of training for and prosecuting a war, Basilica and the 256th assumed control of the eighteen-thousand-soldier-strong joint task force of National Guard forces that eventually responded to Louisiana from all fifty states and three territories. The dramatic homecoming and long recuperation many of the men had imagined had been dashed. The soldiers not affected by the storm went straight to work against Mother Nature's wrath. Men who had been patrolling downtown Baghdad in August were now patrolling their own city in September. When Hurricane Rita landed just a few weeks later, Basilica's Tigers were fully committed to their State mission.

Large numbers of soldiers from the Fighting 69th volunteered to deploy to Louisiana in support of their blood brothers to the south.

But the State of New York sent fresh soldiers, allowing the Wolf-hounds to return to their families. The soldiers flew in several plane-loads from Kuwait to Fort Dix, New Jersey, by way of Shannon, Ireland, where the Fighting Irish hydrated liberally with pints of Guinness and Harp. Slack flew home with the Banshees on the last plane out of the country, arriving at Dix in the early morning darkness of September 10, 2005. Exactly four years had passed since 9/11, and the men of the Fighting 69th were more than ready for the mission that lay ahead—going home.

AFTERWORD
THE OPERATIONAL RESERVE

SAINT PATRICK'S DAY 2006

On March 17, 2006, Sergeant Jay Olmo woke in his apartment in Queens just after 6:00 a.m. He glanced at the clock, realized he was late for the parade, and decided without hesitation to go back to sleep. *What are they gonna do, send me back to Baghdad?*

Though he had fought with the Fighting 69th and seen his entire squad killed or wounded in the regiment's uniform, Olmo still wasn't about to march in that damned parade. Far from instilling some romantic attachment to the regiment's Irish ancestors, Olmo's combat experience with the 69th made him more certain than ever that the parade was a waste of time. He didn't budge from his bed until 9:00 a.m., when he finally pulled on his desert-pattern fatigues. With his Combat Infantryman Badge in place, the veteran didn't even worry about making up a story about why he was late. He strolled confidently into the armory around 10:30 a.m. and headed up to the NCO club, where he met several other Scouts who had also skipped the parade.

At the same time, Major Charles Crosby was leading the veteran battalion in front of the reviewing stands on the Upper East Side. He carried the commander's blackthorn stick in his left hand and saluted the dignitaries with his right. The new battalion commander's staff marched one rank behind him, with Captain Chris Daniels in the front as his executive officer. In addition to Daniels, the staff included the entire team from Iraq. An honorary "special staff" followed, which included Geoff Slack, who had been promoted to full colonel and now worked at the headquarters of the 42nd Infantry Division, and General John Basilica, fresh from command of the Hurricane Katrina and Hurricane Rita National Guard task force. Captain Mike Drew and First Sergeant Richard Acevedo marched at the head of the Assassins. Lieutenant Joe Minning marched as the senior platoon leader near the front of the Banshees. Behind the New Yorkers, a small contingent from the Blacksheep that flew north for the parade marched behind two officers. With a heavy limp and unsteady gate, Major Mike Kazmierzak marched up Fifth Avenue with Captain Mike Melancon, who took over after Kaz was hit by the car bomb. After months of surgery at Walter Reed Army Medical Center in Washington, Kaz was back on regular duty with the Louisiana Army National Guard, where he served as the aide-de-camp for the adjutant general. Once written off as dead by a brigade commander of the 10th Mountain Division, Kaz was very much alive and engaged to be married to the sister of his former executive officer, Lieutenant Dan Fritts, the man who helped save his life in a race against time in Baghdad.

When the unit returned to the armory, the soldiers filed through the great doors to the cheers of the officer corps before making their way onto the drill floor, which had been lined with seats and a massive stage for a formal welcome-home ceremony. Once the regiment and other guests settled in their seats, the official party marched onto the drill floor to the tune of "Garryowen." Kaz followed behind the dignitaries, having linked up with other wounded soldiers to present the 69th's 24th Campaign Streamer to the Task Force Wolfhound commander. Staff Sergeant Hefflyn Lalite, who was wounded by a mortar round on Route Irish, carried the streamer for Horrible Company. Specialist Felix Vargas, who had been wounded in the attack in Taji that killed Engeldrum and Urbina, carried the streamer for the Assassins. Sergeant Sam Cila, who had been wounded while clearing an IED in a *muhallah* near Route Irish, carried the streamer for the Banshees. The four men marched down the center of the armory, flanked by thousands of soldiers, families, and friends. When they reached the dais, the soldiers presented the streamer to Colonel Geoff Slack and Major General Joe Taluto, who had led the 42nd Infantry Division in Iraq and was now the adjutant general of New York.

Slack had once bristled with excitement at the chance of adding another battle streamer to the 69th Infantry Colors. But the Iraq pennant now represented more than simple martial glory and Army tradition. The red, black, white, and tan cloth was an emblem of the sacrifice of the wounded, guys like Kaz, Lalite, Vargas, and Cila. It represented the loss of the nineteen soldiers killed. It represented the pain and suffering of those who waited at home. As an honor guard lowered the regimental colors for the former commander, Slack could see through the hanging streamers of wars past the families of the 69th men killed in Iraq. They had come to the armory for Saint Patrick's Day from across New York and Louisiana, and sat stoically in the front row, some watching the ceremony, and others staring forward blankly. The nineteen soldiers killed had left behind sixteen children, many of whom were alongside their mothers. The streamer represented them, too, perhaps more so than all the others. Every generation went to war so its children wouldn't have to. Yet the rippling campaign credits from 150 years of conflict that hung from the 69th standard seemed to indicate the children might also have to fight at some future date, on some far-flung battlefield, or perhaps in their own backyard. Would the Fighting 69th still be around? Would the regiment be ready? Would it have the best equipment? Would the unit's leaders be well trained and educated? Like the Wolfhounds, the children would go to war with the Army they had. But with any luck, it would look a lot more like the Army Geoff Slack and the other 69th veterans brought back from Iraq than the hollow Army the citizen-soldiers found in desperate shape without nail, shoe, horse, or rider on the eve of 9/11.

After Slack and Taluto affixed the streamer, the former commander visited with each family member. The colonel once allowed the thought that he might complete his tour in Iraq without losing a single soldier. But the reality of what the Army was calling "The Long War" made that impossible in Iraq, and Slack believed the sacrifices were likely to continue. There had not yet been a V-I Day or 11th-Hour Armistice. Combat still raged in Iraq and Afghanistan. Threats from Islamic terrorists still came over the intelligence nets. And the United States Army was not getting any bigger. The National Guard had been an underfunded strategic reserve on 9/11. It was now an operational reserve, and plans already existed to send soldiers from New York state back to the front.

The rumors began as whispers that Saint Patrick's Day as the soldiers hoisted pints of beer and stomped their feet to the "Garryowen." The whispers evolved to hypothetical discussions; the discussions eventually became plans and oaths of allegiance. New York's 27th Infantry Brigade would go to Afghanistan to oversee the training and advising of the Afghan army in January 2008. The Fighting 69th was now part of the brigade and was expected to contribute forces, as other New York battalions had contributed forces for the 69th in 2004. Several soldiers had volunteered for the mission, but most were like Jay Olmo, who went back to work and family, pledging to do whatever the Army asked but seeing no need to press the issue. If they had to go, they would, but short of that, they wanted to stay home for a while. Mike Drew and Rich Acevedo also passed on the mission. In fact, the two soldiers and dozens of other combat-tested veterans had gotten out of the National Guard completely. Their time in boots was over. But Lieutenant Joe Minning and scores of other Fighting 69th veterans of Ground Zero and Iraq did accept the challenge.

The Banshee platoon leader took command of the Scouts when he returned from Iraq. The unit spent three weeks in early 2007 along the Mexican border in response to President Bush's pledge to strengthen security in the Southwest. When they reached home, the men learned they were tapped for Afghanistan. All told, some three hundred soldiers from the Fighting 69th would be scheduled to deploy to the other desert campaign. Though not a single regimental color was going overseas, the battalion would provide more soldiers for the mission than any other battalion in New York state, embodying the Wolfhounds' motto: "Who Never Retreated from the Clash of Spears."

Minning's first drill with the Fighting 69th had been at Ground Zero following the attacks of 9/11. The experience had left a deep imprint on his soul, and the soldier pledged his support for any military effort that was designed to protect the United States from future terrorist incidents. But the mustang had always harbored a special hate for the Taliban and Al Qaida in Afghanistan. They were the bastards who started this whole thing, and Minning, who was promoted to captain in late 2007, wouldn't mind a little payback.

"Besides," he told a fellow officer over a pint of beer in 2007, "if we don't go, who will?"

ACKNOWLEDGMENTS

This book would not have been possible without the assistance of scores of people. Dozens of Fighting 69th veterans sat for interviews and dug through their records to help provide both an accurate picture and a historical archive for the Regiment. For their regular counsel, their backing, and their primary role in shaping this narrative, I wish to thank Colonel Geoffrey Slack, Colonel Carl Pfeiffer, Lieutenant Colonel Charles Crosby, Major Chris Daniels, Captain Adam Headrick, Captain Mike Drew, Captain Mike Dunn, and Sergeant Jay Olmo. I also extend special thanks to Lieutenant Colonel Les Melnyk and his team from the National Guard Bureau's History Office, who documented the Fighting 69th's response to Ground Zero; to author Peter Quinn, who helped me find the connection between today's and yesterday's 69th Infantry; to James Ashcroft, author of *Making a Killing*, who provided background on the defense contracting industry in Iraq; to Staff Sergeant Luke Chiarenza, Sergeant First Class John Koch, Sergeant First Class Gary Carroll, Specialist Jonathan Rothwell, and Specialist Thomas Deleo, who provided volumes of historical data; to Captain Steven Flores for his enduring friendship and detailed background on the Big Army's train-up for duty in Iraq; and to Major Chris Cerniauskas, Martin Lueck, and Günta for their logistical support.

I also wish to extend my sincere debt of gratitude to all the soldiers of the Louisiana Tiger Brigade, Task Force Wolfhound, and Banshee Company, especially First Sergeant Frank Tooker, Lieutenant Brian Rathburn, and the entire crew of B-6: Sergeant Sam Cila, Sergeant Rene Rivera, Corporal David Webster, Specialist Dave Barry, and Sergeant Brian Tippet. I don't recall fondly the campaign, but I miss the team I toured with.

Finally, I thank my family, especially Lori Ann, Hudson Michael, and Lucia Ann, for their unwavering support from Ground Zero through Baghdad and since.

INDEX

Page numbers in *italics* refer to maps.